different strokes

robert rosenthal
bernard bruce
faith dunne
florence ladd

different strokes
pathways to
maturity in the
boston ghetto

a report to the ford foundation

westview press
boulder, colorado

To the young men of Roxbury and North Dorchester who joined in Project Pathways—this is their book, far more than ours.

Copyright 1976 by The Ford Foundation.

Published 1976 in the United States of America by

Westview Press, Inc.
1898 Flatiron Court
Boulder, Colorado 80301
Frederick A. Praeger, Publisher and Editorial Director

Library of Congress Cataloging in Publication Data

Main entry under title:

Different strokes.

Bibliography: p.
1. Afro-American youth—Massachusetts—Boston—Case studies. 2. Boston—Social conditions—Case studies. I. Rosenthal, Robert Alan.
F73.9.N4D53   301.43'15'0974461   76-7952
ISBN 0-89158-036-0
                                        ISBN 0-89158-047-6 pbk.

Printed and bound in the United States of America.

Acknowledgements

Dozens of people worked on Project Pathways—so many that it would be folly to try to thank them all individually. Many volunteered their time out of commitment to the Project, others worked long and hard after the money ran out to keep Pathways alive. We are grateful to all of them.

We are also grateful to the agencies and institutions who generously supported the Project and this book: the U.S. Office of Education, the Ford Foundation, the Harvard Graduate School of Education, and the Research Institute for Educational Problems. A longitudinal project extending over more than eight years requires of a funding agency and a sponsoring institution a difficult and consistent faith that it will, someday, be finished. We feel fortunate to have had sponsors willing to sustain that faith. At the same time, of course, the responsibilities for the analysis and conclusions are entirely ours.

In addition, we must express our gratitude to our families, who helped us through long months of writing and revision, to friends who read and re-read drafts, to colleagues who counseled and edited.

We would especially like to thank a few people whose unflagging support has made this book possible: Marjorie Martus of the Ford Foundation, who believed that nineteen file cabinets full of raw data could be transformed into a manuscript; Daniel R. Stein, without whom that transformation would not have taken place; and especially Henry S. Dyer, consultant, editor, angel of the writing project since its inception.

But, above all, our thanks must go to the Roxbury and North Dorchester families who asked us into their homes and their experiences, sacrificing both time and privacy so that we could help them tell the stories of young men growing up in Boston's ghetto. We only hope we have accurately conveyed their lives.

174497

Contents

PART III   SO WHAT?

PART I

WHY AND WHERE

Chapter
1
Introduction

Our study of the lives of black youngsters in the Boston ghetto began in 1967 and ran through 1974. When it began, the Great Society programs of President Lyndon Johnson's War on Poverty were in full gear. The Economic Opportunity Act of 1964 had appropriated money for vocational training at schools and colleges, the establishment of work-training camps, neighborhood centers for poor youths, and aid to a wide variety of community action programs. The Medicare bill of 1965 allowed hospital and nursing-home aid for persons over 65. Following up on the Civil Rights Act of 1964, a strong voter-rights bill was passed in 1965 that abolished literacy tests and other voting restrictions and authorized federal officials to register voters where discrimination existed. In 1966, the Demonstration Cities and Metropolitan Development Act ("Model Cities") provided funds to help 60 to 70 selected cities to rebuild their blighted inner cores. Federal responsibility for aid to education was also accepted by the Congress, and a series of complicated laws gave assistance to states, school districts, and local boards of education. Most of these pieces of legislation required local participation in the allocation and distribution of funds. Among the most prominent and widely-known programs developed were the Title I programs under ESEA, Upward Bound, and Head Start.

During the same decade, along with rising expectations among both black and white poor, there was increasing tension in the black ghettos. Uprisings in the Watts area of Los Angeles were followed by similar riots in the black slums of many cities. The assassination in Memphis, Tennessee, in April 1968 of Dr. Martin Luther King, Jr., triggered a new series of urban disorders.

Maybe we were naive to expect the federal government to subsidize a social revolution, or members of state and local governments to share hard-won political power with the poor or with blacks. Some now say that the federal anti-poverty program was badly conceived and thus foredoomed, that the field workers were innocent, opportunistic, or intractable. Some now say that the effort was too limited to make a serious dent in the economic inequities which burden the nation's poor.

Whichever hindsight interpretation one chooses, several things stand out. First, the early and mid-sixties offered a climate of hope for black people, augmented by new opportunities for broader participation by blacks in community planning and decision-making. This made black people more willing to struggle for their just share of resources, and gave many of them experience in power politics and bureaucratic functioning, proving once and for all that political strategy was not the mysterious and private preserve of the white man. Demands by blacks for community control and black power grew from the experience gained and the expectations raised during the 1960's.

Second, it became clear that no program could succeed without the participation of those whom it was intended to benefit. The Pathways study was based on that realization. In the early days of the War on Poverty, the federal government put large sums of money into poor communities in the form of educational and vocational training programs for the "disadvantaged." Many policy-makers, planners, and educators were unprepared for the sudden availability of program money. They were forced to generate programs based on sparse and shaky research. Some were distressed by the lack of solid data. Others never doubted that they knew all they had to know about poor and black communities even if they had never seen one. They depended on

4

meager descriptions by researchers, some of whom had only the most minimal contact with the people they described, rather than on direct reports about black people coming from black people themselves. Despite the wealth of novels, stories, and journals through which blacks have communicated the richness of their lives, and their uniquenesses as individuals, administrators and planners often relied on a few available surveys and clinical works, generally by whites which tended to lump together all poor blacks. Some programs developed for poor, black individuals used a social science version of "they all look alike, anyway."

The educational and economic problems of blacks have been a major national concern for forty years, but the number of studies exploring *individual differences* remains minuscule. And the number of studies which allow black people to express themselves in their own language—rather than responding to pre-selected categories devised by white researchers—has been minute. It is, therefore, inevitable (if ironic) that even the sympathetic educator or social scientist may have to depend on crude and stereotyped images of black people.

"Enrichment" programs assumed that black family and community life was emotionally and culturally impoverished. The assertion that black youth generally lacked self-esteem justified programs designed to "boost egos" without providing any genuine chance to develop talents or gain control over their own lives. Vocational programs assumed that black teenagers' job aspirations were either too low or unrealistically high.

The Pathways project had two goals. First, we wanted to demolish some of the myths and stereotypes common in social science and education, myths which were being translated into inevitably flawed programs and irrelevant and sometimes harmful school experiences for black youth. Second, we wanted to build a more accurate picture of poor blacks who live in the northern urban ghetto based on black descriptions of their lives and of issues they decided were important to them. Specifically, we wanted to repaint one of social science's most blurry and

5

unarticulated portraits—the image of the poor northern urban black teenager—splitting the undifferentiated profile into a series of pictures of complex, changing individuals. We wanted to comprehend how the black teenager saw his own range of options, and how he developed strategies for getting what he wanted from life.

THE DESIGN OF THE PROJECT

The Pathways project traces the individual development of a number of black young men from poor families who grew up in the Roxbury/North Dorchester ghetto between 1967 and 1974. We watched each of them develop a sense of what was possible and desirable for him. We traced their uses of various resources and pathways to try to reach their goals. We discussed with them aspects of self-perception and black identity. These complex issues required some knowledge of how people important in the lives of each boy perceived him, what they hoped, expected, feared for him, what resources they offered or impediments they erected. Therefore, we used the "focal cluster" method, which required intensive interviewing of each young man supplemented by a coordinated series of interviews with his parents, his closest brother or sister, his best friend, and two teachers—the one he worked with best and the one he had the most trouble with (see Kahn et al, 1964). The "focal child" was interviewed about all aspects of his life—home, school, friends, work, racial experience, and self-perceptions—while the members of his cluster were asked about all areas in which they had experience with the boy.

The school we chose to study was a *de facto* segregated public junior high school in Roxbury, Boston's black community. We will call it the George F. Ryan Junior High School, a pseudonym. To preserve the anonymity of the young men we studied, and of their families, friends, teachers, and schools, we will use pseudonyms throughout this book. Where specific descriptions might lead to the identification of individuals, we have altered locales and sequences.

The study got under way during a turbulent time for the Boston schools. The school system had just been vivisected in the media and in two widely-read books (*Death at an Early Age* by Jonathan Kozol and *Village School Downtown* by Peter Schrag). The ensuing publicity angered both parents and school officials, although for very different reasons.

We approached members of the School Committee with some trepidation, because we were asking for access to school children in an inner-city junior high school. We said that we were not out to gather material for another "shame of the schools" series, but that we did intend to ask students for detailed descriptions of their experiences with racial and other issues affecting their school life. We were greatly encouraged when the school board allowed us to go directly to the most tormented school in Boston, the 96 percent black Ryan Jr. High School. No attempt was made to limit our access to material or personnel.

Having located our school, we then began to select the young men we were to work with. Because our primary interest was to break down the stereotypes of the black urban poor, we asked the families of all of the poorest male adolescents in the seventh and ninth grades to collaborate with us. In all but one case, the parents and their sons agreed to work with us. Sixty-one young men and their focal groups were interviewed extensively in 1967 and 1968. In 1971, we re-interviewed fifty-five of the youths; the rest had moved far away, or had simply disappeared from the Boston scene. Finally, in 1973, we located fifteen of the young men who represented the variety of the original group and interviewed them again at length.

The Sixty-One Boys and Their Families

By studying *all* of the poorest boys in two grades in a neighborhood school, we hoped to encompass as wide a range as possible of attitudes and behaviors among poor urban black male adolescents. Because all of the boys lived in the same neighborhood and attended the same school, we achieved a rough similarity in the social and educational conditions each boy encountered. By studying both seventh and ninth graders we covered a greater span of adolescence than if we restricted ourselves to one age group. Furthermore, the follow-up studies into high school and beyond into college or work gave us important additional information.

All of the families of the sixty-one boys were clearly poor. However, there was some variation within this group not only in family income and in parental occupation, but also in "intactness" of family structure. Thirty-two out of the sixty-one boys were from households which included father, mother, and offspring. Of those households without fathers, separation accounted for thirteen, divorce for seven, three fathers were dead, three mothers had never married, and no clear understanding could be obtained about the absence of three fathers.

The median weekly income of the families was $90.25. Because most families included three or more dependents, the average per capita income was quite low. Table I shows the distribution of family weekly income. Forty-one of the sixty-one families said

TABLE I

Family Weekly Income

Income	Number of Families
$70 or less	12
71-85	13
86-100	10
101-115	6
116-130	10
131 or more	6
No clear data	4
Total	61

they subsisted on earned income, six said they got partial support from AFDC,* and thirteen said they got full support from AFDC. Data were unavailable for one family.

Parents' educations and occupations varied but most were at the lower end of the scales. Nineteen fathers had eight years or less of schooling, another nineteen attended high school but did not finish, and thirteen were high school graduates. Of the high school graduates, two attended but did not finish college and two completed college. (No data were available for the others.) Twelve of the mothers had eight years or less of schooling, twenty-nine attended high school, and eighteen were high school graduates. (No data were available for two mothers.) Four went on to college, but none graduated

The fathers' jobs included construction work, unskilled labor, and a few white collar positions. The twenty-four working mothers included domestic workers, factory workers, and a few white collar workers. Table II shows the occupations of parents by category.

TABLE II

Occupations of Parents by Category†

Occupation	Fathers	Mothers
Laborer (Unskilled)	19	3
Service	8	8
Operative (Skilled)	10	8
Craftsman	9	2
White Collar	3	4
Professional (Salaried)	1	1
At Home	–	34
No Data	11	1
Total	61	61

*Aid to Families with Dependent Children
†Note: The fathers whose occupations were not coded were either deceased or out of contact with the family for several years.

9

The Interviews

The initial interviews with the boys required from ten to twenty hours for each boy in sessions of two to three hours spread over a two month period. The re-interviews at Times II and III ranged from one to six hours. Interviews with family members, friends, and teachers also ranged over many hours. The boys and the members of their focal clusters were collaborators in our study, and as such were paid for the time we spent interviewing them. All interviews were taped and transcribed in their entirety.

The interview schedules for the boys were flexible but included a wide variety of topics: personal health and history, family relationships, friends, nonschool activities, school and work experiences and attitudes, self-concept, ideas about personal strengths and weaknesses, racial awareness, and attitudes toward neighborhood and home. Interviews with members of the boys' focal clusters centered on their relationships with and perceptions of each boy.

A variety of devices was used to elicit information. For example, to get at each boy's ideas about himself, we asked "The Spy Question:"

> Let's pretend you wanted to disappear from the scene for a while, but you had to get someone to take your place so that no one would know you were gone. You have to teach him, like with a spy, how to act like you so that no one would know the difference. How would you tell him to act around home? With your friends? At school? (etc.)

This question produced many rich responses, some of which are cited at length in the case histories in Part II.

The Time II and Time III interviews with the boys followed the same rough outline of topics, but focused on changes in the boys' attitudes and behavior and on their new experience.

Selecting Six Cases

Six cases were selected to present in detail because the material was so rich that to describe more of them would be unwieldly. In fact, enough material was gathered about each boy and his focal cluster to fill a good-sized book. The six cases finally selected are not a "representative sample" in the ordinary sense of that abused term, but rather are *illustrative* of the range and complexity of the data about the boys on many variables and dimensions.

Our goal was to select a manageable group of six cases that would illustrate the diversity of the total group and also demonstrate the complexity of each individual. We believe that the six cases presented in Part II achieve this goal, displaying a variety of family patterns, styles of coping, adaptations to school and work, self-esteem, attitudes towards race, and willingness to move in the white world. Although we use tags to identify each boy (e.g. "going under," "getting over," and the like) these should be thought of only as shorthand reminders of the boys' experiences. We chose the case method of presentation precisely because we wanted to convey clearly both the diversity we found among the sixty-one boys and their individuality. It is our hope that by pointing to the innumerable ways in which these boys differ, we will help the reader to see more clearly how great is the challenge and how compelling the need for genuinely individualizing the education of the young, especially in the urban ghettos.

From the outset, we were determined to work in collaboration with the community—not to impose our templates on their actions, nor to record and run. Boston's black community is surrounded by colleges and universities. By 1966 the black community was fed up with univeristy-based research and with white researchers who, like white landlords and shopkeepers, seemed only to take from the community. Community people had begun to say they were tired of "being put under a microscope and looked at like we're some kind of germ," and that "all you people want to do is take our words, leave, write another book, make your reps, and that'll be the end of it. Nothing will change, we'll still be in the 'Bury [Roxbury] and nothing will be better."

We felt that involving community people in the design of the project from the beginning would establish the mutuality necessary to identify issues genuinely important to black people in Roxbury. So we began the project by circulating copies of the initial proposal to community-based educators, asking them to help us. At every possible point, we tried to move closer to reality by engaging the expertise of members of the Roxbury/North Dorchester community.

COMMUNICATING THE BLACK EXPERIENCE

White people have trouble hearing the truth about black people. We do not think this is because they have not been told. Blacks have told the story about the black experience with realism, force, and creative power. Nor do we feel this is necessarily a matter of insensitive or biased readers. Some of the most sympathetic readers simply don't know what to do when confronted with the strength and complexity of black Americans.

One manifestation of this problem is the tendency of some program developers and educators to think in terms of groups rather than individuals. Instead of talking about working with Lorna, Josh, and Sonny, they consider "how to teach *these kids* to read" and "how to deal with *troublemakers*." They will readily agree that it is important to break down stereotypes, but they will say, "O.K., so you've shown that black kids aren't all alike. I still have to develop programs for large numbers of black students, and with inadequate funds." Some programs sensitive to individual differences have been designed and are operating—mostly untouted and unknown—around the country. We believe many more are needed. But even if some form of categorizing is required, the categories should be based on existing diversities rather than on fantasied uniformities.

It is difficult to give a balanced picture of both the strengths of the black community and of the chronic hazards that overshadow the lives of black people. If we stress the privations, conflicts, and brutalities imposed by racism and squarely discuss the price

12

blacks pay for enduring these conditions, we risk supporting the stereotype of the ghetto as pathogenic and of blacks as deviants. But if, on the other hand, we stress the strength of black people under the most adverse circumstances, we may minimize the ills which the dominant culture has imposed on black and poor people, and thereby weaken the arguments for the expensive public measures needed to establish a measure of social and economic justice through provision of adequate social and educational services.

We attack these problems by being as direct as possible. The black people who worked with us knew from the beginning that they would be talking, through us, to you. Although they also knew that our values would inevitably somewhat bias our presentation, they also hoped that the portrait we painted would be as vivid, as communicative, as real, as possible.

STRUCTURE OF THE BOOK

This book focuses on the lives of six young black male Americans as they moved from early adolescence to young manhood in Roxbury/North Dorchester from 1967 to 1974. The six young men we chose are both unique and representative. They are distinctive individuals, but any other six we could have chosen would have shown the same diversity and complexity. These six young men and their families are very different from one another. But, like the rest of the sixty-one boys whom we studied, these six have much in common. They are all black, all raised in the Northern ghettos, all from poor families. And they all attended the same *de facto* segregated junior high school.

The book is divided into three parts. Part I contains this introductory chapter and the "Ghettoscape," which sketches the history of Roxbury, describes the physical and social environment in which the boys grew up, and introduces the George F. Ryan Junior High School. Part II contains six biographies tracing the lives of the young men from 1967 to 1974. Primarily in their own words and the words of those close to them, we explore the hopes they have realized, abandoned, or retained; the changes they have undergone. Part III, "So What?" uses material from the interviews with the young men, their families, friends, and teachers, to raise issues important both to the black community and to the larger society: self-confirming and harmful stereotypes and myths about the black family, black youngsters, and the ghetto; the significance of education as a road to upward mobility, the good life and the good society; how teachers, administrators and the rest of us can use the insights these young men provide to make schools and schooling humane and productive.

We do not "speak for" the Boston black community, or even the youngsters and families we studied, much less for blacks in general. We are reflecting an experience with some three or four hundred people whose lives touched because they were all involved with someone who attended the George F. Ryan Junior High School in the late sixties. How representative are the people whose words and experiences we have recorded? We cannot answer this with confidence, and would rather err on the side of conservatism. Black people for too long have been lumped together in facile and erroneous generalizations. But it would be ingenuous to claim that we do not believe that the facts of black life and death in Roxbury are similar to those of life and death in other northern ghettos. The problems seem universal; the range of options seems everywhere constricted; the degree of ingenuity shown in getting by from day to day seems everywhere astounding.

14

Chapter

2

Ghettoscape

One hundred and twenty-five years ago, when the unofficial borders of Boston went only as far as a man could comfortably walk to work, Roxbury and Dorchester were sleepy country villages serving nearby farms and the occasional estates and "businessman's cottages" in the surrounding area. Then the horsecar lines were extended out of the city, and the two towns became fashionable suburbs, offering new homes and green spaces to the middle- and upper-middle-class merchants and professionals no longer able to find comfortable, reasonably priced living quarters in the central city.

By 1900 Roxbury was a brief, ten-cent ride from the center of Boston. It offered the space and serenity of a prosperous suburb, at prices lower than those in the central city. In Lower Roxbury, nearer to the city, builders began to put up blocks of three-deckers for sale and rent. Upper Roxbury and some of Dorchester had mostly wide, tree-lined streets of single-family homes. This area was known as The Hill. According to Sam Bass Warner, "The new streets of Roxbury were laid out with an eye to being easy to get through and easy to clean. Each house had a full set of modern plumbing facilities, gas for light and often gas stoves as well. . . The new three-deckers and two families were extravagant of space . . . lot sizes were adequate, and green space allotment of the new houses exceeded that of the contemporary Back Bay house." (Warner, 1970)

Photographs of Roxbury-Dorchester from that period suggest a close-knit community, partly lower-middle class, small businessmen and workers with aspirations to the comfort and luxury of The Hill, and partly The Hill itself—Upper Roxbury and North Dorchester—where the quiet, rough-paved streets provided a tree-shaded setting for the large homes, luxury apartment buildings and well-kept yards which were the pride of their owners. According to Warner, Roxbury "differed from other suburbs in its higher concentration of professional people and its larger number of households with resident maids." (Warner, 1970, p. 113)

By 1967, the beginning of our study, the suburban peace was gone. Maids still resided in the Roxbury three-deckers, but they traveled to work for families in the white suburbs of Brookline, Newton, West Roxbury and the like. Most of the elegant homes had become crumbling hulks, and the old trees shaded vacant, littered lots and aging alcoholics drinking wine from bottles wrapped in paper bags.

Sixty years had brought great changes to Boston. The first residents of Roxbury, those who bought or built the fine new homes, were predominantly white, native-born Protestants. Then, as immigrant groups found their footing in the city, their more successful members made their way out to this desirable area. Roxbury and Dorchester became predominantly Irish, and then Jewish.

Between World Wars I and II the old middle-class apartment buildings and triple-deckers in Lower Roxbury were increasingly rented to blacks moving out from the center of Boston, and moving up from the South. They were poorer than the earlier residents, and the neighborhood began to deteriorate. By 1940 many middle-class blacks had moved into Upper Roxbury. They bought large, attractive houses and considered themselves worthy successors to the fashionable folk who had lived there in the 1900's.

In his autobiography, Malcolm X captures the character of this neighborhood as he saw it when he moved to Boston in 1940.

> So I went walking around the neighborhood . . . which is something like Harlem's Sugar Hill . . . I saw those Roxbury Negroes acting and living differently from any black people

16

I'd ever dreamed of in my life. This was the snooty-black neighborhood; they called themselves the 'Four Hundred' and looked down their noses at the Negroes of the black ghetto, or so-called 'town' section where Mary, my other half-sister, lived.

What I thought I was seeing there in Roxbury were high-class, educated, important Negroes, living well, working in big jobs and positions. Their quiet homes sat back in their mowed yards. These Negroes walked along the sidewalks looking haughty and dignified, on their way to work, to shop, to visit, to church.

I know now, of course, that what I was really seeing was only a big-city version of those 'successful' Negro bootblacks and janitors back in Lansing. The only difference was that the ones in Boston had been brainwashed even more thoroughly. They prided themselves on being more 'cultured,' 'cultivated,' 'dignified,' and better off than their black brethren down in the ghetto, which was no further than you could throw a rock.

(Malcolm X, 1964)

In the mid-forties, Roxbury was still dominated by the trolley line. But the horsecars had been replaced by the elevated train, and Dudley Station had become the heart of an increasingly black community. For many years, "Dudley" was black Roxbury's major shopping center. Between Northampton and Dudley stations, a string of commercial establishments catered to every local need. Under the giant canopy of the elevated train were pawnshops, beauty parlors, barbershops, bars, restaurants offering fried fish, clams, chicken—the works. There were cut-rate drugstores and discount furniture stores, butcher shops where you could buy the whole pig or the feet, ears and belly; grocery and fish stores which offered porgies, butterfish, greens, yams, even plantains for the West Indians. It was a lively, noisy area, conversation and sales interrupted only by the regular, maddening screech of the train roaring overhead.

17

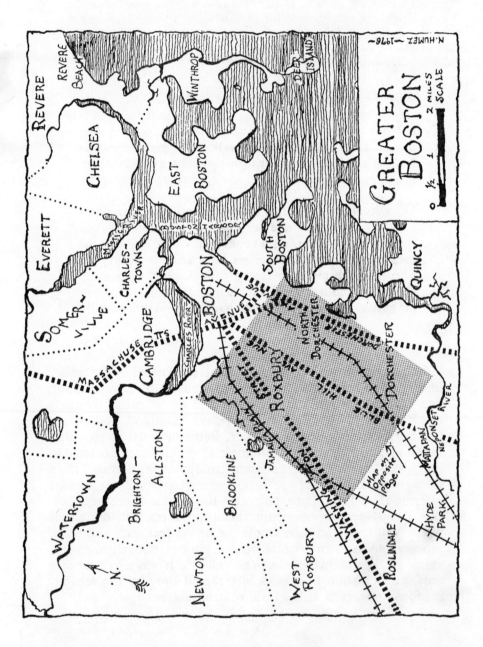

GREATER BOSTON

SCALE

2 MILES

~ N.HUMEZ ~ 1976 ~

REVERE

REVERE BEACH

CHELSEA

WINTHROP

EAST BOSTON

DEER ISLAND

EVERETT

BOSTON HARBOR

SOMER-VILLE

CHARLES-TOWN

MYSTIC RIVER

SOUTH BOSTON

BOSTON

QUINCY

CAMBRIDGE

MASSACHUSE TTS

CHARLES RIVER

TUNNEL

DORCHESTER

NORTH DORCHESTER

ROXBURY

WATERTOWN

BRIGHTON — ALLSTON

BROOKLINE

JAMAICA PLAIN

Map on opposite page.

MATTAPAN

NEPONSET RIVER

N.

NEWTON

WEST ROXBURY

WASHINGTON ST.

HYDE PARK

ROSLINDALE

18

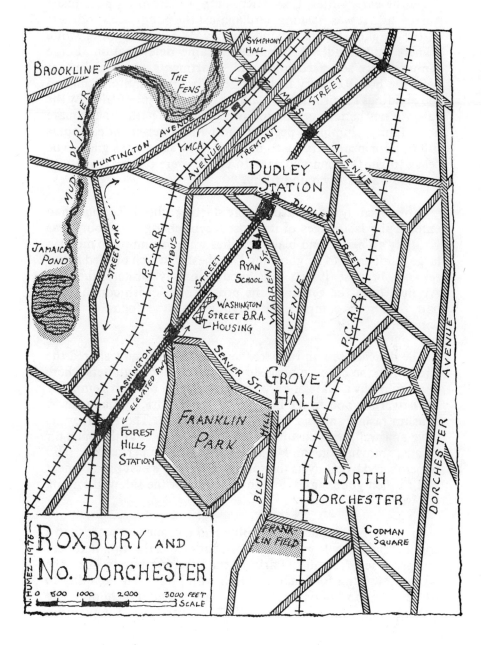

BROOKLINE

THE FENS

SYMPHONY HALL

MUDDY RIVER

HUNTINGTON AVENUE

YMCA

AVENUE

MASS. STREET

TREMONT

DUDLEY STATION

STREET CAR

JAMAICA POND

P.C.R.R.

COLUMBUS

STREET

RYAN SCHOOL

WASHINGTON STREET B.R.A. HOUSING

DUDLEY STREET

WARREN ST.

AVENUE

AVENUE

P.C.R.R.

SEAVER ST.

GROVE HALL

WASHINGTON

ELEVATED RWY.

FOREST HILLS STATION

FRANKLIN PARK

BLUE HILL

NORTH DORCHESTER

DORCHESTER AVENUE

CODMAN SQUARE

FRANKLIN FIELD

N. HUMEZ — 1976 —

ROXBURY AND No. DORCHESTER

0   500   1000   2000   3000 FEET
SCALE

By the early fifties, Lower Roxbury was Boston's poor black ghetto, and it was pushing hard against the middle-class borders of the neighborhoods beyond Dudley. With the flight of white owners and middle-class residents came deterioration. Large families were squeezed into small apartments which had never been the best Roxbury had to offer; absentee landlords milked the buildings for profit, maintaining them only minimally. By the early sixties better housing followed the same path—inadequate heat, faulty plumbing, peeling lead paint, over-crowded rooms full of poor people trying to make do. The streets designed to be "easy to get through and easy to clean" were left by the city to become trash-strewn and filthy.

When the boys in our study were starting school, Roxbury had entered the last stages of its most recent change. Roxbury was virtually all black, and black families were beginning to move in large numbers into neighboring Dorchester, which offered better services because it was still predominantly white. Blue Hill Avenue, once the center of the prosperous Jewish community, had begun to compete with Dudley as the focus of black commerce.

The delicatessen and the kosher meat market now shared the street with the cut-rate pork shops and the lunch counters where you could buy a plate of barbecue and greens. Muslim Temple 11 took over a wood-frame house near the old brick synagogue. A Muslim restaurant and school soon followed. The Avenue was alive and well, with customers buying vegetables at the open air stands, moving in and out of Morse's supermarket (still remembered by many as the source of the city's best buys in meat and canned goods) and greeting friends on the sidewalks along the way.

In the early and mid-sixties, Blue Hill Avenue was more than a commercial strip. It was also a corridor of social action that held the promise of change. Early in the morning busses lined the Avenue, waiting for black children who journeyed each day to white neighborhoods and, presumably, better schools. The bussing program began in 1962 and was called Operation

Exodus. Initially it bussed children from overcrowded ghetto schools to under-enrolled schools in other parts of Boston. It soon expanded to bus inner-city children to sympathetic suburban school systems who made room for them and helped defray the costs. By 1966, six suburban school systems had banded together to form METCO—The Metropolitan Council for Educational Opportunity—to bus inner-city children to their schools, with financial assistance from the United States Office of Education and the Carnegie Corporation. Both Operation Exodus and METCO will reappear in Part II of this book when we describe the education of two of the six young men.

In storefronts and offices over stores, multiple service agencies, black and proud, put up their posters and offered aid to the neighborhood. The Roxbury Youth Alliance, the Boston Action Group, the Northern Student Movement moved into action, with homegrown leaders based in the community giving the organizations their vitality and purpose. They ran tutoring programs and job-training programs, clean-up campaigns and fights against substandard housing and absentee landlords.

Local merchants soon became aware of the need to be socially conscious, and to contribute to *ad hoc* causes as well as the more obviously established community organizations. Those who were slow in their awareness learned through the pressure of selective patronage campaigns, sit-ins, boycotts. It was an exciting time in a community just beginning to get a sense of its own power.

The Roxbury we came to in 1967 displayed elements from its unusual history. It was no typical urban slum ghetto, full of high-rise public apartment projects and disintegrating shopping centers. Turn a corner in Upper Roxbury and you could think you were in Newton. The homes belonged to poorer people, but they were still owner-occupied and proudly kept. In another section of Upper Roxbury, the Washington Park middle-income apartment complex rose—a group of low, wood and brick modern buildings that would sit comfortably in any rich suburban town.

But look again, and you would know where you were. Overflowing garbage cans sat under the old trees, waiting for the sanitation trucks that rarely came. Empty lots were filled with litter, trash, glass, and abandoned cars. Rats, mice, roaches feasted frequently and well on the refuse that collected in the dark hallways of apartment buildings. The spring clean-up campaign was a poor substitute for erratic municipal services. Abandoned, burned-out buildings were boarded up too late to prevent the theft of copper and iron scrap, highly prized and valuable. Broken panes in doors and windows were covered with tattered plastic. Everything needed paint.

Most of the boys in our study came from a neighborhood which borders the once-elegant Hill district. Their neighborhood had been substantial and middle-class in the 1900's, but never luxurious. By the late 1960's it was one of the poorest areas in the ghetto.

The majority of boys who worked with us lived in the triple-deckers. The most graceful of these have open porches front and rear, with stained glass over the entry, and wooden scrollwork around doors and windows. The less pretentious have only sagging rear porches and few decorative touches. The best of these buildings were shabby in 1967. The worst suffered from peeling paint, falling shingles, drain downspouts pulled away from the walls, causing hazardous icicles in winter. The "extravagant space" which lured tenants from Boston at the turn of the century became a drawback—the large rooms were difficult to heat properly, and landlords were reluctant to spend money to heat them.

No one with money or influence cared about Roxbury any more, and the suburb which had been pulled out of the nineteenth century countryside had become a twentieth century slum. The well-tended refuge of the upwardly mobile minority merchant and professional was now the neglected and confining black ghetto.

Ghettoscape

THE ROXBURY/NORTH DORCHESTER
NEIGHBORHOOD: 1967

"My neighborhood is not the best. Matter of fact, I'm trying to get out of there now; I'm trying to sell my house, and get away. Because, doesn't seem as though last three or four years, a lot of people get out there on Sunday morning, they drink whiskey and . . . loud talk and stuff like that. And I don't care about living around these kind of people, that's why I've been trying to sell my house. I don't think much of the neighborhood, tell you the truth. When I first moved here, about eight years ago, it was pretty nice. But now, it's gone down trail."

- Mr. Mitchell, Parent, 1967

The families of the Pathways boys did not live in a slum because they wanted to. Almost no one does. Mr. Mitchell's story parallels the tale of many families, who move from neighborhood to neighborhood looking for a stable, decent place to live, but never find it. Andrew Garrison's father talks about moving to southern Dorchester, but decides not to, because he predicts that it will be allowed to deteriorate over the next few years as the blacks move in and the Irish out, just as his North Dorchester area has disintegrated over the past decade. Brian Henry's mother lives out of perpetually packed boxes, symbolic of the urge to keep moving, keep getting your name on waiting lists, keep looking for the warm and pleasant quarters you are unlikely ever to find or to be able to afford.

Many of the parents are bitter about the neighborhood, and about the flight of middle-class residents—black and white— which has left it less than it used to be, less than they would like to make it. Mrs. Battle tells the age-old story of the black family seeking comfort and respectibility, only to have it snatched from them. She was the first black women in her apartment building and "all the rest in there was white Jewish families and they were old people. And boy, I went through a lot of red tape to get this apartment, but they let me have it because I guess they figured, well, now here is someone that has nice kids. I knew the landlord, see, he was a Jewish landlord from Brookline. He said, 'I will be responsible for her and her children because I know her and I know what she try to make her children do.' They gave me the apartment. I paid my two months rent. And when we moved there, it was so quiet, you could lay down and sleep, you could get up and walk out, you could come back in and you feel like you was just in heaven, it was so nice. And as soon as those people know that there was colored people living in that building, the Jewish families started moving out. He start going up on their rent." As the old Jewish families moved out, blacks moved in to replace them, because "they were so glad to get some place to live, I guess they wouldn't care what amount of rent they paid." The Jews could move to Mattapan, or Brookline, "anywhere, because they was white. So they start moving out, and the colored start moving in. And then they started renting to anybody and everything."

Now, she says, "the whole neighborhood is unlivable. The people in there, you hear all cursing, fighting, they is drunk all the time. They sit in front of the store, and they put all kinds of papers and bottles and bags, and cans, beer cans and tonic cans, all out in front of the door all the time. And all night long they stay in the street. It's so dangerous that I keep a chain on my door and my door locked. I went last week up in Dorchester, and I found this apartment, nice apartment, it was six or seven rooms ..." And so the cycle goes.

Even parents whom Mrs. Battle would see as part of the problem feel unhappy and uncomfortable about where they live. Douglas Jones's father, an ex-convict and a man often in trouble, says that he "doesn't feel too hot about it (his neighborhood), within myself." He says that it has the reputation of being a "whore's paradise ... And a bunch of sailors will be over there, and a lot of jitterbugs will come over there, with their parent's car I guess, and pick up a bunch of girls and stay around half the night, with them record players on them steps out in front, you can't hardly sleep." And he adds, "Especially at night, I don't feel safe, period. Because I seen too many guys get beaten up, robbing them and all that."

24

The boys tend to be less negative than their parents about the neighborhood, perhaps because, for many of them, it is the only life they have ever known. They see the same scenes their parents witness, but they make more distinctions. One boy says, "It's peaceful in the mornings, but at night it's rowdy. The police come through here, maybe a couple of fires. It looks like a regular neighborhood. Cars parked on the streets, a few houses all wrecked up, a few dirty backyards and a big open field." To a fifteen year old who has lived in Roxbury all his life, a pleasant neighborhood has only "a few papers thrown around, . . . not a whole lot of trash and things in the backyards, and on the street . . . people are not there fighting very often."

But, despite their willingness to accept their neighborhood for what it is, there is a pervasive sense of fear in the boy's descriptions. "They say you can't walk in Roxbury alone at night without you having your pocketbook snatched, or hit on the head and things like that." Not all the boys agree that what "they say" is true, but many comment on the crime and danger. "A lot of fights, and stolen cars ride through here speeding, some kids get hit, go to the hospital." And one cautious young man, Andy Garrison, summed up the general tension of life in this area when he said he won't go up to Blue Hill Avenue anymore, because "everybody gets killed up there sometime."

The Urban Renewal Dream

Many of the boys had hope for their neighborhood in 1967, based on promises of urban renewal. Over in Washington Park the bulldozers had done much of their work. Dislocated families found new homes. The unfulfilled dreams were replaced by new visions.

The boys we worked with did not benefit from the Washington Park development. Many of them came from families which had been uprooted by the renewal effort, forced to move from mediocre housing into worse quarters. One parent says that he left his former apartment for a house in which "there's nothing I

25

like" because the Boston Redevelopment Authority "moved everybody out of there. They were gonna redo the buildings; the apartments had seven rooms, and they were gonna chop the floors up and make three-and-a-halfs out of them, where they could charge $125 a month . . . they were getting ninety out of me. Why should they get $90 when they can get $125?"

But if these families felt exploited by urban renewal—none of them could live in the new development—it at least suggested what could be done to produce decent living quarters in the inner city. Some boys hoped that it might happen for them, too. In fact, planners for the Boston Redevelopment Authority had, by 1967, examined nearly 4,000 buildings in North Dorchester, and recommended clearance of twenty-six percent of them, plus rehabilitation of the other seventy-four percent.

Boys made specific suggestions which took into account the discrimination which made genuine rehabilitation more difficult. One boy said that when he thinks about his neighborhood, his first thought is, "How you can improve it. Like for instance, Quincy Street, when you get past Columbia Road, the street's all smooth, but when you get down where the colored people live, it's all rocky and rough. Things like that. The houses need fixing up. They need to take care of the rats that are running around in the street too." Another ninth grader adds, "the neighborhood looks all right, but . . . they should try to clean up the place much more better than it is. Get the construction people to do it . . . to clean it up, or write a letter to the governor. Tell the people who knock down the houses, clean it up, or put something there—build a new house there. Have somebody—put a playground there, cause we don't have that much playgrounds around where we live . . . The houses around there, they should board 'em up . . . and wait . . . til if they're gonna clean it up, or make a new house out of it, or knock it down. They should do it pretty fast."

In 1967 there seemed some promise—at least in the eyes of these young men—of recreating a semblance of the Roxbury that existed at the turn of the century. These boys, like most people, had a vision of a neighborhood in which they would like to live, where they would be proud to raise a family. Ladd (1972) found that the boys had a remarkably uniform dream of the ideal home, a dream of a single-family house, painted white with green shutters, surrounded by lawns and trees. They dreamed of a place which Roxbury had once been and where, by 1967, only splintering shells remained.

THE GEORGE F. RYAN JUNIOR HIGH SCHOOL: 1967

Ryan Junior High School is a red brick structure that looks more like a besieged fortress than a school. Built in the monumental style of the 1920's, it was never an inviting place, but it must have once presented a certain grandeur. A double set of granite steps leads up to the raised entrance to the auditorium. Carved stone decorations, now partially eaten away by pollution and time, once enhanced the front of the building. But, by 1967, any attempt at elegance had been abandoned in favor of a variety of protective measures intended to preserve the school from the young people it was supposed to educate.

A sturdy, wrought-iron fence ran the short width of the decorative front of the building, opening into the school yard at one end to admit students through a guarded main entrance. Windows on the upper stories were covered with heavy-gauge wire mesh screening sprayed yellow or cream, depending on the sub-contractor who installed them. Ground level windows had added protection—heavier gauge steel screens, metal-framed and secured with a number of padlocks. The auditorium doors were locked and chained from the inside, and only opened for such special occasions as graduations or public assemblies.

The school had lost its appearance of dignity. Lights that once illuminated and decorated the main entrance were now iron stumps; no one thought it worthwhile to replace them. The playground never had been more than a narrow strip of blacktop which provided only an access route to the main door. High chainlink fence and remnants of iron fencing separated the school building from the rear porches of deteriorating triple-deckers in

27

varying stages of neglect and backyards filled with abandoned cars, tufts of overgrown grass, broken glass, rubble, and rats scampering visibly from one pile of debris to the next.

Inside, the Ryan was dark and oppressive. Institutional tile covered the walls to a height of seven feet (higher than a boy can reach with a marking pen). Cracked and dirty paint stretched from the tile to the high ceilings. The building was not designed for modern school life. There were no lockers along the tiled walls, so students had to wear or carry their heavy coats from room to room in winter, although the classrooms were often made stiflingly hot by the erratic radiators. Physical education had become a state requirement, but the Ryan had no showers in the gymnasium. Winter classes smelled of steam heat, of stale sweat, of damp wool.

Trying to get into the Ryan at that time was like trying to enter a medium-security prison. All doors other than the main entrance were chained and padlocked to keep students from leaving school, and to keep outsiders (dropouts, graduates, truants) from coming in and disrupting the classes. Once school began in the morning, the main door was locked, and a student or teacher was assigned to monitor the entrance. To get in one had to ring a doorbell, and when the bell was out of order—as it was about half the time—a strong fist and foot were required to make one's presence known. Visitors had to register with the principal's office, and assistant principals kept up a steady patrol of the halls in an effort to keep up a semblance of normal school order.

Inside the classrooms, not enough was happening. Classes were comparatively small—there were approximately 22 students for each teacher, and classes were frequently made much smaller by truancy and absence—but many of the teachers had difficulty managing their classes. The Ryan staff was predominantly white, while the student body was 96 percent black. This in itself caused some tension. Many of the white teachers had been at the Ryan since its heyday as the pride of the old Dorchester Jewish community. Some didn't understand the black students who now came under their charge. Some feared them, disliked them, and

28

considered them uneducable. Some older teachers were reassigned and replaced by young, inexperienced white teachers, often well-meaning and sometimes very successful, but not always able to turn their energy and their desire to communicate into much-needed education for their students.

Some of the young white teachers felt betrayed by their assignment to the Ryan. Those who had grown up in Boston thought of Dorchester as the white middle-class area it had been. They were unprepared for the school they found, unprepared for the spread of the black population out of Roxbury. One teacher says, "I applied to the Boston school system as a provisional teacher, and they said, 'Would you like to teach at the Ryan' and I had no knowledge at all of the situation there and they told me it was in Dorchester, which was a fallacy. I guess that was to get someone there, I don't know. I guess in the school bulletin it is Dorchester, but it is now in Roxbury." The Ryan is geographically in Dorchester, but in 1967, in the minds of many whites, black and Roxbury were synonymous.

The few black teachers and administrators on the Ryan staff were more able, for the most part, to maintain rapport with the students than were the whites. Although a few white teachers were repeatedly praised in student descriptions, the majority of the boys we worked with preferred the strict, demanding, old-fashioned black male teachers. A black assistant principal, known for his necktie requirement and his penchant for paddling difficult students, was among the most widely respected teachers in the school.

Beyond building and staff problems, there were problems with the student body. Families of Ryan students were very poor and had constant housing problems because of job losses, the Boston Redevelopment Authority, and rent-gouging landlords. Many students moved, often in the middle of the year. Teachers were faced with classes that seemed to change with the tides. A teacher might have a class of sixteen students in one course, but they would rarely be the same sixteen for two days in a row. Transfers, illness, and truancy insured lack of continuity. Students were in an equally precarious situation; teacher turnover was so high at the Ryan that a single class might have four or five teachers in one school year.

In this situation, tensions inevitably mounted within the staff, between the staff and the students, between the staff and the community. By 1967 the school had exploded into front page Boston headlines, with stories of assaults on teachers, and a widely publicized union demand for "combat pay" for Ryan staff. After the Christmas recess, in January 1967, the school was tense, apprehensive. Teachers, students, parents, administrators were worried, waiting, wondering what was going to happen next. Fights erupted daily among students; crowds of kids milled around after school waiting for excitement, entertainment. Police cars patrolled the streets during dismissal hour. A dangerous, frantic atmosphere hung over the Ryan. Formal classroom learning virtually ceased.

By April the tension was so high that it was clear to everyone that something had to be done. An assault on a teacher brought demands from the school department that armed policemen patrol the school corridors. Community groups and parents met and decided to establish a coalition to work jointly on the problems of the Ryan and the Burns, a similar junior high school. On this note of mingled hope and desperation, the school year ended.

BLUE HILL AVENUE AND THE UPRISING: 1967

We came to Roxbury/North Dorchester in a pivotal year: the year of the urban uprisings. The pressure of the Civil Rights Movement had mounted, until confrontations with whites were inevitable. Urban uprisings ranged from Watts to Newark.

The major issues in Boston (as in many other cities) were education, housing and public services, and rights of welfare recipients. Operation Exodus had become a powerful community force, expanding its bussing program, and becoming increasingly concerned with improving the quality of local schools. Exodus and other groups organized demonstrations intended to force the School Committee to improve conditions in the predominantly black schools. These demonstrations culminated in a series of boycotts and "stay-out days." During the boycotts, "freedom schools" burgeoned in the neighborhood.

Other groups were concerned about tenant's rights, demanding that the Boston Housing Authority provide safe, sanitary, and adequately heated apartments in the projects. Still other organizations grappled with the continuing problem of police brutality.

But it was the fight of welfare recipients for adequate support and decent, dignified treatment that brought on the first full-scale confrontation between the community and the police department. As with other uprisings across the country, this one began with a relatively minor incident. In June 1967, a group made up mainly of welfare mothers held a sit-in at the offices of the Overseers of Public Welfare. They were ordered to leave. They did not go. The police chained the doors, and violence broke out, flooding down Blue Hill Avenue from Grove Hall to Quincy Street. Policemen panicked and began to beat and arrest onlookers, looters, and passers-by, indiscriminately. Some white-owned businesses were laid waste by flame and looting. "The Strip"—Blue Hill Avenue—was hard hit. Shoe stores, television and radio outlets, liquor stores, and stores which sold the fashionable "knits" were systematically cleaned out.

A number of community groups set up their own emergency services. Operation Exodus set up a center in its office and sent out calls for food, first aid supplies, and volunteers to help police the area. Representatives of community organizations went to the police stations to guarantee the safety of people under arrest and to keep an eye on police proceedings.

After the uprising, the community settled into an uneasy peace. A group of black community organizers founded the Freedom Security Patrol which enlisted volunteers (some of them boys from Roxbury gangs) to protect the neighborhood against violence. But many of the white store owners, who still formed the business backbone of the Avenue, packed up and left—first the shoe store, then the kosher markets. The burnt-out, looted furniture store never reopened. The stores that remained seemed tentatively ready for business-as-usual, but the possibility of flight was ever-present.

One ninth-grader described his experience during the disturbance:

> . . . I heard a rumor that there was something on Blue Hill Avenue, but I didn't know what. So I took one of my friend's bikes. I was going to buy a record at the record shop, I went down Blue Hill Avenue to the record shop, then I saw all these Negro people, just throwing rocks. The friend and me, we went—75 policemen, all in a circle, each with helmets on. I was scared, and I was still on the bike. Then a fat policeman came over to me and he had a billy club in his hand and he said, 'come here!' All the Negroes said, 'Run, run!' Then I jumped off the bike and he threw it at me, and I ducked down and it hit the submarine shop and broke the window. I just ran and kept on running. And he chased me through this yard. I jumped a fence. He was big and heavy and I knew he wasn't going to make it. Then he turned to go back out and all I could hear was screams. I guess they beat him up. I went back to see what was going on, saw them carrying a few colored boys, their heads all bashed in, so I went on home. I came back with my brother.

THE ROXBURY/NORTH DORCHESTER NEIGHBORHOOD: 1968-1974

Many of the boys who worked with us still live in the ghetto. Some got out—they were beneficiaries of the federal and local programs which promised so much to the black community. They are in college now, or in the armed services, or job training

programs run by downtown businesses or suburban manu-
facturers. Others are in prison. But many remain in Roxbury/
North Dorchester, living, as they have for years, within a few
blocks of their old junior high school. One of our histories
describes a young man who lives in a low-income housing project
in which he was raised. Others still live at home, with no plans or
prospects for living elsewhere, or, in fact, for doing anything but
repeat the different poverty cycles of their parents.

These young men no longer feel bound to Roxbury and North
Dorchester as the focus of their lives. In junior high school they
knew little else, but now they have been to other neighborhoods
for school or work or other activities. Some have rejected
Roxbury, their old neighbors, old friends. But most still think of
their old neighborhood as home and have become more critical of
its condition as they have had the chance to compare it with other
urban and suburban realities.

They have plenty to criticize. Perhaps the most remarkable
thing about the boys' neighborhood today is how little it has
changed. The war on poverty seems to have passed by this area.
The only indication of its passing are the devastated battlefields
formed by unfinished forays into urban renewal. Dozens of
deteriorating houses were emptied, and many were torn down,
waiting for massive rehabilitation funds that never came. Now,
the number of dilapidated buildings that are abandoned, boarded
up, or demolished is on the increase. White landlords feel trapped
by plummeting resale values and take out their anger on the
houses they own, lowering maintenance standards which would
have seemed impossible to lower. The few people who try to preserve and rehabilitate (mostly middle-class blacks) are faced with
inevitable failure and frustration. They cannot get mortgage
money, the police do not protect the houses while work is being
done on them, the insurance companies will not insure against
fire or theft or vandalism. And the community cannot protect
itself against drug-based crime. Roxbury/North Dorchester
today seems a neighborhood abandoned by the city, destined to
remain a slag heap and a trash barrel for Boston.

Today, there seem to be more empty and littered lots than in the mid-sixties; city services are as inadequate as ever, and suburban support for community demonstrations seems to have dwindled. Cockroaches and rats are a continuing, visible nuisance. A few new playgrounds and blacktopped basketball courts dot the neighborhood, but they seem only to highlight the bleakness, poverty and despair of the area.

THE RYAN JUNIOR HIGH SCHOOL: 1968-1974

The Ryan closed for the summer in June 1967 in an atmosphere of acute tension and incipient riot. It opened in the fall, after the summer's uprising, with the tensions deepened, not alleviated. Fighting continued through the winter among students and between students and staff. Teachers' cars had their tires slashed, their windshields smashed. With the assassination of Martin Luther King, Jr., in April 1968, and the subsequent rioting, nerves reached the breaking point. The school was on the brink of going completely out of control.

The Boston School Committee had to take action. Skimming the surface of the problems, they concluded that the Ryan's dilemma could be resolved by renaming it after black Revolutionary War patriot, Crispus Attucks (thus "recognizing" the needs of the predominantly black student population) and reorganizing it as a middle school (thus eliminating the ninth grade "troublemakers" who were assumed to be the cause of most of the problems). They soon discovered that more complex issues were involved.

In the meantime, the Attucks-Burns Council began to take action. Funded by both the Boston School Committee and the federal government, the Council had a commitment to community involvement and a determination to restructure the education offered at the two middle schools. One of its first demands was that black principals be named to the two schools. After much debate, the superintendent gave in, and two assistant

34

principals from the Attucks became principals of the two schools. They were the first black principals in the city's history. Everyone was hopeful.

It didn't work. The fall of 1968 began a hectic school year with student disruptions that brought the Attucks school to its knees within weeks. A series of false alarms, wastebasket fires, fights, and assaults forced the new principal to close the school at midday on October 23. It reopened, tentatively, the next day, but by October 29 chaos was rampant, and the school was closed for two days. The staff clearly needed help, so the Attucks-Burns Council planned a two-day conference for early November. In the midst of the conference, the black principal of the Attucks resigned, claiming nervous exhaustion.

At that point some community groups decided that it was time to take over the Attucks School. They formed the "Attucks Cabinet" and developed a series of curriculum, staffing, and administration packages, intended to resolve some of the school's chronic difficulties. They presented their programs to staff and student body and were rejected. For months Attucks struggled along in panic and confusion under the bewildered and distressed direction of an assortment of acting principals and acting assistant principals.

A Day at the Attucks, 1968

The office. Harassed and haggard teacher-administrators trying to maintain the appearance of calm and control. Students line the walls, waiting for disposition of their individual cases. The art teacher is escorted into the room wan and drawn, clearly in a state of shock. She had been writing on the blackboard when two seventh-grade boys assaulted her in front of the class. She smooths her skirt nervously. The two boys, small and quick, are being pursued through the corridors by several assistant principals. A group of ten or fifteen boys are, in turn, pursuing the assistant principals. A boy is cornered in the second floor stairwell, but as he is led

35

to the office, the student posse tries to rescue him. A full-scale fight ensues.

The superintendent added to the confusion and conflict which reigned at Attucks by appointing a white principal over the objections of the Attucks-Burns coalition and other community groups. The situation continued to deteriorate. There seemed to be no bottom to the pit of chaos and confusion.

Even in Roxbury/North Dorchester, where school disruptions were common-place, the Attucks became notorious. The entire community was upset by the disastrous atmosphere of the school. Parents, students, community organizations and school officials offered a wide range of prescriptions. But it was too late, and there was too little substance or power to offer. By December 5, 1968, the Attucks had to be closed. Community and concerned staff set up Learning Centers throughout Roxbury/Dorchester, and the Attucks-Burns Council began plans to reopen the school.

By the end of January the School Committee began to insist that the school be reopened and agreed to follow a Coalition plan to phase-in students by grade levels, starting with the youngest, and completing the process by early February. The plan worked briefly, but the destructive atmosphere reasserted itself, and by March armed policemen patrolled the halls during the school day. Nothing could stop the disruption. By mid-April, students were starting wastebasket blazes and setting off five or more false fire alarms a day, each requiring evacuation of the building. It was virtually impossible for the school to function.

The Lunchroom

Lunch period is dreaded by everyone—students, faculty, lunchroom workers. The lady at the cash register sadly shows her scarred, black and blue arms, the result of fending off attempted assaults on the cash box. A heavy steel mesh grill divides the boy's side of the lunchroom from the girl's side—symbolic to students of the school's attempts to control and repress any sense of options they might have. The room is

noisy, echoing with fights, obscenities, kids banging on the
screen. Everyone is tense, guarded.

At the end of the school year the white principal decided that it
was in everyone's best interest if he transferred. His request was
accepted, and a variety of groups pressured the school department to hire a black replacement. After much maneuvering and
negotiation, a black principal was finally hired and given a free
hand to rebuild the staff and make the physical changes that he
and the Attucks-Burns Council believed would make the school
more attractive, functional, and significant in the lives of the
students.

The new principal invested enormous energy in improving the
physical plant. He had new lights installed, inside and out, and
expanded and remodeled the library to dispel its tomblike
atmosphere. The library became a schoolwide project. Students
built mobile bookshelves in their woodworking courses; the
administration provided new, attractive furniture for the room
and had wall-to-wall carpeting installed. The steel dividing grill
was removed from the cafeteria, so that boys and girls could
actually lunch together. For the first time in recent memory,
students were permitted to sit where they wanted.

The combination of firm leadership and visible action seemed
to work. The Attucks School began to settle down. Teachers were
more relaxed, students more interested in learning than anyone
could remember or had dared hope. There was a general sense
that demands were being met, that everyone was being consulted
about procedures which affected him. The 1969-70 school year
had its rough moments, but it was generally considered exciting
and productive.

It didn't last. The superintendent, who recognized remarkable
talent when he saw it, decided that the principal was too valuable
to waste on the Attucks. In a move that stunned the entire
community, he promoted the black principal to area superintendent. The principal accepted the job, and, once again, the
Attucks was faced with the problem of adjusting to new
leadership.

37

After much weary debate, a new principal was chosen—a black woman assistant principal from the Attucks, who was thought to have the advantage of some previous experience with the school. But she was not able to maintain continuity. Morale collapsed under the weight of too many changes and too little leadership. Teachers became tense and worried about their authority; classes were disrupted; fire alarms again plagued the administration. The principal never left her office without the protection of a male teacher aide. Issues of building security dominated, and ultimately smothered, all educational questions.

By 1974 many of the young, highly-qualified staff recruited during the staff reshuffling of 1969-70 were gone, and many of the teachers who remained felt incapable of being more than custodians of children. The students were not as destructive as their predecessors in the late sixties, but there seemed to be little interest in classroom activity and still less hope that things could change and learning flourish. Periodic outbreaks of false alarms and teacher-student scuffles kept tension high. One outbreak, in late 1973, ended in a fire which destroyed the beautiful new library, which the students themselves had built.

During the 1973-74 school year, the atmosphere at Attucks was guarded. Teachers and students seemed to be marking time, waiting for the year to end, being careful to stay out of each other's way. According to a cafeteria worker (one of the few who weathered the last ten years of turmoil), the cafeteria was less often disrupted than it used to be, but students did what they pleased, when they pleased, and no adult dared to try to stop them.

PART II
SIX YOUNG MEN

Chapter
3
Norman Mullen —
Keeping Cool

NORMAN AT FIFTEEN —
COOL AND CLEAN AT THE RYAN

Looking out, neat and serious, from his eighth grade class picture, Norman Mullen gives one little sense of the boy within. He appears to be a clean-cut, rather ordinary boy—medium-sized, a rich, dark brown in color, dressed in nicely pressed chinos and a pullover jersey that buttons at the neck. In fact, in the world of the Ryan School, Norman is far from ordinary. He is informal class leader, practical joker, smart aleck kid, with a rap for the girls and the word for the fellows, respected by teachers for his brains, but a constant source of exasperation because of his self-proclaimed, thoroughgoing laziness.

The "clean" look is no casual concern of Norman's; he cares a lot about his appearance, about the impression he makes. He washes his hair every morning before school, and insists that his clothes be clean and pressed. Not one to volunteer for household tasks, he will iron his own slacks if necessary, and one chief source of fights with his older brother, Junior, concerns the unauthorized borrowing of Junior's knits. Norman rarely misses school—he has too much fun there—but he will refuse to go if he doesn't look right. His mother recalls a time when "he went to the shopping mall at six in the morning, and they said the presser had got in an accident. And they didn't press his clothes. He was so disgusted. He just said, 'Ma, I can't go to school this morning.' I said, 'Now, don't you think that will be a poor excuse if I have to tell the teacher that you had your pants in the cleaner and we couldn't get them out?' All he did say was, 'I'll tell him.' He didn't go that day."

Under the neat knits, all but hidden from view, are terrible burn scars, left from a serious childhood accident. The scars disfigure Norman's back, and small, square marks show where skin was taken from his legs for grafting. But Norman does not seem particularly sensitive about the burns—he says it was an accident, "playing with matches, I really don't even remember too much." His mother says that he has to avoid contact sports "because his back busts loose; his back was real delicate," and notes that he rarely wears shorts on the streets. But neither his back nor his appearance has kept him from developing expert diving skill, and he doesn't seem the least reluctant to show off his swimming abilities in a brief bathing suit.

Nevertheless, Norman's accident was a significant family event, and they all refer to it in discussions of Norman's growing up. If Norman has forgotten nearly everything except the hospital, his mother recalls the day in detail: Norman was five, a kindergartener, with strict instructions to come home, and stay there, after school. Instead, he "came home, took his school clothes off, and he went back out and he didn't put on his coat. It was one of those nice days in October. The doctor said that I better be glad that he disobeyed, 'cause if he had had on more clothes he'd a got burned to death . . . he was swallowed in blaze. That's what saved him, he didn't put on his coat, his heavy coat."

Norman went out to play with a friend, a white boy who lived in the neighborhood, in some sand behind a building on their street. "He told us that he was sitting down, playing in the sand," Mrs. Mullen recalls, "and he said he knows the little boy came behind him, but he didn't know what he did. He felt himself burning, he grabbed his clothes right there and jumped up and he run about two blocks. He went upstairs, and I had left some baby diapers what I had kinda soaking in bleach in a deep part of the sink and he took a glass and put himself out."

The child then—calmly or in shock—carefully changed into a clean T-shirt, and got into his bed, where his mother found him a few minutes later when she returned from shopping. "I looked over that bed," Mrs. Mullen says, "and I discovered him, so I say, 'Well, he must have come home and went to sleep,' that's what I said to myself. So, I went back down to bring the things up, cabbage and stuff, and he was looking at me. I said, 'What's the matter with you, child? so he said, 'Well, Joey burned me.'

"So I say, 'What burn?' I gently come up back of him. He had this big old blister sitting up here, and then I grabbed him up and I looked at his back. It was just like a piece of baked potato. I hollered and I run out of the house and I run straight to Station Nine. I say, 'My child burned at 212 Wells Street,' and that's all they could get out of me. I just run right back, didn't even look for traffic, just jumped out the steps of Station Nine and kept going."

The police rescue team rushed Norman to the hospital, his mother holding him in the back seat of the police car. She had wrapped him in a thin blouse which she had just finished ironing, and she held a tongue depressor in his mouth so his chattering teeth would not bite into his tongue.

The doctor said the boy was "burned down to the last layer of skin," and that he might have to spend as long as two or three months in the hospital. "But he took it so calm, the doctor say that he never experienced a child that have a burn as bad as he did and went through it as calm as Norman did. It was just a mystery."

Norman's calm and self-possession in this crisis was typical of him. As a tiny baby, Mrs. Mullen says, "He cried less than anyone I had, and I always wondered about him, since he was small. And, he'd always be always watching. Sometimes, I thought something's wrong with his eyes, 'cause he'd always be looking around. And he would sleep for hours and hours at a time.

It was important to Joan Mullen to have a quiet child; there was little enough in her life to make things easy for her. Born and raised in North Carolina, from a poor family, she has struggled all her life to make things better for her children. As a girl, she had her own ambitions. "I just wanted to be a high school graduate, and I wanted to be a teacher," she says, "But I didn't see nothing in the way of money. My parents couldn't hardly survive from one week to the other. I had so much interest in school. And I feel that if you didn't have education you just couldn't make it. You just wouldn't be able to fit in the trend of the world."

But college and the dream of being a high school teacher were out of reach for Joan, and she married instead. Freddie Mullen worked on the railroad, and together they moved from Pennsylvania to North Carolina to New Jersey and finally to Boston, where they settled into uneasy family life. "He didn't want the family," Mrs. Mullen says. "He didn't want to stay with the family, but I tried to keep the family together."

Finally, after ten years of marriage and four children, Mr. Mullen left town, leaving Mrs. Mullen on welfare, which she hated. She had the total responsibility for the household. When Norman was eight, Mr. Mullen came back, asking to patch things up. "I felt if he don't live with me and don't straighten out, damn if I'm going to support him. But at that time I wasn't concerned about nothing but the children. And I was concerned about no other man, so I said, 'Why not give the children's father another chance, 'cause they really need us both.'

"My sister, Christine, said that she would just come and stay around the house and we both could work. I got a job out to a school—that's where I made the first pay to send for my sister. I wanted somebody to be responsible, you know, in case somebody come down looking for the parent, there'd be always somebody responsible for them. I sent and got her and I started work, and I got pregnant with Linda. I told Freddie, I said, 'Well, you better get on your job and stay, 'cause I can't take care of this whole family with just that little $50 a week that I made.' And he said, what did I want him to do about it if I'm now pregnant, just what did he care. That was so bad to say. . ." And again he left.

44

At that point, Mrs. Mullen struggled along, telling the social worker that her husband was still with her, because "lying is better than that $126 every two weeks I would have got." But it was impossible to survive on the $50 a week and the Mullens went back on the welfare rolls. Mr. Mullen comes by to visit when he is in town, but he is no longer a regular part of the family unit.

When Norman was nine, his family moved to an apartment on Claremont Avenue: two rows of decaying triple-deckers, facing each other across a littered street through the remains of neglected trees. Claremont had never been an elegant street, although other streets in the immediate neighborhood showed signs of past affluence. The Mullen apartment is in one-half of a double, brick, six family dwelling. If anything, it is less pleasant than the surrounding structures—dirtier, worse kept, and therefore emptier than the others. By the time Norman entered the Ryan School the house was almost empty; only the Mullens lived in that side of the building. The landlord had long since given up even the most routine maintenance; later that year he was cited in a newspaper series for his neglect of his buildings— the Mullen's building was singled out as one which was unfit for human habitation.

Nevertheless, in Norman's ninth-grade year, six humans inhabit it. The Mullen apartment is decayed and bitterly cold. Plastic wrap flaps at the broken windows; the radiators are cool to the touch. Mrs. Mullen keeps her seven-room home neat and clean, but the cheerful throws she puts over her few pieces of overstuffed furniture fail to disguise its worn out condition.

Mrs. Mullen complains about the "scrapples" her five children get into, but they are clearly a close-knit family. Freddie, or Junior as he is called by the family, is usually away; at Norman's age he won an academic and basketball scholarship to a New England prep school. Now, during the academic year, he is in New Hampshire and during most of the summer he attends a program in North Carolina. When he is home, he and Norman are very close. "I'll be with him most of the time," Norman says. And his mother adds that Norman is "lonesome for Junior."

45

Lena, a year younger than Norman, shares with him some friends and party acquaintances, enough so that they tease each other about boy-friends and girl-friends. But, Norman says, "I talk with her a lot, but I don't do much with them, really. She gets mad at me and I have to, you know, put her in her place." Lynette, at ten, is the butt of jokes and teasing from the rest of the children, especially Norman. When Lynette walks through the living room, Norman says, "Ooo, look at those skinny legs." But Lynette comes back at him: "Ooo, look at those long toes," and so starts an argument. Then, Norman says, his mother starts yelling " 'Why don't you two shut up,' or something like that. But, you know, you don't hurt nobody by arguing."

Only Linda, the baby, is not part of the general contention. Norman says a little scornfully that his mother "always babies the youngest one—just about all mothers do that." But even he, who will not go on a shopping trip with Lena or Lynette, will take Linda along, putting up with her continual demands that he buy her everything she sees.

The Mullen children have many friends, but they rarely bring them home. In the afternoons, after school, Norman plays a little basketball with his buddies, especially Frankie Fletcher who is his best friend when Junior is away at school. But then he comes home, "I sit with my sister, bring out a record player, one of those portable ones. Play records." They feel that their apartment is for the family. The most frequent guest is Mrs. Mullen's brother Lou, who is "like an older brother," to Norman. Everyone likes Uncle Lou, the children because "he takes them to the show and everything," Norman says, and Mrs. Mullen because he gives her advice and support on family affairs.

Norman says that he would like to live near his family when he grows up, "so we can all help each other," and adds that if he gets into any kind of trouble, the person he would want to depend on is Junior. The Mullens seem able to accept one another for what they are. They may require a little pushing around now and then to keep them shaped up, but individual integrity is respected. Junior, for instance, says that Norman is a little lazy, but it is almost impossible to get him to name any way in which he would want him to change. Mrs. Mullen has nurtured the dream that all her children will go to college, but she is willing to accept Norman's reluctance to take a test which might win him a prep school scholarship. "After he didn't want to go, I didn't want to force him into it," she says.

But sometimes this hands-off policy in family affairs bothers Mrs. Mullen. She worries about her children's safety. When Junior is home, she says, "He and Norman go to these house parties. I never did like these house parties, 'cause here when I see them coming out and fighting and beating on young innocent boys, you know, all that stuff. And then the first thing jumping in my mind, mine would be the victim of the same thing." But, she adds, the boys say, " 'You got to let us go and trust us,' but I be thinking something would happen to them, you know? And sometime they say, 'I'm no little baby now.' " And, in the end, she always lets them go.

Mrs. Mullen is unquestionably the center of her family. She is a woman with strong ideas about what she wants, and she is a fiercely devoted mother whose devotion is reciprocated by her children. The two oldest boys regard her with undisguised affection and respect. Junior says, "She's really, she treats us really nice and sometimes she gets frustrated when we get all—when we get on her nerves and all that. But most of the time she's all right. I don't really have the words to explain her. You know. It's love, I guess." Norman agrees, saying that he cares more about his mother than about anyone else, and that she is the person who cares most about him. On another occasion, Norman looked at a picture of an obviously hungry and miserable family. Asked what he thought the mother was thinking about, he answered, "Her children . . . should get something to eat . . . some heat." He cannot envision a mother who thinks first of herself.

The boys' vision of Mr. Mullen is different. Looking at another picture of a family at dinner, Norman says that he thinks the father is "anxious to eat," while the mother is concerned about whether the family is enjoying their food. His father, he says, is a "nice guy," who "doesn't hardly ever get upset." But it is his

47

mother who "feeds me, clothes me . . . gives me money and everything." Junior sums up the boys' feelings about their father: "He doesn't like to work, you know . . . he's just like me. He likes to talk about things. He talks to me a lot. We sit down and have a discussion or something, and—I don't know—he's—I think he's mixed up or something, 'cause sometimes he tells us he loves us and everything, but he doesn't want to do anything for us. And I just don't—I don't understand that part about him."

Although Mrs. Mullen is bitter about much of Freddie Mullen's behavior, she respects his concern for the children. She allows him to stay at the apartment when he visits Boston and encourages Junior to visit him in Newark. If she is constantly telling Junior and Norman not to be lazy like their father, she also compares Junior to him with some affection. "Always talking, always trying to find out something, happy-go-lucky, just like his father is." And, in the midst of a discussion of all the times her husband failed her, Mrs. Mullen breaks off to note that "he would go away and he stayed months at a time, but if you say one thing, he always stay right behind us, you know, keep close check on them (the children)."

NORMAN IN THE FAMILY—
JUNIOR HIGH SCHOOL CHANGES

Norman has always been the quiet, watchful child in a family of talkers. "Compared with the other children," his mother says, "he didn't do a whole lot of crying, and just wasn't too much trouble, having never been too much trouble." But now, in junior high school, he has begun to talk more, to fight more openly and effectively with his sisters, to talk back to his mother. Junior attributes his change to his beginning "to mess around with girls." His mother says "he's kinda hard to get along with" these days and says it is because he misses Junior. "He's always saying, 'Mom, you think I'm a little old bitty boy now,'" she sighs. "And I don't know how to get at it, he's so big you know."

Everyone (including Norman) agrees that he is lazy—both in school and around the house. Junior says, "He doesn't want to do anything around the house. He doesn't even want to take out the garbage." Mrs. Mullen modifies Junior's judgment, saying, "He does a lot of things for himself, like he washes socks out. And there was the time when the washing machine wasn't working, he'd say, 'Ma get the clothes together; I'll take them to the washer.'" Her appreciation for his offer was somewhat tempered by her knowledge that Norman's own clothes were in that load, and he wanted them done more than she did. But she recounts the incident with good humor—Norman's reluctance to help with the household chores is accepted as a fact of life.

But, during his junior high school years, Mrs. Mullen has seen in Norman a kind of withdrawal and independence that goes beyond the ordinary adolescent reluctance to help with chores. She says that, unlike Junior, Norman never seemed to want much affection or attention from her. "He don't care too much about it. Norman just wants to be Norman and don't want you to put nothing else around. And he don't like pity. He don't like to be pitied." Once, a teacher at the Ryan sent home a note, on the back of his report card, saying that Norman "needed more love and affection." According to Mrs. Mullen, "I said, 'What does she mean, Norman? I wonder what she means about that?' He said, 'I don't know.' And he asked me what did I think."

Norman withdraws from displays of affection. He also has trouble asking for any kind of help, even from Junior, who is his best friend as well as his brother. "He don't want to have the idea that his brother can help him," Mrs. Mullen says. "He don't want Junior just telling him how to do his homework. He'll say, 'Oh, I know that, I know that.' They'll be playing around, and Junior tell him, 'Oh no, you don't. If you knew, you'd have it on that paper.' Norman said, 'Yeah, you're right. If I knew it I'd put it on that paper.' Then he'd say, 'Let's see how you got that.' He didn't want to admit that he really didn't know it, you know, because he don't think his brother's smarter than he is."

Norman keeps more to himself now. "I see him in his room, kinda being quiet, all alone by himself," Mrs. Mullen says. "He don't want nobody in there with him, and he just laying there, seem to be in there thinking, you know, with his eyes shut, he just be in there thinking and don't want to be bothered by nobody in there." Sometimes Norman locks the door to his room and paints; sometimes he just lies on the bed for hours, not quite asleep, making plans.

Norman With His Friends

Norman on the street, at parties, rapping with girls, is a different person. He says he is "kinda quiet" with his mother, but with his friends he likes to hook classes, play jokes, or go to parties with "a lot of people gettin' around, dancing and talking. And some of them are drinking."

His sense of caution and control, however, remains. The young people Norman parties with do not fight much—"a couple, sometimes, little ones . . . fists, not cutting or nothing like that," and they are careful about their relationships with girls. Norman says that his friends do not talk about sex very much "because that's your own personal business. You don't say nothing," and adds that he does not go out looking for sex, because "that stuff gets you into trouble." With some sympathy, he describes one member of his crowd whose girl had a baby, but there is a touch of disdain for "that white boy" who didn't have enough luck or sense to keep himself in the clear.

Norman's friends tend to stay away from trouble—they play basketball and flirt with girls, but they do not get into heavy drinking, heavy dope, or serious theft. Norman and his friends restrict themselves to picking up an occasional tie in the local discount clothing store.

Norman's group of friends is loose-knit. The group has no rules, Norman says, and no leader—they are simply a group of guys who grew up together and graduated from playing 'One-two-three, cop on me, o'lario' to more adolescent games. They get together, Norman says, and "everybody, they make any suggestions, and then say—'Yeah, let's do that' or 'Why don't we go to that party?' or something. Or someone will say, 'Let's go over to the basketball court.' And then whoever want to go there, they say 'me,' 'me' and whoever want to go to a basketball court will say, 'me.' "

Within the group, Norman's only deep personal attachment is to Junior. Mrs. Mullen says that "Junior, when they were small, never would go nowhere that he was running around unless he had Norman by the hand. And then I used to look out there, and I know when I didn't see one, they both were lost. And when, whenever you find them, he would have his hand, wherever they would be. And he couldn't have a chance to play because they were going along with other children, he was standing holding Norman's hand. And if he were playing, sit Norman down on the side of him, to play a while, then he'd take his hand back." This protective relationship has lasted, although Junior says that Norman sometimes rebels against it these days: "He looks up to me. Sometimes, he acts like he doesn't like me. Most of the time he'll fight me—tell me he doesn't want to do this. But he looks up to me, I know that. Just the way he acts. If he gets in trouble, I'm there to help him. If he's in trouble, I'm there. If I'm in trouble, he's there to help me." Norman agrees. He says he likes Junior best of anyone, that he would like to be more like his brother, and that Junior is the only person in the family who really understands him.

When Junior is gone, Norman has another friend, Frankie Fletcher, who takes over as his running buddy. Frankie and Norman have been friends since they were children on Claremont Avenue together. According to Frankie, Norman "started going out, trying to be a big bully. So me and him had a fight, and he beat me up and my mother brought me and him upstairs and started talking to us, talking about we should be good friends, shouldn't fight, get to know each other much better and have more fun."

They do have fun, shooting the breeze, smoking reefer together from time to time, playing pool. Frankie says that Norman is a tease, constantly looking for victims for his jokes. Frankie will ask Norman for a cigarette when he has run out; Norman says "no," and then smokes one in front of him. Frankie is watching television; Norman will pass through the room and switch it off. Frankie says that Norman is selfish, but he accepts the teasing and the selfishness. He is the follower, but he says that if he were in trouble, Norman would be the person he would trust most.

Norman in School

"Norman, I think, is average ability," says Mr. Hyland, the popular black history teacher who is Norman's favorite at the Ryan. "Somewhat lazy; he needed prodding, but he could do good work when prodded. Wasn't the type of child that would go out independently and *do*. Even when it came time to take a trip to the UN, while all the students were asked to bring $2.00 and the other money was being paid through outside sources, he was lazy, I would say, too lazy to bring the $2.00.'"

Mr. Hyland says he doesn't know what Norman's I.Q. is, but "I would be able to take a guess it would probably be average. But again, this would probably be gauged on the day that he took the exam, how he was feeling about it. It would be a sleeper as far as I.Q. is concerned, because here is a kid who would give you the impression if you didn't know him or hadn't over a period of time, that, you know, he was just there. But you would know that he wasn't stupid by a long shot."

Norman would agree about the laziness, about his ability to do better, about the limitation of his ambition. He has flatly refused to take college track classes, despite his statement that his mother and his teachers think he could and should go to college. At the beginning of ninth grade, he was a candidate for the Independent School Talent Search Program—the organization that had sent Junior to prep school. His mother came to school to check out application procedures and Norman filled out the application. But on the day of the test, Norman withdrew, telling the teacher in charge of the test that he had lost interest. The teacher, who had been excited about Norman's prospects, was disappointed, but said that he "found it typical. Maybe it's my attitude towards these [black] kids, but they just don't want to expend themselves any more than necessary."

Mr. Hyland, as a black, explains Norman's behavior somewhat differently. "I would say he doesn't really know that he has the ability," he says. "Then again, I might be wrong. This might be a part of what I call passive resistance. But off the top of my head, I would say he gives the impression that he doesn't believe he has the ability."

Norman has his own reasons. He doesn't want to go to college, he says, or into a college-bound program, because "college costs money." He would prefer Dorchester High School, because it "got a good art course . . . a lot of girls." Junior might prefer a private school in the boonies, with no girls and only six other black boys, because there he can find "teachers who care about you." But Norman is Norman, and he doesn't especially want teachers caring about him. He is unwilling to give up his familiar surroundings.

"School's essential," he says, "I know that. You have to have it, if you want to be around the world. But if you didn't have to take school, you know, if school wasn't necessary, I sure wouldn't go." And his chief desire is to get the essentials over with as painlessly as possible. "I guess I can do the work better . . . I just don't want to," he says. "You know, an A you have to do all that stuff. And a B's just like it. So is a C. You pass with either one. So I just do as much as I can get by with. A lot of people, they break their backs trying to get an A. It's just the same thing. You just get a piece of paper says the Honor Roll."

Norman's strategy of "getting by" in school started early. "It was mostly playing in kindergarten," he recalls, "Having fun. And when I got to first grade, I thought it was gonna be hard . . . like you go to one grade, if you pass that, I thought the next grade would be harder. But it seems easier. Like, in the second grade, you just go over most of the things you had in the first grade. The same with all the other ones, too. Like, in the seventh grade we went over the things we had in the sixth grade about half the year. And then we started with square root and stuff like that. So I just sat the eighth grade out. And in ninth grade, the only thing different was algebra."

His junior high school classmates and teachers are well aware of the ease with which Norman coasts through classes. Brian Henry, whose grades are far better than Norman's, describes him as "a regular genius. He always got questions right. I'd say he was right around 99% of the time." And Mr. Hyland says that "if you called on him, prodded him, and got him up out of his seat, he could give you some form of answer, an answer that would be one which he would be pretty sure was near what the answer to the question was."

But Norman does not really care about that—not now. He goes to school, he says, "mainly for gym . . . and playing around with the girls." He has no objection to classes—in fact, he prefers the tougher teachers, like Mr. Hyland and Mr. James, who "give you the paddle if you don't do the homework . . . you have to pay attention there." But the true pleasure of school is that "it's like an adventure, you know . . . hooking class and stuff, hoping you won't get caught or nothing like that." And it is this kind of fun that he is looking forward to continuing, with the old Ryan crowd, in Dorchester High, while Junior slaves over his books in New Hampshire, and Lena does her endless hours of homework for her METCO high school.

Norman has not yet made any connections between going to school and preparing for a career. He things vaguely of being a pilot, "learning how to fly a plane and the different parts. Say, like you're going on a mission tomorrow. You have to study the flight pattern and everything . . . just where to go and how to get there and what to do when you get there." He adds that he might want to be a gunner instead, like in the "war pictures," or maybe an "electrician in the Air Force or something like that." He briefly considers airplane maintenance (he knows someone who does that), but rejects it. He says he does not want to do "manual labor."

Mr. Hyland feels that Norman is the "type of kid who'll get by at whatever he decides to do. He could be a draftsman, hold down any blue collar job, and with a little effort he could a professional person, a good engineer." He adds that he could also do "good work with teenagers, or with children, as he seems to be patient, easy-going and everything."

But Norman, like most fourteen-year olds, lives from day to day. As for the future, he says, "I don't wanta do nothing. To tell the truth, I just want the money to come out of the skies while I just sit home, enjoy myself. But I know that won't happen."

Norman's Sense of Racial Identity

Although Norman is not clear about his future, he has, at fourteen, some deep suspicions about whites and a strong sense of his own blackness. His mother attributes Norman's dislike of whites to the time he was burned by his little white friend. "I can remember when he got burned, and he was there and he kept saying this little white boy burned him. And he said, 'But he was my friend; but he was my friend.' And I wonder did he, as he got big and he read about the race strife, and I wonder was that a barrier in his mind. He really—that wasn't really his friend, you know, and I wonder did that take an effect on his thinking now. That he thought he was so close and he was so dear, but yet he tried to destroy him."

Norman, she says, is far more anti-white than anyone in the family. He teases Junior about being "always up there with them whiteys," and avoids any interracial contact when possible. But he shares with Junior and his sisters a pride in being black carefully nurtured by Mrs. Mullen. She never allowed the word "nigger" to be used in her home; as the children came home, in their preschool years, asking what the word meant, she says, "I told mine, I said, 'Don't you worry about your skin, because you're great, we're a great nation,' I tell them all that. I say, 'We're proud to be black.' And I say, 'And one day, you'll find out.'" She adds, a bit ruefully, "But I haven't seen no way—no kind of possible way, you know, nobody being great, but I always use that word. I just have great trust or something. I don't know. I don't want them to live to feel they were less superior."

The lesson has been learned. The girls tease Junior about the darkness of his skin. Mrs. Mullen says, "Lena says, 'Old Black Junior,' and he say, 'I'm proud to be black,' and put his arm up against hers." Norman says he feels that Negroes are "just as good or even better," than whites, but that the white world "just don't give us a chance." He feels called upon to defend his race frequently, and reports those incidents with more glee than distress at the racial slur. "At City Point, one day," he says, "some white boys came up . . . 'Hey, niggers' . . . We chased them, beat the shit out of them, took their money. We used to always beat up white boys."

Norman is one of the few students at the Ryan who feels that the school should be entirely re-designed around the tastes and needs of black students. "Get all the white teachers out . . . and the white students . . . for one thing. Give better lunches . . . no white people's food. We want soul food—corn bread, pork chops, chicken, stuff like that." Unlike several other boys, Norman says that he would rather be taught by black teachers than by white, in any subject, because "the Negro, he knows how to get along with you, while the white one, he just wants to be a boss and everything."

And the school that he would design to replace the Ryan, is his idea of the black junior high school student's dream: "Chemistry laboratory, about three gyms, shops . . . I wouldn't have any algebra teachers . . . or physics. Have Negro history . . . not all that American stuff . . . all Negroes, no whites. In the cafeteria, I wouldn't have all that dried up stuff in the can. I'd have the home-cooked food. And I'd have a swimming pool . . ." He leans back, imagining. "Benches all around outside . . . kids wanta just sit around . . . talk."

NORMAN AT DORCHESTER HIGH

Two important things happened to Norman in the summer between junior high school and high school. First, the family moved from the run-down triple decker on Claremont Avenue to the Franklin Hill Housing Project. Second, Norman got his first regular paying job.

The move from Claremont Avenue to the project was Mrs. Mullen's idea, and it is not especially popular with the rest of the family. "They don't like it down there," Mrs. Mullen explains. "They don't like it down in the project, that's what they tell me. They say nothing to do down there. It's not nothing but the skating rink down there that they go to, or in the summertime when the municipal swimming pool is open down there, they go for swims. They say, 'Ma, we want to move back to Roxbury.' I'd been waiting—I'd been trying to get in that project for about ten years."

Unquestionably, the Franklin Hill apartment is easier to live in than the one on Claremont Avenue. "I like the heat," Mrs. Mullen says. "I like it because I've got plenty of hot water, and when you pay one rent you pay your light bill and gas bill, everything go in one bill." The new apartment is warmer and more comfortable than the Claremont Avenue place, and it has some new furniture, including a television set.

But Norman misses his old friends, and spends a good deal of time back at Claremont, "hanging around" and occasionally going over to the "Y" for some basketball practice or a swim. Further, he doesn't like integrated Dorchester. When he thinks of his new neighborhood, he says with some distaste, he thinks first of "white people." He adds, after some thought, that the neighborhood is "pretty clean," but that is the only good thing he has to say about it.

Norman says, "I'm not always at home, and when I am, I don't stay too much," so the move has not affected him as much as it has his younger sisters. In the summer between Ryan and Dorchester High, Norman's days were absorbed by work, his evenings by his friends. He worked in the Vacation Bible School at a local church, a job acquired through the influence of his mother, who works as a teacher's aide for the church school program. Norman liked the job, which involved "watching all those little kids, read the Bible to them, teach them arts and crafts. . . stuff like that." Norman earned $25.00 a week at the Bible School, thereby freeing himself from total financial dependence on his mother. He liked the priest who ran the program, and the time in the afternoon when the little children had gone home, leaving the student aides to their own devices. "We had fun during that time," Norman says. His primary objection to the job had to do with his immediate supervisor, a woman whom Norman describes as "Bossy . . . you know, she wants everything just right."

Evidently, Norman did enough things "just right," to be rehired by the church program during the school year. Now, as a Dorchester High School student, his life is packed with activity. Norman leaves for school early, to give himself some time for "walking around school and letting everybody see me." After school, he has to put on speed to get to the church by 3:30 for the beginning of the after-school program. Evenings are devoted to the cultivation of his social life. He is home hardly at all, and when he is there he is not the slow-moving boy his mother remembers.

"I crack jokes," Norman says of his home style. "I eat a lot. Sometimes I act mean towards my sisters—yell at them a lot, call them names, slap them around once or twice every now and then, just to let them know who's the boss. I always tell Junior how to do things. I'm always sayin' 'What's you doin'—that ain't cool.' I'll always be straightening him out." He adds that his mother and he fight more than they used to. "My mother's always gonna yell at me. Soon as she starts to yell, I always have something to say— 'that's right'—something like that. I just straighten her out, just say my little piece and then stop. She keeps going on, so all I have to do is say, 'I'm going to bed' and then stop and listen to her . . . or don't listen to her, or whatever."

Norman's fights with his mother over old issues—his reluctance to help in the house, his desires for more money, more clothes, more freedom. Mrs. Mullen has always been careful with money, as much from principle as from necessity, although the necessity has always been there. She has given the children any spending money she could spare, and Norman has gotten his share. "Like every morning I would give him 50 cents," she says, to cover carfare to school and lunch, "but some mornings I give him a dollar and on Sunday I give him a couple dollars to go down to the skating rink or to a movie." At the same time, she feels that the children must learn to respect money, and to respect the scarcity of the family resources.

"A lot of the time they ask me," she says, "I don't give in. Money's so hard to hold onto and I know the value of not spending it so much. I figure, if you can do without something, do without. When I can't open that pocketbook and get food money out of there or I can't open that pocketbook and get clothes money out of there it's bad conditions, and we have to limit that money."

She is delighted that Norman now has steady work. "If he didn't have that $12 or $14, he'd be copping on me every week about it—'I need this, I need that,' but now I just say, 'You're making that down there and you're going to use it for some of the things that you need most.' Then that's where I'd be mean. Now I make him use that to help himself out."

But Norman sees his earnings as a supplement to the money he can get from his mother, not a replacement for it. "He can have a dollar in there," Mrs. Mullen complains good-humoredly, "and tell me, 'Ma, I need my lunch money.' And then I say, 'Well, what you gonna do with that dollar?' He says, 'Don't ask me how I use my dollar,' and he'll be gone. I suggest, 'Why can't you use that?' and when I make that suggestion, he say, 'Well, that's okay, Ma, if

59

you're going to preach about it, I'll go ahead and use it.' She imitates Norman's huffy, put-upon tone as she quotes him, and then laughs.

Mrs. Mullen is delighted with Norman's job for more than the money it brings in. She is more enthusiastic about his work than he is. Norman says, "On the job, I just do what I'm supposed to do; I don't do no more than what I'm supposed to do." But, he adds, "When I do what I'm supposed to do, I want to do it right." According to his mother, "He does a beautiful job, the education director told me. She say when he gets down to his work that he's really good, because he have conferences with the education director, twice, I think it's twice a week. They make lesson plans, go over lesson plans with the head teacher. And so far, I mean he don't miss no time, he's always on the job." She laughs. "Whether it's the money involved, I don't know, but he does a beautiful job with the children."

The after-school program is more demanding than the summer Bible School. The tutors "help with just about all subjects that the children have in the fourth grade. Reading and arithmetic." Mrs. Mullen says that Norman "barely says anything about it," but he did ask once or twice for help on his lesson plans. His supervisor is the white "bossy lady" from the summer, who "makes me sick," sometimes, according to Norman, but whose demands seem to produce results. Mrs. Mullen says, "I think she was kind of tough on him, but I can see the reason because I work, I help out down there in the afternoon program and there's so many of those children, if you just go in without any discipline, they'll just take over." Norman, who is not as sympathetic, says, "She wants everything done her way . . . she's always bossing you, telling you what to do."

Little as he may like it, Norman puts up with being bossed, because the money he earns is essential for his social life, now his central concern. Girls have become important to Norman, and his "rap" is one of his most cherished skills. "I rap some dynamite stuff," he says, "especially with girls. I don't know what it is about me; it's just that a lot of people are scared to say certain things. I just say anything, 'cause I don't care what they think about it. I figure—if I say so and so, they'll think this and that. I say, 'Well, I think I'll say it, 'cause I want them to think like that.' So I go about that and they give me an answer and I'll answer them. I'm not scared to say anything and I just say it—meaning it or not meaning it—I'll just say it and try to make like I mean it.

"With my girl friend, I can be real loving, but whenever she steps out of line, whenever she does anything that's out of the way, then I straighten her out. Like if she gets loud—I can't stand a girl who gets loud—so I tell her, 'Hey, wait a minute, you got to be cool!' With girls—I always give them compliments and stuff, play with them. I know what to say to con people, to get what I want, especially the girls, I blow their minds all different kinds of ways. I got various ways, various techniques. Depends on the girl and how she is."

But he is against any permanent relationship. "I always tell them I'm interested in the present," Norman says. He adds that he has never gotten a girl pregnant because "I ain't got no time for no babies right now . . . no time at all."

For all his interest in girls, Norman's most serious relationships are with his running buddies. Junior is still his closest friend, and Frankie Fletcher is next. The composition of the crowd has not altered with the transition to high school. Norman and his friends "do something together every night. Last night we went out to the party and got high, talked to the girls . . . then we went down to Sack's Steak House and stood around there for a while." Norman never drinks—"I can't stand it," he says—but he frequently smokes marijuana and, late in high school, experiments with harder drugs. "Heroin, once in a while . . . I smell a whole lot of coke. I act the way my friends act," Norman says, "They all act like me anyway. We talk a lot, we talk about money and girls and what we going to do when we get older."

Mrs. Mullen is increasingly alarmed about Norman's friends, he says, and disagrees sharply with their values. "Like with drugs," he says, "I think reefer is nothing, but she thinks it's something big and dangerous. My friends think it's nothing. Staying out late . . . she thinks that's something real bad. I don't think it's nothing . . . my friends don't. She don't even like me going down to the pool room and all you do there is shoot pool. But she thinks there's something else. She's a real nice lady," Norman adds. "It's just that she's not too hip. She's not too down with what's going on today."

Norman in the Classroom—Mr. Cool

Throughout his high school years, Norman seems to view school as an extension of his social arena, a less interesting version of the Sack's Steak House scene. Some of his friends, he says, dropped out of school soon after junior high, "I guess because they got tired of going. A lot of times I felt like stopping, but I never did—kept on going. I liked school. I didn't like the work, so if I got out of school I couldn't just stay home all the time, 'cause that'll be boring too, so I just fool around in school. I had fun.

"Around school, I like to get a lot of play. But when I'm in school, I be pretty cool. I don't say too much or do too much. I just go to my class, sit in the back of the room and I sit there the whole class. If the teacher happens to call on me, I'll say, 'Well, the answer is this and that' or if I don't know the answer, I say, 'I don't know' and I just sit there."

Norman's cool has not endeared him to his high school teachers any more than it did to Mr. Hyland. "Mrs. Carmichael, my business law teacher, seemed like she just always pick on me," Norman complains. "She'd ask me a question—I didn't know nothing about business law anyway—I could never understand what she was talking about. I'd say, 'I don't know' and she'd come right back and ask me again, and you know I'm going to say 'I don't know.' She just keeps on asking me, thinking that it's going to make me feel stupid. But it didn't. I didn't care. If I say one thing to somebody, she'd jump right on my back—'Mr. Mullen, be quiet'—or 'Shut up'—or this and that. It was funny when she'd be picking on me, because I'd always be laughing. And I'd crack a joke and everybody in the class would be laughing at her, and she'd feel like a fool."

Norman's native intelligence did not get him as far at Dorchester High as it did at the Ryan. "I used to get A's and B's," Norman says, "Then I got in high school and I started going down. I don't think I did any homework in business law all year; I failed that anyway. I did English homework because that was real easy—I did that in school. Bookkeeping I copied from somebody, usually." Norman says that his mother is concerned about his marks, " 'cause everybody in my family was getting good grades."

Despite his poor academic performance, Norman reports, the Dorchester High School guidance counselors "thought I should go on to college. But I was in a business course. I wasn't thinking about going to college then. I always told them I would go to a business school after I got out of high school. I don't know if they believed me or not . . ."

By his senior year, he has come to feel that "I want to graduate from college, but I don't want to go to school for all that many more years." So he is considering a variety of shorter programs which might help him achieve his work goal: "a job that is something that I know how to do—something that they are paying me for knowing how to do, not something that they're going to tell me, say, 'This is what I want you to do and I want you to do it like this.' I want them to say 'Do such and such, you know how to do it, you just do it the way you know how.' "

Norman has never had a job that fit his description. After the church after-school program and summer Bible School, where he was told what to do in great detail by his white supervisor, he went to another job in a U.S. Army Housing Supply Warehouse in a Boston suburb. Norman says that was the best job he ever had, although he adds that he left because "I couldn't take it. It was boring. I didn't do hardly nothing. We slept on the mattresses most of the time." Occasionally, the regular workers would take a truck to pick up furniture, leaving Norman to "sit at the desk and answer the phone. We sit down with the sergeant and the other airmen and we'd all sit down and be laughing and joking and drinking coffee and stuff—this was in the morning. Then we'd go to lunch and come back. They have to find something for us to do so we could say we did something that day. Or like when one of the officers come in, he'd say, 'O.K., go on everybody, and look like you're doing something.' Sometimes we just disappeared.

"On Wednesday, a big truck will come in and we have to load furniture on the truck and then we have to go with the truck to deliver the furniture. I hated that day because this was the day we worked. I was glad when they told me I was working in the laundry on Wednesdays, 'cause all I did was sit there. But that was real boring, 'cause it was so easy. I hardly did anything.

"I want a job where I learn to do something at it . . . that no one else around me knows how to do, so that no one could tell me how I'm supposed to do it. And I want it to be something that's in demand, that if something happens with the job that you're not working any more you can always go and find another one. They'll be looking for you instead of you looking for them."

By the end of his senior year at Dorchester High, Norman thinks he has found a career possibility which would give him the independence he wants and the money he needs. At first, he says, computer programming appealed to him, but then a representative from a local business college "told me about that court stenographer—it's that man who sits next to the judge with that little machine and be taking down everything. That's pretty cool. It sounded like it might be pretty nice. You only work ten months out of the year and the other two are paid vacation. You're not doing anything—that's nice—I like that. And it might be interesting to hear all those different cases every day." Norman thinks that life would suit him. The only problem he foresees is that "I know I'm not going to like getting up in the morning to work."

Norman on Race—Increasing Bitterness

Norman sees discrimination, not lack of training, as the major barrier between him and a good job. He has chosen court stenography as a career partly because he thinks it offers an open opportunity for blacks. In his opinion, few other fields do. "This is a white man's country," Norman says. "You can get better jobs being a white, better homes, a whole lot of things. Being black slows you down. It stops you from getting ahead. I can't see no advantages in being black . . . none at all. All I can see is disadvantages."

Neither does Norman see much hope in the Black Power movement—either the militant or the nonviolent wing. He is aware of a variety of groups, ranging from the NAACP to the Black Panthers, but he holds himself aloof from their activities. "I don't go for it myself. I mean, it's groovy, and if they can do it, it's a good idea, but I don't think that too much is going to come out of it." No group, he says firmly, speaks for Norman Mullen. "Actually, I'm just for myself, to tell the truth. I'm just out for me."

Norman says that he participated in the 1968 riots in Roxbury, but not because he thought he was striking a blow for black power. "I just looted," he says, "to get something." Nevertheless, he thinks that riots may hold some small hope for the future of blacks in America. "Maybe this rioting and protesting will make them stop and think things could be made better." But he sees no role for himself in that effort. "I never found a cause that I wanted to support," Norman says. "My voice wouldn't be heard . . . they wouldn't hear me if I tried."

AFTER HIGH SCHOOL—NORMAN IN A FUNK

At high school graduation, Norman looks very different from the super-clean, open-faced ninth grader who had entered Dorchester High. He is taller, thinner, more lethargic. His skin is sallow and unhealthy; he looks as though he hasn't been out in the daylight for a long time. Dressed for a hot summer day in a tank top and a pair of shorts, Norman looks just slightly unkempt— hardly noticeable in another young man, but unusual for Norman, whose appearance has always mattered so much to him.

"Ain't nothing been happening," he complains in the summer after his high school graduation. "Ain't nothin' goin' on. It's a drag. Except that I graduated from school. That was it. Now I don't do nothin'. I'm lazy now, see. I don't want to work. I don't like to get up. I usually don't get out of bed until around four o'clock.

"There's nothing to do now. I be day dreaming sometimes. Sometimes I just try to go back to sleep. If I can't, I just go ahead and get up. But mostly, I keep dozing off. Usually I be day dreaming, day dreaming about money. Then all of a sudden I stop day dreaming and be on my way. Or somebody comes to get me up. There's just nothing to do. If somebody comes by, then I'll have something to do, so I do it. But if not, they'll be down to the poolroom, and that's just sitting around, shooting pool. You go right out of your mind."

If going out during the day is unattractive to Norman, staying home is not much better. His relationship with his mother has deteriorated. She is worried sick about him, and he cannot bear her badgering. "She's always yelling at me, and there's no time to talk in between that yelling," Norman says. "So I got to be ready to go whenever she starts that yelling. She yells about work, tells me to get a job. I say I can't find no job. She wakes me up at 8 a.m., tells me to get a job. I don't want to get no job yet, and it's hard to find a job this time in the summer, but she's always bugging me, keeps on bugging me."

She compares Norman with his father, which hurts him. Although he thinks of his father as a "cool old man who knows what's going on in the city," he does not want to be like him. Asked what his father wants him to be, Norman explodes, "I don't know how that fool feels! I never talk to him." And so it hurts when his mother "tells me I take after my father. She says he was lazy and she's always calling me lazy.

"I can't think of anything that she likes. She never tells me she likes anything about me. I heard her describe me to people before—calling me a worthless this and worthless that, but I don't think she means it. Maybe she's just fooling . . . I don't know what she was saying seriously . . . I don't know. She'd say 'He's my second oldest boy, but he's lazy and he only thinks of himself.' I don't know." And even in his funk, Norman defends himself. "I'm not lazy," he says, "and I'm not worthless, and I don't only think of myself."

Norman and his mother still argue over money. "Once in a great while she used to give me money," Norman says. "But now that she keeps getting on my back about getting a job, she says she's not going to give me money." He gets some money from his girl friend now, and some from an occasional hustle. "I go boosting sometimes. You usually get something and then you sell that. You get about five pairs of pants and sell them for about $8 apiece and you have $40." But, unlike Doug Jones, Norman does not like the risk of stealing. When he looks toward his future, he says he plans to "work hard. I want to have a house and a nice car, money in the bank, good job—then I'll be happy. Everything I have now is not mine—it's my mother's."

During this unhappy time, Norman is sunk in lassitude, drugs, and gloom. His pupils are dilated, his movements slow, out-of-touch. He rarely leaves the house, almost never during the day unless his mother screams him out. But even lying on his bed, day after day, until 4, 6, 8 p.m., Norman's mind is working. "I have to be always planning something," he says. "Always planning something—always planning to do something, scheming. Scheming to get around somebody, scheming for all different kinds of things. Every time I go some place there's something I got to scheme on . . . something always comes up that I have to say, 'Well, somehow I got to do this,' 'How am I going to do this?' See, I'll get from so and so, or this and that. If I really want it, I usually will get it . . . somehow, if I don't have it myself."

Many of his plans involve a grand future; a house in Beverly Hills, "with a Rolls Royce, garden, a swimming pool, a chauffeur. I'd like it to look like a palace, but it probably won't. I'd like to have gold chairs, velvet cushions, carpets on the floor, rich paintings all over the walls; expensive furniture, a maid to do the work, a butler to answer the door. Outside, I'd just want the building to be together, not falling apart."

One thing the future does not contain, Norman says, is a wife. He says firmly: "I wouldn't want to marry no one. I don't need marriage—what am I going to get out of marriage that I can't without being married? Marriage never crosses my mind. That is the farthest thing from my mind: marriage and dying. Two things I never think about."

GETTING OUT OF THE FUNK—
MOVING ON TO COLLEGE

Looking back on that bad time, from the perspective of three years later, Norman says, "There's never going to be another year like that one for me as long as I live. That was terrible, wow!"

The long summer of 1971 slid into fall, and Norman was less and less able to move. He drifted more deeply into drugs—"Different people turned me on to it . . . I tried it and liked it . . . see, how it was, I didn't want to miss nothing." The entry date for the court stenography course came and went; Norman was no longer interested.

"I really wasn't too interested in anything, really. I was just loafing around all the time. All that year, during the school year, from September to, what? June, I wasn't workin'. The drug problem was somethin' in the city, and I was into that a little bit. I guess that was probably one of them things that was slowing me down, making me not do anything, 'cause I think that throughout my life I was pretty active, and I was a pretty busy cat until that year, when everything just went zzzzup, just wasted for the whole year."

Norman says he was never really hooked on heroin, "but I'd have it now and then, maybe three or four days in a row, but I think I was always smart enough not to do it too much, even though I was dumb in that sense for getting into it in the first place. A lot of people I knew was snorting heroin, shooting heroin, the rest of them things. I think I was still young, and pretty immature, and I was going along with everybody else. I had a lot of things on my mind I had to figure out, and maybe I didn't want to think about it. When I had dope, everything was mellow, where I didn't have to think about nothing. That's mainly what it was, I was trying to figure out what I really wanted to be doing, and when I was messing with the dope, it just took my incentive away."

During that year, Norman lived from hand to mouth, getting a little money from his girlfriend, a little from dealing dope. "I even had a whore at one time," he says. "I did a little bit of a lot of stuff on small levels, never nothing on a really big level, because it was too much of a hassle for me. I really wasn't into that kind of thing. I really didn't want to do nothing like that."

He thinks, now, that his status as a petty hustler may have kept him from becoming really strung out. "My woman, she used to always take care of whatever I needed, that was one thing she was good about. Whatever I needed, I could always come to her for it, so I'd never have to go out and hustle for it. That's probably the main reason why I wasn't too hung up in it, because maybe if I went out and hustled for it and made a hundred dollars every two or three days or so, every time I got that money I'd go out and get some dope. But this way, I'd get twenty dollars from her, I might go out and get two bags of dope, but it was never nothing strong."

Finally, as Norman began to sort out his plans, he began to move away from drugs. "I always liked to buy clothes," he said, "and that money that I was spending on dope was taking away from that, and that was another consideration. I always like to have money to do what I want to do. When I get ready to go out, I like to have some money in my pockets. While I was doing that, while I was messing with the dope, I couldn't be getting things I wanted. I just decided that I really don't need that and I really don't have the money. I really don't want to be deprived of other things just to have that. And it eventually came to the thing where I just figured I didn't want to spend my money for something like that. I wanted to spend money for other things. I never really got my mind all tangled up in dope. I always kept my mind clear, my head clear."

And his concern about his appearance went further than clothes. "After a while, I really didn't like shooting up dope, snorting dope," he says. "I just didn't like to do it because I didn't like to look like I be looking when I'm doing that. People can see it on you, and I never like for anyone to see anything negative that has anything to do with me."

Coming off dope, Norman also dropped most of his hustling and took one last dead-end job, as a messenger in a hospital. He says he was "one of those messengers that brings test tubes and stuff to different departments in the hospital. I worked there for a week and just didn't come back until I got my check. I said, 'I'm never gonna get another job like this; if I ever have to get another job like this, I'm gonna have to go out there and knock somebody in the head."

That deadly job gave him the final push into action. "I always thought I was a pretty bright cat," Norman says, "so I decided maybe I'll go to school." He consulted Junior, who was then an undergraduate at the University of Pittsburgh. "He'd been going for quite a while and he seemed to be quite interested in it and all during school. I really never had any big problems with school. Only thing was I didn't like gettin' up in the morning. So I decided I'd go ahead to college."

Norman sees school as the route to what he wants—access to the white world's luxuries without the risk of the hustle or the dangers of street life. "I've seen blacks that are in the slums, in the ghettos," Norman says. "I seen them and I seen how they act and what they got. And I seen other blacks that have been to school and have good jobs and things and I found out how they did it and

I realized that they'd been to school to do it. Now the government has got all this money and these different agencies for people who don't have the money to go to school. Everybody doesn't realize that the money is there. Somehow I happened to find out that it was there and what kind of benefits it'd have for me and now I'm just taking advantage of it. The other alternative right now for me would be to what—get a job right now, and the job I get now would be a fucked-up job where I know I'm not going to like it, because I had the only kind of job you can get just coming out of high school and I couldn't stand it. I worked maybe two weeks and then quit. So I just quit, you know, and I just loafed some more and I said, 'Hey man, I can go to school, and if I go to school I be doing something you know that would benefit me and something that I really don't hate too much, you know, that I really can put up with.' I heard about college kind of environments, I experienced them visiting my brother's campus. I thought it was pretty nice atmosphere where I could be doing something to benefit myself and I wouldn't have to be doing that other kind of work that I wouldn't be able to stand. So I decided I'll go ahead to school and try to make it that way."

Once he made his decision, Norman found the rest of the route fairly easy. Junior and his mother knew almost everything there was to know about the educational resources available to Boston blacks in the early seventies, and they were pleased that Norman was at last ready to take advantage of those possibilities. Junior, Norman says, "knew all about how to get the money and who to see. So I just hooked up with him and he told me how to do it. I went on down there and took care of it.

"From my brother mainly I knew that I had to apply to a school, mainly that was the first thing you had to do, to make sure you got some money from the school. Then the next thing to do was apply to Mass. State, because that was almost guaranteed if your family income was below a certain level. So that's a few grand from those two sources." From Junior, Norman also learned to mine the NAACP and Christian Scholarship funds and "a whole list of others that, depending on what category you're in, you could get some money from. I picked the ones that

71

were suited to me, like your family had to be making under a certain amount, you had to be a resident of Massachusetts for such and such a time. I picked scholarships like that, "wrote to 'em, got applications, filled them out.

"At first, I was surprised that you get that money so quick. At the time I didn't know. People say, 'Shit, you can get money from all these agencies, man.' I said, 'Man, who's gonna be giving you all this money? Man, you must be crazy!' When I finally did it, I got a letter saying, 'Mr. Mullen, you been awarded, your application for financial aid has been approved, and you been awarded such and such—four hundred, five hundred, six hundred, a grand, two grand.' I say, 'Wow! shit! I can get all this free money, man, to go to school. Let me get into this thing!' Shit! Well, I can get money to go to school, then get money for expenses too, and plus I be doing something that's going to benefit me, rather than going to work now and getting into a job where I'm just gonna be working? You know, just going there, just waking up at a certain time in the morning, going to the job, going through that routine and coming home and getting paid on Friday. That ain't *enough*, you know? Soon as I got a whiff of that money, I said, 'That's it.' I'm gonna get some now and do what them people that got the money to do it is doing. People that got the money to do it, they're spending their money to do that thing. There must be something in it if they're gonna spend all that money for it. Now I can get the money for nothing . . . shit, I'm gonna get some of it."

Where he went, with "all that money" was Fillmore Junior College, a two-year program which provides both academic and vocational training. Fillmore, which is a school accustomed to being the first rung on the ladder out of the lower class, was a good choice for Norman. "For a while there," he says, "I was kind of worried . . . you know, *college,* but I thought it was cool, and junior college is really nothing anyway.

"I went through those two years like nothing. I was even on the dean's list a couple of times. I know I could have been on the dean's list all four semesters, if I really applied myself, but I didn't

72

do that. The first two semesters—the first semester I was adjusting; the second semester I was pretty well in the groove, but I still wasn't dead up interested in really what I was doing, in the whole process of school, until by second year. The first semester of my second year, I really was getting much more mature and really started . . . I really didn't apply myself all the way, but I made an effort to do better than I was doing and I got on the dean's list that semester and the following semester until that was over."

When he started at Fillmore, Norman's career plans were still vague. He took the marketing course at the junior college, but he continued to cast around for other, more interesting options. "I got a little bit of talent when it comes to art," he says now, "and while I was going to Fillmore, I thought about maybe not going on in business, maybe to go ahead and try to do something in art. I had opportunities before to do things in art, but I didn't take advantage of them. Like one time when I was in high school, my instructors used to encourage me, saying I had talent, that they could help me get into something in art. I thought maybe in business I could get something better out and make some more money, so I dropped out of my art course and went into business.

"And I got out of school, and I went to college for business, and I said, 'Well, it's cool, and I think I can get out of school and I can work in it for the rest of my life.' But now I got out of Fillmore and finished that business course, and I found something that was related to business and to art, and I put the two together and that's something I like."

What he has put together is a scholarship to the Fashion Institute in New York, in a program that combines art and money, merchandising and fashion management. "Like half the credits you earn would be art courses—fashion drawing, fashion figure sketching, things like that. Different art courses would be half of your credits to earn the bachelor's degree. The other half would be like business courses. The business courses, I had taken most of them at Fillmore already, so if I transferred into that course, most of the courses I would be taking at the Fashion

73

Institute would be like art courses. I thought that was pretty cool, and now I applied and I got my money together. I'd already been accepted, and everything is cool now. Now I'm just waiting to go."

Norman heard about the Fashion Institute program on "Transfer Day" at Fillmore "when representatives were coming from different schools to talk to the seniors." A number of schools appealed to Norman, but the Fashion Institute seemed to offer a combination of qualities he felt he needed. "It's a pretty unique course," he says. "It's the only one in the country where you can earn a bachelor's degree in merchandising and fashion management."

But there were other compelling reasons for choosing the Fashion Institute. "I know I could have transferred, I could have gotten into Boston College or Boston University, but I didn't want to go to school in Boston really, because I wanted to get away. I want to see other places, I want to know about another city than just Boston. I don't mean just one other city, I mean a lot of other cities—I'd like to travel. Mainly, I was just tired of the Boston atmosphere."

More important in Norman's eyes than the need to travel, is the need to get away from old companions, old temptations. Norman feels that going to Fillmore got him off the street, and he does not want to risk backsliding. "There was a time," he says, "when the main bulk of people I knew were people from the streets. I got to college and I started meeting other people with the same kind of ideas I have and shared the same kind of interests I have. When I'd come home, I'd get into an environment with the old people I knew, that weren't into no kind of college scene. They were just in the street. That would stop me from doing the important things I had to do relating to school.

"While I was at school, everything was cool because I had a different kind of head. I was around people who were into the same kind of thing I was, and out for the same kind of goals and things. I think when I'm around those kind of people, I think I'll

really make it, but when I get around niggers from the street
again, everything starts getting depressing. I mean *really*
depressing. Like this summer, it's really been a depressing
summer for me because I'm not around the kind of people that
can really help my mind. Everyone I'm around is them same old
people that will get me into the same old shit. I don't want to
know none of the street niggers in New York City. Don't even
come up to me, because I know just what you're up to. I know
what you want. I know what you're doing."

School, and the ultimate benefits of school have become the
center of Norman's life. "I'm always planning something new," he
says, thoughtfully. "And it wasn't like that before. I think now I
know how to get the money, and I know who I got to get it from,
and it's not out here in the ghetto. Ain't no money out here in the
ghetto unless you going to take it from everyone else out here in
the ghetto and they ain't got nothin'. You goin' to have to take
from everybody to get enough.

"Now the white man he got plenty money, all you got to do is
get into his system and find out how you can get it from him. You
already know how to take it from your own people and the white
people around here, you already know how to get it from them.
That's small time anyway. As for the pimp, more than one time I
had in my mind pimping and conning and dope dealing and all
that in my mind, but that's behind me, that's from the ghetto fairy
tale books you know. You might see a movie and say, 'Ah, that's
cool. That's what I want to do.' But it ain't like that. If you want to
be big time in anything, it's going to take a whole lot.

"Now I figure if I wanted to be big time out in the street I could
probably do it, but I don't want to go through all of those hassles.
I figure I can make it if I go to school and get a job like whiteys is
doing. They going to school and you know they getting good jobs
and making some kind of money in their future and I figure if I do
that somehow I'm going to make some too."

Fillmore gave Norman the opportunity to clarify and refine his
own ambitions, to take his old love of money and quality and

focus his energies on practical means of obtaining it. "I know that I like things," he says. "I know that I like good things, quality things. When I'm around dirty things and cheap things I don't feel right, you know? Like living in the ghetto, I don't feel right when I'm trying to get out of the ghetto, you understand, because all of this is around me and it's reminding me of things you know, that I really don't want to be reminded of. Like if I'm in an atmosphere where everything is nice and clean I *feel* like money. When I have money I feel better; when I got nice things I feel better; when I look good I feel better; when I feel better I do better, you know?

"I might be kinda swollen headed and conceited and shit like that, but that's me, you understand? If I act to people around me, if I act to them like I think I'm better than them, then that's me. I don't care what they're thinking, I know what's going on in my mind and if I feel better than you, I am better than you. People might say that no one is better than nobody else but that's crazy! I really think that I'm better than a whole lot of other people and I think that I can get to be better than some of the people that I'm not better than now."

Norman says that nothing will stop him from going on, getting better and better than the people he leaves behind. "Sure," he says, "if I walked out there and got hit by a truck or a bus right now, or if someone shot me through the head . . . but other than that, I doubt that there's anything that's going to stop me from going to school, because I got my mind set now on going to school and finishing that before I do anything else. Right now there's no way in the world I'm going to stop going to school and decide maybe I'll get a job now, no way in the *world*. As long as I can get the money to go, I'm going. It would probably be different if the money wasn't available, then I'd have to figure out some other way, because I ain't got the money to pay to go to school. But it's there now, I know how to get it, I'm gonna get it and I'm gonna put it to use. And, eventually, things are gonna work out somehow."

In the drive to go to school and beyond, some things have to be left behind. Norman says he has no best friends now. "I try not to be around anyone that much. I know him and I know him and I know her and I know her, but I never really get into any kind of relationship with too many people that I know around here. But there are a few people that are real tight with me, like people that I know since I was really small." Frankie Fletcher is still one of Norman's close friends—"We always been like brothers, you know"—and Junior and Norman are still solidly behind one another. But Norman keeps his distance from others.

Norman's girl, to whom he never refers by name, has had a baby, "a son who's six months. Fine little dude, too," Norman says, "fine little dude." But he does not feel that the child gives the girl any permanent hold on him. "I plan to take care of my son, and I want him to always know who I am," he says, "but we don't have to get married for that. There may have been a time before when all of that was a must, but it's not now.

"She doesn't want me to go to school really, being away from Boston, but I feel it's something I got to do and that's it. She got to understand. I guess she'll eventually understand it. I'm not even thinking about marriage. That's completely out of the question. I really can't understand a lot of these people that are getting married and raising families and stuff now . . . they ain't got nothing established yet. Maybe it's because I'm selfish. But I know I'm selfish, see? I really think that's good and I think it's good that I know I'm selfish. Because the fact that I am selfish means that I'm gonna try and get something for *myself.* You can't get nothing for no one else until you got something for yourself."

Norman feels that he knows himself, both his faults and virtues; that self-knowledge is the route to self-control. "I try to examine myself," he says. "I'm always trying to figure out all my faults and all of my good points. I don't want too many responsibilities other than myself. Because it's so hard now just taking care of yourself. You understand. If I had a family, then that would just slow me all down, because I wouldn't be happy, I really wouldn't be happy. Like—I like my son now, but I really don't think I could have him around where I got to take care of him all the time and stuff, because I don't think I'm that kind of person. Unless I *had* to do it, if it boiled down to where I had to do it, then without hesitation, that's an obligation, I have to do that.

"But if it came down where I got married and had a family, she'd have to be an out of sight chick to get me into that kind of situation from jump street. I don't think there's no broad out there that's that bad that's going to make me change my goals *now*. I don't think it's possible."

Norman's relationships with the old street crowd are deliberately casual now. He and Frankie "get together with our women, or sometimes on Sunday he'll bring his son over and I'll get my son and we'll go out and take pictures or something, get high together. I'm talking about smoking," he quickly adds, "I ain't talking about nothing else." But that is as close as he gets to his former closest friend; his school relationships are even more formal. But he feels they are better for him, more productive, aimed in the right direction.

"When I'm at school and when I'm with my friends at school, mainly we're talking about school and talking about what's gonna go on in the future. Usually, everything we're talking about is related somehow to school. When I'm around the city with my friends from the city we never talk about school. All we talk about is what's happening right *now*. I like to think about what's going on later, rather than really what's going on now.

"When I'm around people at school it's more interesting. I'd rather talk about things related to school than things that's going on in the street, the pimps and the whores and the dope pushers and all of them. I'm not interested in them no more."

Norman feels a little sorry for his old friends, and perhaps a bit contemptuous of them. Frankie, he says, is planning to get married, "so I guess he's not going to college. He's working during the summer and he sells weed, and that's it." But he thinks there is a limit to the amount of direct influence he can bring to bear. "Everybody I know out in the street that I'm pretty tight with, I try to tell them," he says. "I say 'Listen man, all that money is out there.' If he didn't finish school I say, 'Man, go ahead and finish school.' Usually it's only one more year they had to do. I can't understand why they don't go ahead and finish that one year, because *nowadays* if you don't have a high school diploma you might as well forget it! I mean at least a high school diploma, even that ain't nothing, a bachelor's degree really ain't nothing, won't be nothing in four years, you know?

"And just think in 1980 what it's gonna be like if you ain't got a high school diploma? You gonna be in a hell of a jam! Everybody is going to have something; you ain't gonna have nothing! I be tellin' these cats that. There's a couple of people I told that and they really made an effort to do somethin' about it, and there's one cat that goes to U. Mass. and I think I influenced him to go there, you know? But everybody I'm pretty close with that's not goin' to school, a lot of them, some of them just say, 'Oh yah, I been thinking about it, man, but, you know, so and so and so and so, I don't like school this, I don't like school that.' Do your own thing, I can tell you what might be cool, if you don't want to do it, do whatever you think is best but that's what I'm gonna do."

Why is Norman different from so many of the boys he grew up with? He says, "I don't know. Maybe because they didn't like school, so when they was in school they was getting bad marks and things like that. When I was in school, I was gettin' pretty good marks, even though I didn't study too much, and my brother, he was going to school—he was always interested in school—and that had some kind of effect on me. My mother, she was always interested in teaching—I guess that had some kind of effect on me.

"If I got a problem you probably wouldn't know I had a problem because I wouldn't look like I had no problem. If I had something on my mind I'll come in a room and I'll close the door and I'll sit and turn on the TV or radio or something and I'll start thinking about it and figure things out for myself. I'll never have that grim look on my face where people will know what's going on in my mind, because I'm not like that. If something happens that's bad for me and you know I made the wrong decisions or something what I do is I say, 'Well, c'est la vie, comme ci comme ca, so what? It happens, tomorrow is a new day, let me make tomorrow better. This day is already gone by.' "

Norman feels that his capacity to keep his private self very private, while developing a variety of public styles, has helped him live in the two worlds of the street and the college. "With different people I act in a different kind of way, you understand?" he says. "Like if I'm talking to a nigger out in the street I say, 'Hey man, so and so and so and so, what's happening, what you been up to, man? Let's go and do so and so and so and so,' and I deal with him on that level. If I'm dealin' with a cat out of college there, a black cat out in college I say, 'Hey so and so, how you doin', man? Is everything cool?' and I'll rap in a way suited to how he sees things. If I'm talking to some whitey, some business man, I sit down and say 'So and so and so and so' and I'll talk in a way that's more up to their level, you understand?

"And no matter who I'm talkin' to I try to talk to them in a way that they're used to hearing someone talk, and talk the kinds of things that they want to hear, rather than actin' one special way with everybody, because you have to deal with people and you got to know how to talk to different kinds of people."

Norman on Counseling

Norman attributes his own ability to "get over" to qualities of his own family and personality, and feels strongly that the schools he went to did not adequately encourage his development. "I think if I had of got good counseling while I was in high school, I woulda went straight to college," Norman says. "I wouldn't have wasted that year. I didn't have any counseling at all; I just went to school."

The last statement is clearly untrue. Norman, in high school, reported that guidance counselors tried vainly to pressure him into switching from the business to the college program. Mr. Hyland says that similar efforts were made at the junior high school level. But Norman goes on to describe the kind of counseling he thinks would be effective, and it is far more complex than anything he ever got in school.

Because he had completed most of his course requirements before his senior year in high school, Norman was able to take a minimal load his final year. And, he says, it was not even necessary for him to attend the few classes in which he was enrolled. "No one even—it seemed like no one even cared that I wasn't going to those classes or nothin', so I thought it was cool. I used to stand up at the Square, we standing up there until twelve o'clock, until someone decided whether we was going to hook school or whether we was going to class. Most of the time during the last few months of school we'd just hook school, we wouldn't go to school at all, maybe the whole week. But I still, whenever there was a test, I'd get just a good enough mark on the test to get me a "C" and a lot a times I was lucky and got a "B", you know, without even trying."

Norman feels that Dorchester High was wrong to allow such a possibility to exist, and blames the guidance counselors for not being more aggressive in their advising. "When I was in high school they had two white counselors, all you see them was walking around the school. There was never no time for you to come in for a consultation or nothing. All you do was seeing them walk around the school. You never knew really what their job was."

Norman would like to see more black counselors, whose "aim is specifically for black students," whose job would involve making young people aware of what really awaits them in the outside world. A lot of his contemporaries, Norman says, "just think that what they got to do is just get out of high school, and then 'I'm ready to go get me a job, man, and make me some money.' You ain't gonna make no money just going out of high school and getting no job. You got to look ahead, and you got to look far ahead. You can't just be thinking about what you going to get Friday, when the check comes in, because that ain't nothing, because next Friday it's going to be even less. And you're gonna *feel* like even less.

In Norman's design, the counselors would make the alternatives available and clear. They would "let them know what's going on in terms of the future and the job market—in other words, if you get a high school diploma, what you can look forward to, if you got a college degree, what you can look forward to. They should know that, they should know that there is money available if you want to go to college and they should know how to get it, they should know what schools that there are to go to.

"Like in a lot of high schools they don't tell the black people this, they don't know nothing about all of that. A lot of places when it comes time for you to select your course of study in high school like say a business course or college course and stuff like that, all they do is give you a slip of paper and say fill out what major you want to major in, you know? They don't tell you nothing about what's required and what's gonna happen, what that can be applied to when you get out of school. All they tell you is pick what you want to major in."

Norman feels that his notion of becoming a court stenographer was a more-or-less random choice, stemming from "off-the-wall counseling." He says that he didn't know what he wanted to do when he graduated from high school, and grasped at the first idea that came along. "When I was thinking about court reporter, I was just thinking about some kind of training." Now, armed with the things he has learned in college, he feels better equipped to make a sound decision. "Now I been to college for a while, and I've met people that are working in that kind of area, and I got a little idea of what kind of things I could get out of going into fashion," he says. "My mind is pretty set on that."

Norman and His Family

Norman's new attitude toward life and his future has firmly re-established him with his family. He says he has a "dynamite" relationship with his parents and his brother and sisters now. Junior is still gone most of the year, but he plans to come home to help Norman move his belongings to New York in time for the beginning of the Fashion Institute's school year. Norman says that he and Junior are still very close, although now that they see so little of each other, Norman has grown more and more fond of Lena. "We always been kinda pretty close," he says. "With Lena, it's the sort of relationship where she looks up to me, and with my brother, it's the kind of relationship where I look up to him. You know—he helps me and I help her."

Lena is now an undergraduate at the University of Massachusetts' Boston campus. Lynette has followed her into the METCO program and is doing well in a suburban high school. The family has never been in better shape. "I think it's mainly because we're pretty tight here," Norman says. "When I speak of family I'm speaking about my mother, my brother, my sisters and myself. I'm not speaking about cousins or uncles or anything like that because to me family is just the people that are in this house.

"Like my cousins and things—I'll see them out on the street, I'll say, 'Hey cous' so and so and so and so,' but it's just like to me they are just some other dude that just happens to be related to me through blood or whatever. Family, when I talk about family, I'm talkin' about people that's livin' like in the house and we stick pretty much together."

Norman does not include his father in his family list, although Freddie Mullen is around more—often staying in the Mullen apartment, and Norman says that their relationship too has never been better. "We get along like . . . like he might be my brother," Norman says. "And that came about in a strange way, just"—he snaps his fingers—"just overnight. Like one day I saw him and it was still that father-son kind of thing, where I still had that kind of, leery kind of feeling. But now I see him and I say, 'Hey, what are you doing, so and so and so—what's happening?' We sit down and smoke, whatever we going to be doing, just like he might be some friend I know from the streets—something like that."

Norman says that his father approves of his plans, but he does not consult him about them, one way or the other. "We never really—I was never the kind of son that would do a whole lot of

83

talking with him. My older brother, he'd always be talking to him, but I hardly ever would talk to him. I'd like, usually I just keep whatever was on my mind, I usually just keep to myself and hardly no one would know. But I never hardly ever talked to him—I'd nod, I told him I was going to Fillmore, he said, 'Yah, that's good, what are you studying?' I told him I was studying what I planned to do and things, he said, 'Yah, that's good.' He never really says anything negative, everything is positive. I think everything we do, me and my brother, to him is positive, because I guess he figured we might turn out a little different, you know."

But it is Norman's relationship with his mother that has changed most since the difficult time of his "wasted year." Norman says, "We have little arguments and things, but she understands my nature, and I understand her nature. She helps me a lot. I know whatever happens, whatever comes down, I know who I can depend on, and that's one thing for her."

Looking back on his bad year, Norman says, "She always knew I was gettin' high and things but I don't think she really knew what it was, because I always respected her. Whenever I was doing anything like that I just wouldn't come home.

"I wasn't into that stealing and all that kind of thing, so I wasn't gettin' put in jail and stuff. She had those ideas that anyone that was into dope was doing all this stealing and stuff, so I guess she figured, you know, that I wasn't into that dope. She probably figured that maybe I was smoking reefer or taking pills or something like that."

Now, at the other end of his bad times, Norman is openly grateful to his mother for her concern, her persistence—even for her nagging.

"She was always there, and she always was encouraging us to do something other than what everyone else was doing, all the other niggers was doing. She always encouraged us to go on to college, ever since I can remember. Even when I was going to elementary school, junior high and high school, there was times when I'd be *scared,* I'd think at nighttime of how I can get out of going to school the next morning and I'd think that I had the scheme down pat and when the morning came I was ready to run it down but ain't nothing come of it. She'd say, 'Uh uh, get up and get dressed and go ahead to school,' and eventually it got so that I said, 'Well, shit, I'm not gonna scheme nothing, I'm not gonna run that down on her,' and I found that once I got up out of the bed and I was dressed, then I was ready to go, I was game to go. So all it took was for me to get outa the bed. She helped me with that.

"Every morning she'd be right there, right there to wake me up, you know, and wouldn't let me go back to sleep. She'd come in and say, 'Come on. Get up!' and pull the covers off. I'd say, 'Okay, I'm coming.' Soon as she walked out the door I'd fall back asleep. I figured that if I fell back asleep enough eventually she'd be gone on to work herself, I'd just lay on and sleep. That wouldn't work either, she would keep coming right back and when it got too late she'd come and pull me outa the bed so that I'd have to get up."

Norman on Race

Norman's venture into the predominantly white world of Fillmore has not softened his view of whites, but it has helped him to refine and focus his capacities to capitalize on his blackness and to avoid the pitfalls along the route to succes in the dominant culture. Norman says that he might have some difficulty in getting a job in the fashion world because he is black, "unless I get hooked up with the right companies." He would like to work with an all black fashion agency or firm, partly for his own comfort, but also because "in fashion there's more opportunity coming about for blacks... in a lot of different fields the opportunities for blacks are expanding wider than they were before."

Norman is determined to take advantage of these new opportunities, to differentiate himself both from the "street niggers" who will never make it and the militants who will not play the white man's game even though it is the primary route to affluence and comfort. "I see niggers—the black people—not into anything. They really look poor. And I think it's not because they're dumb, and it's not because they're lazy, it's because they don't know how to get out and get something better. They just conditioned, their mind is conditioned, this is the way it *is,* you understand, it's too late to do anything about it now. Well, I'm young now, and I'm seeing all of this stuff now, at least certain opportunities are opening up now that somehow I got lucky and, you know, taking advantage of them.

"And through education I learned a lot about what the world is about, what these white people are about. And when I know what these white people are about I think I can deal with them better. A lot of these blacks around here they don't know what these white people are about. They might read about white people in the Muslim paper, they might read about them in there. Sure they're like that, that's how they are, but you got to deal with them. You got to deal with them so find out about them, live in their kind of world.

"I mean you going to be in your own world anyway, because you're black and you don't think like no whitey, no matter how much you going to be around them you ain't never going to think like no whitey because you know you're black, but you can deal with them and you got to learn to deal with 'em. You can't just deal with them by reading no papers and shit like that, you got to get out really and find out what they're all about.

"And you can't deal with them if you ain't got your education and your head together you ain't going know how to deal with them, because they got their head together. They got all the money and they know what's going on in the country because they're educated. A lot of the blacks aren't educated, you understand, and the ones that did graduate from high school they graduated from a high school in the slums, where they teaching you slum shit.

"If you get into college you know, you learn other things, you learn a lot more about the country than you learn in high school and you can't learn by just staying in the ghetto and staying around all these poor black people, you got to get out with these whiteys and get into their shit."

Norman is irritated at the suggestion that blacks who "get over" forget the ghetto. "You can't just get outa the ghetto and forget about it, because that's just impossible. You're never gonna forget about what it's like in the ghetto. And you never, no matter what you're doing, I don't think, you're never gonna forget your people that are in the ghetto."

But he does not feel that it is his obligation to go back. "If I got some kind of training that's going to benefit people that's in the ghetto, that's gonna get them some, and make them more wise to what's going on, then I think that's where they should come in. Like people in urban studies, people in business, too, if they can get an opportunity to help the people in the ghetto then I think that they really should do it.

"But you can't always find opportunities in the ghetto, like when you're going to college, you're going to make some money, you're not going just to help somebody else, you're going to help yourself. Now, if you can get something out of helping your people, if you can get some money and help your people too, then that's cool. But if you gonna go to college and come back and try to help your people without really making any kind of money, that's just a waste of time!"

Norman's approach to life is detailed, well-focused, and intensely pragmatic. He is not irrationally optimistic about the prospects for wholesale alleviation of the problems of poor blacks. But he does believe that one young black man, ambitious, cautious, well-controlled, can get what he wants from white America.

"I think things are getting better," Norman says. "I don't think that they can really get worse until it comes time when the whitey's decide they gonna kill all the blacks, and I really don't think that gonna come about 'cause I think that they be too many negative things coming out of that if that happened, I mean internationally. So things have got to get better, and they are gettin' better. A lot of the militants and things, they won't agree with that because they got all this separatism ideas in their head, but I don't think that that's gonna happen, you know? No matter where a black person goes it's always gonna be the same when the whitey's there because the whitey's got everything.

"Now you talk about going back to Africa, ain't no way in the world you gonna go back to Africa, because we don't know nothin' about what's goin' on in Africa, we wouldn't know how to deal with it! I know I wouldn't know how to deal with it, all I know is what's happening here, you know, that's all I know, so I got to deal with that here.

"*Everything* is never gonna be cool, but when I got some money and I'm doin' my own thing *in* the system, then everything is going to be cool for me, and I can help who I want to help. I don't want to help everybody. Like they talk about 'help your brothers and sisters.' I can't help my brothers and sisters, I can't help everybody, I can only help myself, they got to help theirself too. But if there's a way I can help you, then I'm gonna try to help you, but if it's gonna hurt me you might as well forget it . . . you understand." He laughs, "Everybody got to do somethin' for theirself, you understand, I'm talkin' about in this world. Even the whiteys, they're doing everything for theirselves too, all of them tryin' to make their own things, that's what I'm trying to do. If I can help you, brother, if I can help you sister, cool, I'm gonna help you, but if it's gonna interfere with what I got to get, then you might as well forget my help."

FOCUS: NORMAN MULLEN—OWNING THINGS

Norman Mullen, strung out on drugs, seemed to be a hard case. His mother's threats, his brother's counseling, his own frustrated ambitions did not seem adequate to pull him out of his "funk." And the pivotal motivation, when it finally came, seemed trivial: "I always liked to buy clothes. And that money I was spending on dope was taking away from that." Norman always cherished his appearance—the thought of running out of clean shirts was enough to drive him to do the family laundry. But it is hard to believe that the prospect of new knits would be enough to entice him away from drugs. And yet Norman, and other young men we talked to, said that their need to buy new clothes was an important incentive to leave the drug scene.

Clothes and other personal possessions are important to most Americans. Our society consistently promotes acquisition as a source of self-esteem, especially among the young. Many a sagging adolescent ego has been bolstered, however temporarily, by a new sweater or a new hi-fi set. And in the ghetto, routine American materialism takes on new power and new functions.

Much has been made of the ghetto family's obsession with things. The Cadillacs, expensive knits, and color television sets in the Roxbury/North Dorchester neighborhood seem incongruent with the dreary apartments and trash-filled streets. "Why does that mother send her child to school with a transistor radio and no glasses?" teachers ask. "Why did that family buy an expensive car instead of saving for a new home?"

Questions like these are often answered with a culture-based argument: poor blacks have a different set of goals and desires from those of the dominant, middle-class white culture. Therefore, their priorities and choices are different. Pro-black theorists can use this argument to argue for the validity of cultural differences; anti-black speakers can fulminate about the "bad values" of the ghetto.

The only flaw in this popular argument is that it does not appear to be true. The Pathways interviews suggest that the dreams of young black men are very similar to those of their white counterparts. Norman, like most of the young men we interviewed, had standard adolescent fantasies about a sudden deluge of money which would allow him to live in Hefneresque luxury. But, barring that unlikely event, Norman and his peers tended to express the most "middle class" of goals—a "clean" job, a house with a yard, comfort and stability.

What separated these young men from their white suburban counterparts was not their perception of what they wanted, but their sense of whether or not they could get it. Young white men could plan for a middle-class future; young black men often believed that they could only dream about it. And in the reality of ghetto life dreams were often more reliable than plans. A young black man could train as an electrician, but find the union closed to him. He could save enough money, perhaps, for a small house with a yard. But he was not welcome in Roslindale, and houses in Newton cost more than he could save in a lifetime. Putting $45 in the bank instead of into a pair of alligator shoes requires some sense that the bank account will ultimately buy you something more valuable than the present pleasures of looking sharp and feeling good about yourself. Looking out at Roxbury and North Dorchester, there is not a lot a young person can see that is worth the risk.

Possessions are very important to people who live in the ghetto. They are a source of self-esteem to those who have few other sources. By what criteria are people judged in our society? Income? Most Roxbury incomes are very meager. Occupation? There is no prestige attached to the manual labor or to the service and domestic jobs which are the staple jobs here. Virtue? Hard work? Only fools would base self-esteem on traits so rarely rewarded. Fame, wealth, glamour, success? Except for the pimp's life, all of these are strangers to the ghetto. When a man is not respected for what he is, there is little left but to respect him for what he has.

To a young man like Norman Mullen, high style has another function. Young blacks have been the style leaders of our country since the 1920's—and they know it. The young men we interviewed had clear confidence in their superiority over whites in dance, in dress, in music, in language. It was one of the few areas of life in our society in which they *knew* they were ahead. Keeping up with the latest style, then, is more than showing you have money to spend—it affirms black identity in one of the few ways the white world respects.

Unquestionably, many blacks in the inner cities spend much of their meager funds on clothes, on cars, on other conspicuous consumables. But to attribute this pattern to cultural difference misrepresents the truth. The buying habits of people in the ghetto are the results of a success-oriented society which will not allow its poor black members to succeed. They have learned instead to be superb consumers.

Chapter

4

Douglas Jones—
Going Under

DOUGLAS AT FIFTEEN: IN AND OUT OF SCHOOL

Doug Jones, slim and quick, slides through the corridors of the Ryan school, evading the patrolling teachers. Down to the boy's room for a quick smoke, a beer shared with his best friend, G. W. Poole; back to a few minutes of class with a particularly baitable teacher; out the locked school door to spend the last school hours looking for something to steal in the local stores. Doug Jones skims the surface of the Ryan—he never really attends.

Doug's real life is all outside the school—at home, in the streets, moving through Boston with his brothers or his friends. He lives with his parents and three brothers, Danny, Daniel, and James, in the Church Road Project, a collection of deteriorating brick buildings plagued from their earliest days by poor management, bad design, and unhappy tenants. The Joneses live on the fifth floor of one of the high-rise buildings. From his bedroom window Douglas can look out at the lights of downtown Boston or down at the glass- and paper-littered blacktop parking area that is their front yard. The apartment is neat, but shabby; the overstuffed chairs show the effects of four active boys. Mrs. Jones has tried to make the apartment attractive, but the dark asphalt floor tiles and the institutional salmon pink paint are difficult to counterbalance. The apartment lights are always dim, and the glare of a naked light bulb in the kitchen casts shadows into the dark hallway.

93

At fifteen, Douglas Jones is a shy, slender, well-developed boy, with a rich brown complexion. He has a nervous way of laughing, covering his mouth with his hand as if attempting to stifle unwanted outbursts of laughter. He walks like a prizefighter; shoulders slightly hunched, head tucked in, as if he were constantly defending himself. He moves as if he were expecting someone to come up behind him—feet gliding close to the ground, body tense and ready, eyes always moving. Douglas is always conscious—of himself, of others watching him, of potential dangers that might strike from any direction.

Douglas defines his relationships with others in terms of attack and counterattack. He describes his brothers. "Now my brother Danny," he says, "he's seventeen years old. So, a . . . once in a while me and him get in fights, like before, when he started gettin' on me about his coat. I accidentally ripped it on the fence. So he started getting mad at me. I lost my temper and punched him in the chest. One of his friends tried to break it up, so I ran in the kitchen and got a knife and a broom. He told me, 'What are you going to do with that?' I told him, 'You butt in again, you'll find out.' I raised the broomstick up and hit him in the neck. He started coming at me and I raised the knife up, then he stopped. Danny told me to put the knife back in the kitchen drawer. I told him to shut up. So my father told me to put it up before he put something on me. I just stood there for a minute, than I walked in the kitchen, set the stuff up, and put it back in the drawer. Everything was all quiet then.

"My brother Daniel, he's 14-years old. He's in the reform school. He wants to mess around with me more than my younger brother [James]. I started pushing on him, twisting his arm and everything. He ran outside, got a brick and a couple of his friends. Like they was gonna do something. I went over to him and grabbed him in a headlock and I threw him over my back. His friends just stood there looking at him. So he got mad—he picked up the brick from the floor, threw it at me and hit me in my ankle. So I grabbed him and threw him against the wall, put my knee on his chest, and I was telling him to say he's sorry 'cause he always

94

messes around with me. He said it, so I let him up. I just went in the room and played the record player.

"James, my younger brother, he's all right once in a while. He gets on my nerves, too. Like my mother say, 'Something's broken. Who did this?' James will open his mouth and say, 'I don't know; Douglas was the only one in the house when it happened.' I run over and slap him in the arm or stomach. My mother gets all mad about it. Then when I come after him, he run in the bathroom and lock the door, start calling me all sorts of names."

Douglas will fight with his brothers, but he withdraws from his father's anger, retreating into his room. His father says, "Douglas is a quiet boy and you don't know he is in the house. Every now and then, he might want to play with you, or something like that. But outside of that, he got a book he's reading in his room. He specialized in those *Life* magazines. He goes for that." Mrs. Jones concurs. "He's quiet, like I am sometimes. We can stay in the house all day long without saying one word to each other. Douglas is like me in more ways than any of my kids. And he looks like me. I don't favor either of my kids, but I really can get along with Douglas better than anybody."

But Douglas has a short fuse, and Mrs. Jones, more than anyone else, can ignite it. When she is drinking, their similarities become deficiencies in her eyes, and she becomes violently abusive to her "quiet" son. She says she used to beat him, but "one time he almost struck me back, and I stopped doing that." Now she taunts him, calling him "black," which she knows infuriates him. Danny says, "Douglas and my mother—they're the darkest ones in the family. My mother even calls him 'black' sometimes . . . he'll get mad at her. And she is the same color . . . she's dark." Mr. Jones disapproves of her treatment of Douglas, but he feels helpless to stop it. "I don't believe in swearing at a child," he says. "Or, just because he is the darkest one in the family, to call him 'black.' I don't believe in that. She got a bad habit of doing that. That make him mad. Sometimes he starts for the door. I say, 'you don't have to go out. Just stay here.' She yells out, 'Get out of my house.' I say, 'You don't have to go anyplace. Just stay here.' But if I don't say nothing, he'll go out the door. You'll see him next morning."

Mrs. Jones says that her husband is right about the most effective way to deal with Douglas. "He tells me to let him alone and don't holler at him. I say that's the only way that Douglas knows that I really mean something, by hollering at him. But my husband, he can just talk so I can't hardly even hear what he's saying, but Douglas hear it, and he'll do it just like that. But not for me." She says that Douglas is his father's pet, and that if she didn't punish him, he wouldn't be punished at all.

Douglas's fights with his parents have a regular pattern. His father says, "He gets a little mean sometimes, but it's not his fault, really. He swears pretty bad when he swear, then he gets pretty evil, and then he takes off, and comes back the next morning. I don't try to stop him because he's right a lot of times." Mrs. Jones describes him as "stubborn." "He'll do and he don't mind, but he just take his time about doing it. When he gets ready. When he's mad . . . he just . . . just let him alone. If Douglas gets mad enough, he'll go out, or go in the room and close the door. Uh, uh, but I know he is mad."

Douglas sees the pattern, too. "I act kind and talk nice to her, but if she start talking mean to you, start talking mean to her a little while and she'll stop real quick. If she stops, I stop too. Because if I don't, she yells at you about five minutes or so." He handles his father in a more gingerly fashion. "I act nice, but if my father starts jumping on me for something, I don't try to fight him back." Douglas chuckles and adds, "That's what I did before. He hit me on my chest before, with his fist, knocked me against the bed. And I got mad, jumped back up like I was gonna do something. He grabbed me and slammed me against the wall and started yelling at me and cursing. So all I do is get near the door, call him a name and run out of the house. Wait till my mother or someone come home. That's when he be drunk. He start all his stuff then."

All the boys are wary of their parents when they have been drinking. Danny, the oldest boy, says, "Well, my father. He's all right at times, except when he starts drinking. He likes to play around a lot. Sometimes you'll be sitting there, watching a good picture, and he'll come in there drunk. He'll start messing with you. Can't watch the picture. You start getting mad, then. We don't say nothing to him. We get along all right. He don't beat us, he just talk to us, gives us things. You know, if we ask him for it, if he got it.

"I think my mother is *sick*. When she starts drinking, that's it. She all right too, but she'll start drinking, she start hollering, she'll call you all kinds of names, she gets mad at you. When she's not drinking, she's kind of evil. She's always quiet. You say something to her, she'll tell you to shut up."

Douglas' view of his parents is different. "My mother don't hit on me or none of my brothers like my father does. She don't drink and get on your nerves like he does. When there is a picture on that we want to see, she lets us look at it. But when we wanna see a picture and tell my father, he say he's looking at this or that. That's why I like my mother more than I like him." Douglas praises his mother for giving him "breaks . . . when I be truant from school. She don't tell my father or nothing like that." But sometimes she lets him down. "Like before, when my brother got in trouble, I tried to help him out, but my mother found out the truth about him . . . she started yelling at me like my father does . . . but she don't hit on me. She thinks I'm too big for that. So, I start yelling back at her. So she got mad and called the cops on me one day. So they came and started talking to me about court, how it was at Youth Service Board and Kirkpatrick. They told me to take a walk so I can cool off. So I did what they said."

Douglas recalls when he was truant from school and his father "started out hitting on me with his fist. I got mad and started cursing at him a little. So he just grabbed me and put me in the room and started talking to me . . . yelling and everything. I started getting mad again, but I didn't say anything to him. I just sat there on the bed." At the same time, he says that he is closer to his father than to any other man, and that they enjoy doing things together. "Like on Friday or Saturday night, we go over one of his friends' house and he buy me this, he buy me that, without being asked for it. . . . Sometimes in the summer he used to take me and G. W. horseback riding too." And Mr. Jones describes their relationship as "just like two brothers. We wrestle in the living room, or something like that. Sometimes he'll walk up and throw a punch at me, and say 'I got you, didn't I?' I say, 'That's all right, I'll get even with you.' "

But Douglas does not mean those threats. He turns his anger on outsiders and on himself. His brother Danny laughs, and says, "You see his hand? He put it through a window. Saturday night, we was drinking. He got mad at me. Me and him had a fight. My father tried to break us up and he swore we were double teaming him. He wanted to fight both of us, so he just ran on out of the house and put his hand through the window. That's happened twice before."

Danny, who is closer to Douglas than anyone else in the family (they share a room, clothes, acquaintances, and escapades) understands Douglas very well. He perceives him as essentially shy, quiet, a loner, who "likes to go in the room and read and listen to the radio by hisself. He's scared of girls. He likes them, but he's just bashful, that's all. When he starts drinking, that's when he just likes to fight. I don't think he would kill nobody anyway. There's times he could have killed me. He tried, but by the way he looked I know he didn't want to. Twice he got mad at me and grabbed a knife. Then he come at me. He would just cut at me. He wouldn't really even try to hit me with the knife, just scare me." Both Danny and Douglas describe these fights with relish.

Both boys will defend each other against outsiders of any kind. Danny describes a time when they were fishing in the Charles River with some other boys. A dispute broke out between Danny and another boy over a fish hook. Douglas, standing nearby, picked up a stick and hit the other boy in the back. The boy turned and began fighting with Douglas, who threw him on the ground. On another occasion, Danny heard noises outside the apartment, and found Douglas fighting with the neighbor's boyfriend. Without hesitation, Danny "grabbed the guy and Douglas just started beating him in the face."

Bad Luck, Worse Times

The Jones children were born to a life of poverty and violence. As a family, they have known little else. Mr. and Mrs. Jones were both born in rural southern families who migrated north in search of better opportunities which never materialized. Neither of them finished tenth grade, and, as young adults, both drifted into the low-life style of the "bucket-of-blood" bars—full of bad whiskey, rentable bodies, and the constant threat of injury or death.

The Joneses met in one of those bars. Mr. Jones was on shore leave from the Navy; Mrs. Jones was out on the town for the evening. Mr. Jones describes the events. "I was in the Navy. And you know how you get leave off a ship? We went to this barroom, me and a bunch of the boys. I don't know, some fight started some kind of way. All of us was carrying pistols and things like that. So when the fight started, I started blowing out the lights. So she ran, she tripped over me, and knocked me down, and when we got outside, that's who I had, was her. It just started like that, kept right on going, right on going. I don't know whether I was drunk or she was drunk, but one of us asked the other to marry him. I think it was her asked me. So we got married on Christmas Eve 1949."

Much has happened to the Joneses since that Christmas Eve. In 1950, Mr. Jones was given a bad conduct discharge from the Navy, after being charged and convicted of stealing $20 by a white Southern officer. According to Mr. Jones, the officer "said he had the numbers off the bills, but I had sent my wife some money, so I stopped the money and let him check the bills. The numbers didn't match, but still I got BCD and they kept the money. That was just a railroad job."

Mr. Jones had been a winch driver on shipboard, but his bad conduct discharge and his race kept him from finding a similar job in Boston. Instead, he worked on the "killing floor" of a slaughterhouse during the day, moonlighting as an office cleaner to supplement his income. Then, in 1953, he was convicted of "abuse of a female child," and spent a year at the Deer Island House of Corrections. Mr. Jones sees this conviction as another "railroad job," the result of a grudge. "Well, me and another boy got in a little argument, we had a dispute. He tried to put a rape charge on me. IIc had some girl up his house. She was supposed to have been a prostitute. Come to find out the girl was underage or something like that. He tried to say it was me. I knew I was home. The wife knew I was home. So him and I, we both used to be boxers, we went to war. I ended up getting a year."

Released from prison in 1954, he began working nights in a Chinese laundry, loading and unloading an extractor. Mrs. Jones didn't like his night work, so he found another job as a furniture mover. Then, in 1959, he got into a serious fight. "I got stabbed in the back and got this hand ripped open," he says. "I was fighting these two fellers, and I hit one of them. He hit the ground and hit his head and he died." Mr. Jones ran, and spent days hiding from the police, drinking heavily, getting more and more tense. Finally, "I went over by the Star Dust Bar on Washington Street, and they were over there. I just turned myself in to them. I was tired of drinking, tired of hiding."

He was convicted of manslaughter and sent to state prison for a four-to-seven year term. At this point his relationship with his wife began to go to pieces. "She started going with my best friend. I never will forget it. They came down there once to see me. She was drunk. He was high." This was Mrs. Jones's only visit to her husband in prison and it hurt him deeply. He says, "That's when I got that 'I don't care' feeling. I got it when I went to the place, there. And she didn't come to see me or nothing. I got that feeling. And I've had it ever since. But I wouldn't advise no one else to have it. Because it's not such a good feeling. You get up in the morning, you look in the mirror, you need a shave, or your face

100

does. And you say to yourself, why should I wash my face? Why should I shave? Who have I got to look good to? That's that old 'I don't care' feeling."

Part way through his prison term, Mr. Jones began hearing rumors from his friends that his wife was pregnant. "That was the worst thing. Them babies. I got a hospital bill, such and such amount of money for the burial of Baby Jones. What baby? Maybe I could have learned to accept a lot of that stuff if she hadn't been too bold about it. You don't . . . just have a child by a man [who] tells you, 'Don't break up my family,' and you take and put it on your husband. That's a little too bold. Seems like you see them laughing behind your back or something like that. See? That's pretty rough to get over with it."

Mr. Jones's main source of pleasure in prison came from visits from Danny and Douglas, who were eleven and nine when their father went to jail. Mr. Jones recalls, "Somebody would put them on the right bus, and then there was an officer down there would let me know when the next bus was going back. I'd make sure they got on it. They'd come down and we'd sit there and laugh and joke. And Douglas always worried about when I was coming home. That's the only thing that hurt me, really. Outside of that, nothing else bothered me. Not even her, that didn't bother me. I felt good when they were there. But when they left, that's when I'd start feeling bad! I'd feel depressed. In the night I'd be laying there thinking, wondering if they got home okay. I'd have to sweat it out two or three days till I'd get a letter from the oldest boy. He'd let me know that they got home all right."

Mr. Jones was released on parole after serving two years of his sentence. But tension between him and his wife continued. Finally, the conflict between the two grew so intense that Mr. Jones decided to violate parole and finish his prison term. "I just didn't want to be looking at her no more," he says. So he stopped reporting to his parole office, and when the man came looking for him, Mr. Jones gave him a "fake hard time." And he returned to prison for another year. By 1967 he was out of jail for more than a year, but his relationship with his wife had not markedly improved.

101

The Jones family's involvement with the criminal justice system continues unabated. In 1967, the three oldest boys are in constant trouble with the law—for car theft, truancy, purse snatching, and ringing cash registers. Mr. Jones is often in court with the boys and feels harassed and humiliated by juvenile court judges. One of them "gave me a hard time down there," Mr. Jones says. "He tells me about I ain't no good and all this because I've been to the station. I didn't owe them nothing. I paid my time. And he acted like I was on trial. And he tells me if I come down there again, he's going to lock me and Douglas both up and things like that."

Mrs. Jones uses the same tactics on the father as on the sons. "Even my own wife, it gets throwed up in my face. She's got a bad habit, every time she gets a drink or two in her, tell her to do something, she say, 'I call the police, send you back where you come from. You know what that judge told you.' And all like that. Just grab my hat and coat and walk out. She slam the door so I don't get back in. I just keep going. I don't come home that night."

Mrs. Jones does more than threaten her husband and sons with the police. Whenever she feels a fight has gone beyond her ability to control it, she heads for the telephone. This infuriates Mr. Jones, who says, "I hate to see a Negro woman, I hate to see them calling the police on a Negro man, just behind an argument, no licks passed, no nothing. The last discussion we had, I got busted behind that, but I spoke my piece anyway. Me and my wife, 'All you do is sit there and get yourself high and call the Man on me. What did I do?' Next morning I am up for assault and battery. I didn't pass a lick. They don't let the boys say nothing in court, they are down there, but they don't let them say nothing. So that's like, I told her, 'All you know you want to call the wagon, go ahead and call them. Get it over with.' "

This kind of life has taken its toll of Mr. Jones's health. He has developed a chronic pancreatic condition which gets worse year by year. "The doctors told me not to drink, not even a beer," he says. But he doesn't stop, and going to the hospital for his weekly check-up becomes more and more of a chore. "It takes so long to go to the hospital. I been sick for two weeks and I ain't right yet."

Poor health, a prison record, and the general disorder of his life have combined to make it impossible for Mr. Jones to hold a steady job. Instead, he has taken over the household from Mrs. Jones, who is drinking more and more. Mr. Jones washes clothes, cleans, shops, makes lunches, and looks after the boys. He has also gained control of the welfare check—their sole source of income—which used to give Mrs. Jones much of her power. "She's been on welfare ever since I went away," he says. "And they caught her two or three times, she was intoxicated, so they took it away from her and put me on it. I just throw it back into the house."

Mr. Jones pays the rent and sets aside enough money for food, clothing, and allowances for the boys. But there is considerable tension about what happens to the remaining dollars. Despite his doctors, Mr. Jones tends to do a "little drinking," on check day, and often becomes reluctant to divvy up the spoils. Douglas says, "When the check comes, my father, he pays all the bills. My mother ain't home and he get her money, he go out, go get some liquor and come back drunk. So my mother asks where her money? So he say, 'You wait until tomorrow,' something like that, and so my mother start yelling, and he start cursing. So my mother don't say nothing else about it. My father just go in the room, and fall asleep. She go in there, try to sneak some money out of his pocket. She can't do it, so she tells me to try and get about twenty dollars out of the wallet. So I go try it. Every time I try to get the wallet, he starts twitching and turning and everything. So my mother said, 'Wait about twenty minutes.' Then all of a sudden he started snoring. I said, 'I think I can get it now.' I went in there, I stuck my hand in his pocket, and he didn't move or nothing. So I took his wallet out. While I was taking twenty dollars out for my mother, I took five for me and stuck it in my pocket." Douglas chuckles at the memory. "I gave my mother twenty dollars, so she said, 'How much did you take for yourself?' I had a feeling she'd know I was gonna take something.

So I said, 'Nothing.' So she said, 'Come over here!' She stuck her hands in all my pockets. Before she could get over to my left back pocket, I reached my hand back there and took the five dollar bill. I stuck it up my sleeve. So she said, 'This is one time you didn't do it, huh!' "

Douglas in the Street—1967

Douglas does well in the street. The legend of his violent temper and no-holds-barred fighting ability makes him known and respected in his crowd. He has a best friend, G. W. Poole, with whom he spends most of his time, and who is his partner in excitement, fighting, and crime. Douglas and G. W. have been best friends since the fourth grade, when, according to G. W., "Me and him was going to have a fight. So we did have a fight. I asked him what his name. He said, 'Douglas Jones.' I said, 'You got any brothers?' He said, 'Yes.' So I said, 'Let's go over your house,' and he said, 'O.K.' So we went over there." They have been running buddies ever since.

Douglas and G. W. have one main game—the search for excitement in any form. Douglas's favorite tales are of their fun and adventures. They relate their successes and narrow escapes with pride and relish. Douglas tells one story of a day when he and G. W. wanted to go the amusement park at Revere Beach. They had no money, so their first ploy was to ask Mrs. Jones for five dollars. She had a twenty dollar bill, but wasn't about to trust Douglas to take it to the store for change. Mr. Jones was asleep, and the thought of waking him to ask for money didn't appeal to Douglas. "So G. W. said, 'Now what shall we do?' I said, 'Name something.' He said, 'How about a pocketbook?' I said, 'I think I know where a place is—come on!' We went downtown to Citymart. I said, 'Instead of snatching a pocketbook, get a bag. We can walk out with one.' So he got a paper bag. I said, 'Behind that counter is a yellow pocketbook. A lady who works behind there always keeps a yellow pocketbook; I always see her put one behind there.' So he said, 'Well, let's get it.' "

Douglas then asked, "Who's gonna get it?" "Let's buck up," G. W. replied. Douglas retorted, "Who do most of the things when we need things most?" So G. W. said, "O.K." Douglas kept watch while G. W. went behind the counter and threw the purse to Douglas who caught it in the paper bag. The boys retired to the subway station, and went into a phone booth. "We took out the purse," Douglas recalls, "looked over the pocketbook. Nothing else was in it. So we just laid it there, put the bag over it. We opened up the little wallet and there was $56 and some change. We divided that up. It was about 4:30, so we just went to the beach."

Excitement and fun for Douglas and G. W. mean trouble for them and for those who are in their way. The housing project is near busy Huntington Avenue, close to the YMCA and Northeastern University. Most of Douglas's street life is focused on this area, because he knows these streets and all the escape routes they provide. Douglas says, "When we go somewhere like on Boylston Street, or somewhere far, cops might see us; we might get chased; we might won't have a chance to get away. When me and G. W. went out for a car alone, G. W. popped it and everything, so I started driving it. When we started going down the street, two cops, they was right in back of us in a car. So G. W., he looked back and saw them. He yelled and said, 'Step on the gas.' So the cops heard him, put on their sirens . . . we got chased. So I made a turn around the bridge and started back into the project. They tried to cut in front of us, but I kept turning so they wouldn't. So I kept going, so when we got into the project I started putting up more speed. By the time they got near us, we jumped, stopped the car and got out and ran in the project building, ran out the other side."

Doug and G. W. like subway stations, where robbery is easy in the quiet hours. Symphony Station, opposite Boston's concert hall, is a particular favorite, because it is both near to home and likely to provide affluent victims. Doug recalls a day when "me and G. W. was in Symphony Station. There was this lady . . . so I said to G. W., 'I wanna get the pocketbook.' 'O.K.,' he said, 'Where we gonna run at?' I said, 'You should know—where do we always run?' He said, 'O.K.' So I snatched, so, you know, I snuck up behind the lady first, and I grabbed it. She started yelling and everything . . . so we ran right under the trolley tunnel. That's where we go . . . but we stay on the side. We started running, the trolley started coming. So there's big holes in the wall. We ducked into one of these and when the trolley go by, we run right out the tunnel. There was $160 in it and so when we met Teddy and them in the project, we went to Revere Beach the next day."

Douglas and G. W. pursue their illegal adventures alone, but they have groups of friends for other activities. They have formed a singing group and club called "The Esquires" with five or six other boys. They practice together, party together, and buy matching ensembles for their shows. They are admittedly short on musical talent and go in for imitations of well-known black singing groups, but they enjoy themselves. The group is a launching pad for the rest of their social life. Douglas describes a typical day. "Harry (the informal leader of the singing group) told us to go home, get dressed, so we could go down there (to the recreation rooms in Building 81). So we all put on our—we all got the same suit, you know. Yellow pants with yellow shirts with gold with it, and shoes that buckle on the side . . . black hats, black leather coats, we'll all put on the same thing . . . black silk socks. So we went over, down 81, so all the other kids and everything started looking at us, yelling 'Look at the Esquires,' and everything. So we said, 'That's right, you like us?' And everyone started laughing. So I said, 'G. W., put a dime in the juke box— play "Stand By Me" or something like that.' So he played it, so we all started dancing . . . and some girls starting coming, all the kids started coming from the back room. They started looking at us, and everything. So we started getting all shy and everything, so we went running out the place. We didn't get back down there, so we all went back home, put back on our dungarees—we kept our leather coats on—so we went in the basketball court, started playing basketball."

For a singing group, "The Esquires" do not seem very eager to perform, but the group gives the boys a way of attracting attention and providing a kind of mutual solidarity. The kind of support the boys give each other usually leads to trouble. The

106

group goes to the Y to practice, and the custodians ask them to show a pass, proving they are authorized to be in the building. The boys jive the janitors, and the janitors call the cops. Then, as Douglas describes it, one custodian "grabbed me by the collar and said, 'Come on upstairs with me.' So he told the other janitor to get G. W. The janitor reached for G. W. . . . he moved and I snatched away. G. W., he grabbed this Royal Crown bottle, threw it at the janitor. I picked up a chair and threw it at him, so Ralph and them starting throwing ash trays and everything. So we ranned out the door and shut the door on one of the janitor's arms. We started laughing and running. We ran all the way to the project."

Douglas's parents blame the trouble on his friendship with G. W. Mr. Jones says, "He hasn't been in trouble lately, just when he is with G. W. Poole and Teddy Brown, then he is always into something. Something like 'follow the leader.'" And Mrs. Jones concurs, saying that she doesn't allow G. W. or Teddy to come around.

Douglas and His Schools—1967

Doug and G. W. want to stay together and will arrange to be transferred to another school or get expelled from class to stay with one another. In fact, the two have spent most of their junior high school careers shuttling back and forth between the all-black Ryan and the predominantly white Murphy Junior High School, which is more convenient to Doug's house.

Doug began seventh grade at the Murphy, but transferred to the Ryan after a round of fights and suspensions. G. W. soon followed and their pattern of conflict and disruption continued. Encounters between Douglas and adults sometimes generate major uproars, even when they begin with the most minor issues. Douglas describes a time at the Ryan when he came to school with his tie hanging out of his back pocket. Mr. James, assistant principal and tie freak, stopped him in the lunch room and, yanking at his shoulder, asked, "'Where's your tie?' So I said, 'It's

107

in my back pocket.' He said, 'put it on, before I pick it out and hang it around your neck.' So I told him to try it. He took the tie out, tried to get it around my neck, and I snatched it out and pushed him. He leaned back on the table and flipped right over it." Two teachers grabbed Douglas and "just, you know, threw me right out the school. Left my lunch money on the table, and coat in the school. I just waited out there about a half an hour, and rang the bell. This boy came to the door . . . you know, he didn't know what happened, so I just walked in the school . . . I went in my room . . . got my coat and everything, went in the cafeteria and my 35¢ was still there on the table." Douglas chuckles, and adds, "I got that, and just went home. Didn't tell my mother nothing." He never really went back.

He tried to get back into the Murphy after that, but they were less than eager for his return. Doug got into one argument with a teacher and was immediately taken out of his classes. The principal assigned him to janitorial work for the indefinite future. G. W., who had followed Doug back to the Murphy, "didn't like doin' no work in school," Doug says. "So he got in trouble on purpose to get down with me." Both boys preferred this to regular classes, since they could work a little, relax a little, and get their orders from the head janitor rather than from teachers.

By the end of the seventh grade, Douglas has nothing positive to say about school, even in his recollections of elementary grades. He talks about school as he talks about his family, about his life—I had a fight with this teacher; the principal yelled at me. He remembers only one teacher who treated him with kindness and respect. "She thinks I am nice, because I never got in trouble with her or nothing . . . when she tells me to do something, I don't give her no back talk." This English teacher took Douglas seriously, called on him for help with classroom chores, and made him feel that attention in that class was worthwhile. "She say, 'Will you please pay attention to me next time, so I could say something proud about you to other teachers?" She is Douglas's one bright classroom recollection.

After a few weeks in the basement, helping the janitor, Doug and G. W. were returned to regular classes and regular trouble. Mr. Jones says, "Down in Murphy they acted like they didn't want him in school, and that made him lose confidence, so he said he was going to get a job." Douglas dropped out of school in seventh grade, seven months before his sixteenth birthday.

Whatever the immediate reasons for his dropping out, Douglas never intended to continue past the tenth grade. Along with all of his friends, Douglas looked forward to sixteen as a magic age, when a person is finally allowed to do what he wants. "When I first get 16," Douglas said, early in the seventh grade, "I want to stay in the house at least until around 12 o'clock, you know, when all the pictures I like go off. Go out, call for G. W., and then go out and fool. We might go to the club house, play music, or go to the YMCA—start fooling around, or play the piano in the room." He wants to "sleep all day," giving a reason why he hates school, "they don't give you enough of sleep. When I get up in the morning, I feel dead and weak and everything."

Douglas's close friends had all planned to quit, although some of them have back-up plans for night school or other ways to complete their diplomas. One friend says that he has to quit, because the teachers get on his nerves, and "if he keeps going to school he just might end up killing one of them." G. W. and Teddy plan to go to night school, because "we have, you know, more fun in the daytime than at night. We have more things to do when the stores open. You know, when the good programs come on TV, like the Beverly Hillbillies . . . stuff like that." Douglas says that he will "do like G. W.'s gonna do. Go to night school." He says that he would like to go through the tenth grade, because by then he'll "know more things than I know now." But what these things are, and whether he expects to learn them in school or on the street, is not clear. Douglas has a vague sense that school ought to be good for something, but his loathing overcomes all other considerations. "I think school's a nice place, you know, to be . . . teachin' things, so the person, ah, get a good job goin' for yourself . . . sometimes I wish that . . . if that man were still living who thought of school, I would kill him . . . something like that. Be thinking that sometimes . . . that if, you know, he never thought of school and no one else did . . . things like that."

Douglas's low educational expectations have been further depressed by the expectations of his parents and teachers. Douglas says that his parents want him to go "about to the ninth grade like my brother Danny did." His father clings to a faint hope that Douglas will finish high school and have some kind of trade. Mrs. Jones bluntly states, "He don't like school, period. But he gotta go. And the teacher told me, he said, 'He's here every day, but he just don't want to learn.' That's it. And so I guess when he gets sixteen he can quit. I'm not gonna make him go." The Joneses talk about the importance of education and its utility for making the necessary connections with the world of work, but they see no way to make the schools work for their boys. Danny left school in tenth grade to join the Job Corps. The younger boys are often truant. And the Joneses assume that the fault lies with their children. Mrs. Jones says that one of Douglas's teachers told her that "Douglas, he put his mind on something, he's one of the smartest boys and he's one of the neatest workers . . . so he had him doing something in his room the other day, and said, 'Mrs. Jones, you shoulda saw how beautiful a job your son, he did.' Said if Douglas wanna do something, he can really do it. But if he don't wanna do it, he don't do it. I said, 'That's exactly the way he is here at the house. You almost have to pet Douglas and pay Douglas to do things. If he don't want to do it, he won't do it."

Douglas speaks of himself as a troublemaker, a classroom clown. His teachers describe him as withdrawn, bored, utterly uninterested in the routine. One teacher says, "I had him in the afternoon all the time . . . he was just quiet and withdrawn. He looked like he was completely bored . . . he was like . . . it was like a psychiatric situation. He'd put his head down; pick it up. Write his name down . . . I'd bring him a pencil . . . then he would put his head down . . . actually no involvement."

Another teacher said she pushed Douglas to perform and felt that he had the ability to do the work. She says he "read beautifully," but that he was not a worker. She saw him as a boy

110

biding his time until he turned sixteen and could quit school. "The future didn't mean much more to him as long as he ate, slept, and had a few clothes on his back," she says. "That would be more his description. I don't think he would give you much trouble—just don't complain. Don't bother him and he won't bother you." This teacher feels that Douglas will be handicapped by dropping out, that he will not be able to get the job he would like to have, "unless he changes. If he changes... something may shock him." As a last resort, she says, "I'm hoping someday they'll come up with something—have a little box they can turn on and it will do this for you. I wish I knew if there was some way you could put a spark plug in them. Try to press a button . . . if the buttons were numbered: ambition, or this, or that. And someone would press the button of ambition, I think he'd make it. Someone else has got to do it. He is not going to do it on his own. But I think that some smart scientist is going to find a way of creating some sort of desire within the human body of some of these slow ones who need a push. Some people are wonderful but you've got to push them all the time."

Douglas Views the World of Work

Like most seventh graders, Douglas lives very much in the present. But he has well-defined dreams for the future. In the ninth grade, he wants to be a salesman in a large department store, "like Jordan's or Sears." He would prefer to work in the television and phonograph department, where he could "turn 'em on . . . look at it . . . something like that, no customers to take care of . . . you know, turn on a hi fi or something like that. No customers to take care of . . . play a record . . . that's what I like about it." He acknowledges that there might be things about the job that he might not like, such as having to deal with a demanding customer, but he feels that the freedom in such a job would compensate because salesmen can "walk around the store . . . do most anything they want to."

He hasn't thought much about what he would have to do to get a job at Jordan's or Sears, but he thinks he could keep it if he got it. "I don't think the work would be hard, and it'd be nice, selling televisions . . . add money all in the cash register, and show that I was working hard and everything. You might have to learn about electronics and everything . . . when you go in, telling everything you know about 'em . . . if you do, you gonna have to sign some papers and everything like that."

Douglas says his mother would like him to be a doctor, but he suggested that she get his brother Danny to do it instead, because he does not want to work around "dead people." "She said, 'Suppose I was sick or something and didn't have time to go to the hospital. And you learned medical things, and everything, you know, and how to cure. You can save my life. Suppose you just don't be nothing,' she say, and I say, like 'I was planning on working in a big department store.' She be saying, 'Well, suppose I be in bed all sick, dying, and you don't know nothing about doctoring?' And I say, 'Why don't you tell Danny or one of them to be a doctor . . . ?' I told her I didn't like that stuff." Mr. Jones says only that he would like to see Douglas get into some kind of trade that would allow him to earn a decent living.

In the meantime, Douglas earns a little money working at odd jobs when he can find them. He stays until he gets fed up with the work, or has a run-in with the boss. "Me and G. W. got one on Huntington Avenue. 'Bout for a week. The man was kinda mean. G. W. just bust a bottle of shampoo. Man started talkin' his stuff to him. Said that cost money, he should take it out of his pay. So me and G. W., we worked that day and didn't come back the next day." But despite his difficulty in getting and keeping jobs, Douglas says he would rather have steady work than depend on the kind of criminal activity that has kept him solvent but in constant trouble.

STALLED IN THE GHETTO: 1970

Life at Home

Life in the Jones household has grown even more difficult over the last three years. Although only James is still living at home, all

112

the family problems have escalated—drinking, quarrels, trouble with the law. Mr. Jones is drinking heavily, and Douglas can no longer communicate with him. "Can't understand him the way he is now," he says. "The liquor is messing up his mind. If he sends you to the store for cigarettes and you bring them back, he'll say he sent you for a box of sugar. Forgets quickly. Before, you could . . . you used to be able to talk with him, ask his advice. But now all he wants to do is hang on street corners and drink—just don't want to be bothered with anyone. You tell him something, he'll say to you, 'Don't you think you're old enough now? Figure out your own problems and solve them.' Just can't talk with him anymore."

Daniel has dropped out of school and is currently in Charles Street jail for car theft. Danny married and moved out of the family apartment and into one of his own in the Columbia Point project. He is drinking more, and his fights with Douglas are more serious. Douglas says that when Danny is drunk, he thinks he can "whip the world . . . He jumps me and we get into fights. I fight with him then till someone breaks it up or one of us is hurt and can't fight any more." James, the youngest, is still doing fairly well, although Douglas feels he suffers unduly from his father's drunken belligerence.

Douglas feels closer to his younger brothers now than he does to Danny. He tries to give them what protection and support he can. "Mother called me up one day," he says, "and told me that my father was drinking heavy and he was beating on my smallest brother for nothing. I went over there and try to talk to him. He just started arguing at me, wanted to fight, so I started arguing back at him. I told my brother that if he hears from the cat, pack up your clothes and come over, we'll put him up." He and Daniel share tales of survival and Douglas says they try to help each other out. "If one of us get in trouble, the other be right there."

Douglas feels that he has changed. He says that he has become more sensitive and short-tempered with his family and his friends. He has been in a "lot of things—fights, jail, arguments—more than I ever had." He attributes this to drink and to his bad temper.

Arguments with his friends begin when, "like they ask me for a couple of dollars and I say, 'Well, you owe me already,' but they say, 'come on, you can do this for me; I'll pay you back,' then when I know they are lying, I just bust out."

Douglas was always a fighter, but he feels his new agressiveness is important and worth being concerned about. "I'm getting a little too fresh . . . talk back to relatives now. Never used to do that . . . Like to be like I used to be . . . in a way. Go to work every day, be more frank with people. Now I am not." He still feels good about his relationship with his mother, "I can talk to her, have a ball with her. Sit down at the kitchen table, ask her advice on something; she'll give it to you if she knows it."

Douglas says he knows what his parents think of him. He says his mother might describe him to someone as being, "O.K., but don't get me rowdy sometimes 'cause then I might cut your throat, something like that, she said it to someone before. She'll say if I have something you ask for, I give it to you, no questions asked." He goes on to say that she would be wrong about saying that he would cut someone's throat, but the rest would describe him perfectly. His father, he thinks, would say, "I'm evil, I don't like people to put their hands on me and what not. Oh yeah, he would talk nasty, just nasty about me. Oh, he'll say I'm a thief. Oh yeah, he'll talk like that, because I heard him before."

His best friend, he thinks, would be more positive. "I think he would say I'm O.K., you can get along with me—get in trouble, I'll help you out. I think he'd tell a person maybe 'keep on guard' that I'm short tempered or something." He believes that the special thing about himself that makes him different is that "I have a short temper . . . I never met anyone else with one." He thinks he is good at some things—being a clown for the pleasure of his friends, "joking around, being funny all the time when I'm drinking . . . they like that about me" and "telling the truth and giving them what they want for them to like me more."

Douglas says that his parents are generally satisfied with how things are going for him. "They're fairly happy now because I'm working, taking care of myself, not hanging around on the streets." His mother has told him "she knew I would make something of myself. She tells me she's glad I got a job because like my brother Danny just stays around the house all the time." Douglas shares his earnings with his parents when they need it, and if he has enough to spare. And they will give him money from the welfare check if he needs it badly enough.

Douglas in His Own Place

Now that Douglas has extricated himself physically if not emotionally from his family, he lives in Roxbury, next to a trolley garage. The apartment he shares with three roommates is on the second floor of a three-story yellow brick walk-up. Douglas contributes one-third of the $65-per-month rent and shares the utility bill. He likes his new quarters because they are relatively peaceful and quiet, with a back porch for barbecues and there are only a "few rats running around." Douglas likes to socialize with his roommates and their friends, but he still needs a certain amount of distance and privacy to collect himself. "Like on weekends," he says, "everyone at the house who I live with wants to go out someplace to visit one boy. I don't want to go, something like that. You know, and I don't know why. I don't have anything to do . . . I don't know, I just like to watch television on the weekends. I just sit around the house and listen to records." Douglas can't explain his reluctance, but says that this creates problems for him with one roommate who gets angry at him for not going along with the group.

As in the seventh grade, Douglas has one close running buddy, now a young man named Billy Rose. Boozing and battling is their chief pastime. They get drunk and fight each other and anyone who interferes. Douglas describes one such incident. "Oh, it was over in the project, around ten at night. We were fighting— breaking out windows, pushing each other through people's apartment doors and what not, so they called the cops. We stopped fighting each other and started fighting them. They couldn't handle us so they called more. They came. They put handcuffs on us, took us to the station. Wow! Gave us a good beating."

Billy has replaced G. W. in Douglas's life, but another friend, Ralph Crown, has become the man Douglas feels closest to. Older than Douglas, and a lady's man, Ralph has drawn Douglas into more social life than he has ever known before. Douglas says he and Ralph spend weekends "riding around in a car, talk to women, have a ball."

They go to many of the bars that Mr. Jones used to frequent, picking up women, getting into fights. Douglas says it is Ralph who "helps me out more than anyone else does when I get in trouble; he always asks me if I want to borrow his rifle . . . blow a person away. Offers to help me in fights—twice when I was going to have a fight with someone else, he ask me if I wanted him to take my place."

Work and Crime

Douglas has been working, off and on, since he left home. In mid-1970, he works as a stockman and shipper for an auto parts department in Somerville—a long way from home. To get there in time, Douglas has to get up at 5 a.m., to get a ride from a friend who works in the same place. But he likes the job, and says that he goes to bed earlier these days and doesn't even need an alarm clock—this from the boy who couldn't get himself four blocks to school in the morning because he was too exhausted. He describes his day with some pleasure. "Arrive, wash-up, sit down and rest before you start, get the slip saying what kind of stock I'm suppose to bring up. Take a break at ten, then work til lunch at twelve noon, then take another break at three. Quit at four. No arguments or nothing with people there." He gets along well with his white boss—"at lunch we've gone to the barroom to have a few beers together."

But this pleasant job is not likely to last. Douglas depends on his friend for the ride, and the friend "probably going to quit, and then I don't know how I'd get there." Douglas's attachment to all his jobs has been tenuous, depending on transportation, how bored he becomes, how much trouble he has gotten into.

Trouble is still the key to Douglas's life, and it has interfered with his ability to make for himself the life he would like. He had a good job, at one point, about a five minute walk from his apartment. "I knew the place," he says, "I was like a supervisor there in a way. I thought the pay was okay. Got along with everyone." But he was sent to jail and by the time he got out, the job was gone.

Douglas has only been to jail once—Charles Street, for two months—but there has been little let up in his conflict with the law. He has been arrested for fighting, for assaulting the custodians in the YMCA, for breaking and entering. The last was the most serious charge, although Douglas does not take it particularly seriously. "There was this store on the corner. Friend said it had an alarm, but I said no it couldn't because the glass was already broken and boarded up. So we got together, pulled the screen off, looked around, then we kicked the board in, waited for a while to make sure everything was all right, came back, got in, went upstairs, grabbed some bags, loaded them with cigarettes, bacon, chicken and what not. On our way out, cops were coming out the street.

"We didn't have time to run, because they spotted us. By the time we turned, there were two coming with their guns drawn out. So we went to run the other way, and there were these two paddywagons. So we had to give up. They grabbed us and hit us a few times. They took us to Station 10; they asked us some questions, like who thought of it. I said I did. They said, 'Why do you want to do that sort of thing? What if it was your own house or something?' I said, 'I don't know. I haven't given it much thought. I needed something, that's all.' He said, 'You need something, you're going to have something.' Kept on calling me black and what-not; started talking fresh with me, trying to get me mad so they would have something to beat me for. I kept my cool."

117

Recently, Douglas's street life had been taking even more dangerous turns. He describes one incident which echoes the events that sent his father to prison for manslaughter. "Happened about four weeks ago. There was this white dude at Washington Street. This was around three a.m. in the morning. I was coming from the Hill. No one was out there. I bumped into him because I didn't see him—it was too dark. So he said, 'Aren't you going to say anything?' You know, he started it. I said, 'You better get the hell away from me.' I didn't feel like being bothered with anyone. So he came up to me and grabbed me and started punching me. So I said, 'Wow!' I grabbed him and threw him down, stomped on him. Just left him there. I didn't even know if he was dead or alive. I knew his last name 'cause I knew him from someplace. Next thing I heard was . . . I saw on the police blotter he had a broken neck."

Douglas in Search of the Good Life—1970

Despite his taste for trouble and his nearly uniform bad experience in school, Douglas connects education, work, and living a good life. He says that when he is older, he would like to be "living good—clean house, good job, good pay, do what I want to do. Have a nice house, car, maybe a wife." And the wife he wants is completely unlike "most of the women I know who go into barrooms every night, mess with different boys." For his good life, Douglas wants a "nice, easygoing girl, not too rowdy, clean."

Douglas now sees school as the route to all this, investing it with a magical ability to transform lives. He wants to be trained in what he calls electronics—repairing televisions, radios, high fidelity equipment. But he is uncertain that he will ever be able to get the education he needs. "I think I would go back to school and get an education really," he says, "But no, I can't, because I am with my friends and have to pay rent." And he looks back at high school as an opportunity lost rather than as an active possibility. He says he is not sure if a person can make more money in his lifetime if he finishes high school, but he adds, "I've gone to a lot of jobs before, and I couldn't get into them because I didn't have a diploma."

He knows about prejudice and the limits it puts on his prospects. He says, "Well, the job business. The boss of the company or something could be prejudice against blacks. Because, you know he's going to be white. He just might be prejudice, tell us, the blacks that he's all filled up, don't need any help. But if a white guy go in behind you, I believe he would get one." And he says that he doesn't go into the white areas "like up in Dorchester, because "you get jumped. But if they come in a black section, we don't even touch them. We just let them walk around, too. We can't go a lot of places where they discriminate without getting jumped."

He doesn't name race as a barrier between himself and the life he wants, but he feels that whites have more access to opportunity than blacks in the ways which lead to the kind of success he would want. "All the white people I've met or I've heard of, they seem smarter, they sound smarter . . . they seem like they have learned more than us, 'cause they've been taught better or something— they pay more attention than us blacks do in their work." I just don't see whites living in ghettos and whatnot like blacks do; that's why I say they are living better." But he feels helpless to change the *status quo*.

DOUGLAS AT TWENTY-ONE—STILL SLIDING: 1973

Although Douglas has moved around a lot over the last three years, he still keeps in close touch with his family and with his old friends. He moves with little provocation—a casual invitation, a friendly atmosphere, a bunch of old friends are enough to make him pack his things and go along. But as he says, he doesn't *really* move into these various apartments, but spends two or three nights in a place, then a few nights at his mother's, and then moves on again. At one point, he moved back home for a number of months until he could find a more stable base of operations.

Douglas gets along better with his family these days. The senior Joneses are now alone in their apartment. Danny and his wife have split up, but he still lives in his own apartment. Daniel is in jail again—serving time at the Framington reformatory for armed robbery (he tried to hold up a grocery store, Douglas says, got away, but "a guy dropped a dime [informed] on him . . ."). James, who had been hooking school more than he had been attending, has left for a Job Corps camp in Kentucky. Douglas worries some about his brothers: Danny has a penchant for drugs and other people's wives; Daniel is on drugs too, and spends a lot of time in court. James is the least subject of concern. He does do a little stealing, Douglas says, but he is slick, and doesn't get caught.

Douglas says his parents are doing fine, but adds that his father continues to drink too much and is disintegrating rapidly. "He gets high . . . he's hearing things. You can be talking about him. Wanna fight and everything else. When he is sober, he is a nice guy, really is. The doctors told him to stop and he did for about two months and he started back up again." About his mother, he says, "She's not suffering from anything, but sometimes she drinks a little too much. Argues with the neighbors about dirtying up the hallways, kids playing in front of her door while she's trying to watch her soap operas." Douglas says that he and his mother don't fight as much as they used to, although they still have occasional battles. "Not too long ago, I brought about three friends of mine upstairs in the house without asking her," he says. "She got pissed off, she really did, started jumping on me. I threw my food on the counter. She pushed me, and I pushed her back. That's the last time we argued. No more after that."

Douglas now sees his parents as warm people, generous with their resources. "You ask for a few bucks, she'll give it to me. She won't lie and say she don't have it like some people . . . My father, he's all right, like if today, right, I would come in, he would say to me, 'You broke?' I'd say, 'Yeah.' He'd say, 'Here's a few bucks,' pull it right out of his pocket and give it to me. They are free-hearted with their money if they have it." He sees a lot of his parents in himself, in superficial and in deeper ways. "Well, my mother," he says, "I'm like her, I'm a television freak, and my father, when he don't drink, he says nothing. He just sit there, don't open his mouth, read a book, watch television, or stare out the window." He also sees how much he is like his father when he is high. Douglas says that when he is drinking, he likes to tease people the way his father does, provoking them to come after him.

At twenty-one, Douglas is finally ready to discuss his old, more damaging battles with his mother—the name-calling bouts that bothered Danny and his father, but which Douglas never mentioned. He says, "I used to really lose my temper, I call her 'bitch' . . . 'get the hell out of my face, or I'll kill you' . . . and shit, really swear. She called me 'sons of bitches,' 'black mother-fuckers,' she used to call me every name in the book; some names I never even heard of . . . sometimes can't even pronounce." He recollects the bitter fights with little rancor, and accepts the explanation of a neighbor. "A friend of my mother said we can't get along sometimes, you know, 'cause we look alike and we both black." And he adds that his mother admits that they look alike, but "she don't believe she's blacker than I am."

After his series of moves from one apartment to another, Douglas has now settled into an apartment with Billy Rose, his old companion in mayhem, and another young man. Billy and Douglas have shared apartments on and off over the past three years, and live in the Church Road Project across the street from the senior Joneses. Douglas is not sure how Billy got into public housing. "I guess he just went and signed up for it. So he asked me did I want to move in with him, and I said 'Okay.' So here we are."

Drinking and fighting are still their favorite occupations, with picking up women a distant third. Douglas recounts a time when he and Billy "got into an argument and started fighting one another. Got disgusted with each other. I stopped fighting, I got so disgusted at it. I back-handed a window. Billy had punched a window out with his hand. We ended up in the hospital for about four days." Douglas's cut hand was so bad this time that it required thirty stitches to close it up. He still has numbness in the hand from tendon and nerve damage. He says he might have made the damage worse because he took the stitches out himself instead of going back to the hospital. And he never went in for the physical therapy he needed.

Douglas says trouble just happens, everywhere he and his friends go. When they go to lounges and bars, one of his friends might talk with a woman and say the wrong thing. She might get upset and start raising hell, he says, and then a fight starts. In the bars they go to—the Patio Lounge, the Party Cafe, and others of the old "bucket of blood" type—when fights start, everyone grabs for a bottle and gets ready to beat someone else's brains out.

But Douglas also says that when trouble doesn't come to them, they often go out looking for it. "You know," he says, "mess with whiteys. I have nothing against them, we just messing with them because they are white, that's all. We don't want to go around messing with our own kind of people. We just mess with them because they are just there. I guess it's because I didn't use to like them, so from there, I just kept picking on them. Yeah, I used to be prejudiced against them." Douglas says he is not particularly prejudiced any more, but he just likes "beating on" whites, "messing around with them, stealing from them and what not. That's the only people we really steal from—the cars—don't mess with any brothers' or sisters' cars. Just them."

Douglas says he is uninterested in black issues and black leaders and says "to me everything is cool. I don't listen or read books on things like that." But he picks his racial responses carefully—he can drink comfortably with his white boss and equally comfortably rob a white shopper.

Douglas ascribes most of his fights with friends and other dangerous escapades to "booze . . . drinking. Just getting in an argument, over nothing really, start to fight for no reason at all. It just be the booze, that's all it is. Wild Irish Rose, Gordon's vodka, and beer. That's really all we drink." But no amount of trouble seems to stop the boozing. The day after Douglas and Billy got out of the hospital, their hands still in bandages, they went immediately to buy "three or four fifths of Wild Irish Rose. The day we got out we started drinking."

Douglas feels that he has full command of his drinking—that he can stop at will. He says he is certain that he will never allow himself to fall into the same condition as his father and some of his father's drinking buddies. He can stop drinking whenever he wants to, he claims, and besides, he takes care of his stomach. "Sometimes I start out drinking before I eat anything," he says. "Once I feel that burning sensation, I get something to eat right there. That would be the booze eating into your stomach. That's one thing I do is eat. I feel my stomach messing up, I would stop drinking right there. I ain't gonna keep drinking like they do."

But Douglas has not stopped yet, because, he says, "when I don't drink, I don't have any fun. Could be a roomful of people drinking, laughing together, I'd be sitting there sometime looking stupid. So I drink too, just to be with them." He doesn't care much for the "sober Douglas," on the wagon. "I don't really go places. I just sit around the house, mostly watch television, don't talk much." But the "drinking Douglas . . . that's when I go out, can't stay in the house. Then I gotta go out and have fun somewhere, hang with the boys, have fun and what not."

He says that he only has fun when he is high because liquor "builds your courage more," gives him the confidence to overcome his shyness. "I guess you build up confidence in yourself—I don't know, you talk more, rap more to people. Specially if you really want to say something to a girl. When you are sober, you can't, because you would think it was wrong, but by the time you get high, you say, 'Well, the hell with it, I am going to say it now.' You say it, it be all right. The girl likes it. They fall for you just like that (snaps his fingers)." When he is sober, Douglas says, he doesn't talk sex to women. "Sober, I don't even talk to them. I stay in the house sometimes, like I did yesterday and like I am doing today." He says he's shy when he isn't drinking, "but when I'm high, I would tire you . . . sometimes women don't want to be with me then."

Douglas Surviving—Back with G. W.

Douglas is currently out of a job and lives primarily on a $134.00, bi-weekly welfare check. His mother introduced him to the welfare system. "My mother brought me up there," Douglas says. "She told her social worker about me and so she told me to go up there. I went and filled out a blue card. And they asked me a few questions ... Had I been looking for work? I had to lie a little and tell them I just got out of jail and I am looking for a job. So they said 'O.K., we'll see what we can do. We'll send a letter telling you when to pick up your check.' It took quite a while. I been getting them every two weeks."

But the welfare checks are not enough for him to live on, and he says, "that's why I go out and try to hustle up some money any way I can." One of the ways is to team up with his old running buddy, G. W. He says he doesn't see G. W. often, but during the summer they "made a nice hit." Douglas describes the incident— an event right out of the old days in the project. "It was 5 a.m. in the morning. We were high, so we were broke. We needed some scratch in our pockets. So G. W. said, 'Let's go over to Columbia Point Station and wait on a white guy ... jam 'im up and rip 'im off.' So we went there, we waited and all of a sudden, one came in. We played as if we were waiting on the train. Time he turned his back, G. W. grabbed him, threw him down. I went into his pocket and got his loose change and a white envelope that contained $600. He yelled out, 'That's my vacation money.' We said, 'We don't give a damn,' and stomped him in his mouth and kept him quiet till we got away. We ended back up in Columbia Point at G. W.'s mother's house and counted out the money there. Evened it out to one another. After that I got about an hour's nap, then I left."

The Continuing Dream

Douglas has not fulfilled any of the ambitions he voiced in 1967 and in 1970, but he still harbors dreams of a good life that he will have someday. He no longer wants to be a television salesman or an electronic repairman. Now he would like to be a plasterer. He works, occasionally, for a friend who has a brother in the real estate business, helping them fix up apartments before they rent them out. Plastering and painting caught Douglas's interest. "I be looking at them, trying to learn. Sometimes I'll pick up the trowel, and do a wall. It turn out all right. I like that kind of work." He likes the notion of being his own boss. Plasterers, he says, have no one to tell them what to do. But he feels uncertain about his skill, and says he would want some kind of on-the-job training program where he could sharpen his abilities while he worked.

Douglas says, "I don't think about the future. Once I get a job I really like, I slack up off the drinking. Like I said, only drink Friday, Saturday, rest Sunday, and be ready for work Monday again. Taking it easy like that." He has no plans for marriage. Although he sees several women, it is "occasionally, only when I am high." He says he would shack up with a woman who would let him maintain his independence, let him come and go as he pleases. But he does not see himself in the husband role and he wants no children. His most constant girl friend is a woman who lives in Annunciation Road, around the corner from his old home project. She has three children, but Douglas says he doesn't mind them. They aren't his own.

This woman has been "real fine" to Douglas, anticipating his needs, lending him money, buying him cigarettes, and treating him well. He says that if he moved in with someone like her, he would do the best he could to help her buy food and clothes for herself and her children. And if he had kids of his own, he would try to "teach them to avoid trouble, less swearing, respecting adults." But then he laughs and adds, "I can't really say, because I have no respect. I wouldn't know what to teach them."

But if he tries not to think about the future, Douglas does think about the past, about the lost education which he thinks is the missing link between himself and success. He blames his friends for his school difficulties. "I used to like it at one time," he says.

125

"I used to be on the honor roll. I had five stars at one time—you know that? Until Teddy Brown and G. W. Poole came in the class. They messed me up right there. All my stars just disappeared. From then on, we started hooking school together. This was in the Murphy. Started hooking school . . . got suspended. Started messing around with the teachers, buggin' them. We used to drink beer in there."

He says he doesn't know if a high school diploma is important, pointing out that his brother has one and he isn't working. But he feels sad that he never got the credential. "I coulda got a high school diploma. I coulda got one, but I never went back there. Like two friends of mine, girls, they came up to my mother's house one day and happened to look at the walls and seen my baby brother James's diploma up there. They asked, 'Where's yours?' I told them I had lost it—embarrassed as a motherfucker. I wish I woulda had one then to show them. All I had to show was a happy and sad face. . . . What you make in woodwork shop."

FOCUS: DOUGLAS JONES—BUYING THE MYTH

"All the white people I've met . . . they seem smarter . . . they seem like they have learned more than us, 'cause they've been taught better or something—they pay more attention than us blacks do in their work. I just don't see whites living in ghettos and whatnot like blacks do; that's why I say they are living better."

The worst thing anyone can call Douglas Jones is "black." His mother taunts him with the color of his skin (and hers), and his brother worries that she has gone too far. Douglas sees whites as aliens; he has no compunctions about taking their money or beating them up. But simultaneously, he sees whites as better than himself. He has bought the myth of black inferiority.

Douglas is far from the only young man in our study to harbor this destructive belief. Even the most militant youths, able on one day to talk rationally about the pervasive effects of racism on

126

blacks in our society, will, in the next interview, confess to believing that whites are smarter, more competent, more loyal to their own communities. And, while they are able to marshall facts and arguments in defense of black strength and integrity, their belief in white superiority seems, sometimes, more deeply felt.

There are powerful reasons for the pervasiveness of these beliefs. To a young person not acquainted with sophisticated economic and political information, the "evidence" seems all too clear. Like most children, Douglas watched a lot of television in the days before blacks were featured in commercials or situation comedies. Douglas saw the "lives" of the white middle class—comfortable, smooth flowing, vanilla pudding lives, with problems that even a fool of a father could solve. Then he looked at the lives around him, racked with insoluble problems—his father in prison, his mother drunk, his neighbors, like his brothers, in and out of serious trouble. What is he to conclude? One well-off white family, one troubled black young man might be luck; an all-too evident world of comfortable whites in rich abundance on the screen, contrasted with an entire neighborhood of poverty-stricken blacks with troubles that cannot be resolved in a half-hour sequence, makes it look as though whites know something that blacks do not.

The "evidence" of television is powerful, and it is heavily reinforced. The whites Douglas sees all have money—teachers, shoppers, even the guy in the subway station who was foolish enough to be carrying his vacation cash with him. Douglas sees them primarily as potential victims, but he sees them also as people with access to funds that he cannot legitimately get.

Further, Douglas has been taught black inferiority in school. Despite token "Black Pride" days, school has taught Douglas that whites "have learned more than us." The books he reads are full of white children doing all the television things, full of white historic heroes, white children cautiously counting their earnings in endless math problems. Further, many of Douglas' teachers believe, at some level, that their black students are inferior—genetically, culturally, because of their family structure, their

127

nutrition, their cognitive style, or whatever. When teachers believe in black inferiority, they communicate it, often wordlessly, to children already primed to accept a poor sense of themselves. Teachers tell them that any decent person can make it in America. But if the child knows no one who has made it, does this mean that blacks are not decent people? Too often, this is the conclusion the black child reaches, unconsciously encouraged by parents and teachers alike.

Among the young men in the Pathways study who made the great leap from the ghetto to the middle class world of college, we found a recurring pattern. Somewhere in their early lives, they had a model—a brother, an uncle, a close friend of the family who managed to break down the stereotypes, to dissipate the destructive beliefs.

But Douglas—and many of his peers—have no such close model to use as a wedge with which to break into the monolithic body of pseudo-evidence which shows only black failure. Black is poor. Black is dumb. Black is something to be ashamed of, whatever Malcolm X might have said. School says so, television says so, the evidence of eyes and ears in the housing project all confirm what Douglas learned, quite literally, at his mother's knee.

Douglas does not know, and the schools do not teach him, that the behaviors he sees as black are associated with lower class life styles both black and white. He does not realize that much of the physical decay and anti-social behavior around him is the product of poverty, low-status, and white racism, not a result of his color. Because he does not understand social cause and effect, he cannot distinguish between Douglas the victim and Douglas the perpetrator.

When we wonder why Douglas becomes a drop-out and a free-style bandit, why some of his peers, who are clearly intelligent and ambitious, have difficulty completing an education, we must remember that the myth is powerful and difficult to combat. Douglas is acting out a role which he believes is one of the few available to black men. When others attempt to lay claims to roles they perceive as "white", they must battle not only their own, often inferior academic preparation, but also their deeply rooted sense that "white" success is not possible for them.

Chapter
5
Andy Garrison—
Keeping Close

ANDY AT THIRTEEN—SEVENTH GRADE

Andy Garrison slips into the classroom, looking around almost uncertainly at the familiar room. Shyly, he puts four neatly written sheets of paper on the teacher's desk—the homework for the last two weeks. The teacher looks over the written work, raises her head to compliment Andy on his accuracy. But he is gone. The other students in the class say they do not know where he went. Most of them never noticed that he had come at all.

Andy is a short, wispy boy who looks younger than his age. He is delicate and very, very thin. The juncture of thumb and wrist forms a deep hollow; there is no fluid flesh at the meeting of head and neck. His high Afro distorts his head size, making it look almost too big for the small body. He wears only a short-sleeved jacket with a sweater underneath in even the coldest weather. In the dead of winter he wears no boots, but rather a pair of black shoes with pointed toes which look two sizes too big.

He smiles a greal deal, laughs softly and often, speaks in a near whisper both in school and at home. On the street, with his brothers and sisters or his friend, Jackson, he is freer. He and Jackson walk very slowly through the city streets, pausing about every fifty yards to have a play fight, Andy leaping into the air to launch a spectacular kick that just misses his friend. But no one at

131

school sees this side of Andy. They see only the shy, reclusive, bright boy who is only rarely involved with what is going on.

THE GARRISON FAMILY

The family is the center of Andy's life, and the Garrisons seems to provide him with all the stimulation, adventure, and activity he needs. There are a lot of Garrisons—Samuel and Barbara Garrison have raised nine children in the last sixteen years, most of them small, delicately built, sharing a strong family resemblance. The senior Garrisons are both in their late forties, hard-working, respectable people, unwaveringly family-oriented. Around them swirls continuous activity. In addition to their nine children and whatever friends might be around, there are always animals underfoot. In Andy's memory, the family has harbored two dogs, four rabbits, a couple of garter snakes, lizards, white mice, cats, pigeons, squirrels, and several hundred fish.

At the center of this tumultuous household is Mrs. Garrison. She grew up in Dorset, Maine, a tiny farming community in which hers was the only black family. There were thirteen children in her family, so there was always someone to protect small, sickly Barbara from the racial taunts of schoolmates. She remembers, "My sister would beat the kids up, and then after that we were friends, they'd come to the house, and we'd go to their house, you know. My mother and father were good, respectable people, and the people and the kids knew that we weren't monsters. They just accepted us." Mrs. Garrison is very proud of her parents: her hard-working father who lost both his feet in a work accident, and her "nice, quiet, friendly" mother who "always had time for us." Mrs. Garrison speaks wistfully of her years at home and, indeed, she seems to have had trouble leaving. She left high school, although she says she loved it, because she began to have fainting spells in class, and stayed home, working off and on, until she was 27, when she left to marry Samuel Garrison, in the hope that they might duplicate the respectable and happy household of her childhood.

After bearing and raising nine children, Mrs. Garrison, in 1967, is a tired woman, frail and often sick. She leaves the house rarely except in the company of her family. The older children do the marketing and other errands. Although she belongs to the parent-teachers association for each of the three schools attended by her children, she rarely has anything to do with their school lives. She says, "I never have to go up there to see the teachers or anything. I've never been up to talk to any of them [except] when they have parent's day, or when they have open house." When the school calls to demand a parent, Mrs. Garrison arranges for Mr. Garrison to go, or deals with the issue on the telephone. But Mr. Garrison rarely manages to keep his school appointments. Something usually comes up, and Mrs. Garrison calls the principal and tells him "that we won't be able to make it."

Mrs. Garrison depends greatly on her children, especially for help in the house. She rates her children by how much they are willing to help at home. She says that Andy is very helpful, especially in contrast to his brothers. "If I ask him to do anything in the house," she says, "he'll always do it," and he is solicitous of her when she is sick, helpful with the housework if he is home from school.

Mrs. Garrison's happiest hours are spent in family trips to the beach or to dinner, and in games with her children and husband. When she needs to escape from the pressures of large family life, she retreats to Maine where her sisters and brothers still live. She claims no other interests. Although intelligent, articulate, and a reader (she once belonged to the Book-of-the-Month Club), she has little to say about black organizations, ideas, or current issues.

Mrs. Garrison does not complain much about her life, although she says if she were starting over she would have a smaller family. But she is distressed about her children's problems with drugs, school, and crime. Her one major effort was to teach her children to be honest, and she finds it hard that one son is in jail, and four other children are continually in and out of trouble with the police.

She tries to shut out her troubles. "All these problems I put behind me, I don't think about them. I feel that if I could sit down and think about it, I could go nuts thinking about the things that could happen to the kids." Instead, she turns her energy to creating inside her ramshackle Roxbury house, the home atmosphere she remembers from her own childhood.

Unlike Mrs. Garrison, who is open and accessible to every member of the family, Mr. Garrison is more reserved. He is a model family man—hard-working, sober. He does not drink, smoke, swear, or consort with women. He finds time to play with his kids and to go on weekend trips with his wife, even while working a full-time job and moonlighting in the evening. And yet, there is something remote about him, a part of himself that keeps separate, even when he is playing or working with his children. One of Andy's teachers says, "I have talked briefly to their father. He's very interesting. There's something mystical about Mr. Garrison. And it leaves me dubious of him." Andy seems to agree. He says that he and his father work together, on the car or on the house, and that his father tells him that it's good to have somebody around to help. And yet, when he talks about whom he loves the most in the family, Andy chooses his mother, saying that he doesn't like his father "that much."

Mr. Garrison was born and raised in the Boston area by his divorced mother who took her daughters and Samuel with her when she separated from her husband, leaving the rest of the sons with their father. Like his wife, Samuel Garrison grew up as the lone black in a white area. He graduated from South Boston High at the end of the depression, and set out to make his way in the white world in which he had been raised and educated.

It has never been easy. Samuel Garrison has always been self-confident and reasonably ambitious. As a boy, he says, "I always thought I would be smart enough to become a foreman or a supervisor, and it didn't matter what type of work, but I could always do things good." His ambitions, he remembers, were not excessive for a bright boy, "carpentry or printing or any job that wasn't backbreaking or filthy." His first job, at eighteen, was both—he was hired to wipe the dust off cars in a garage—and all his jobs since have similarly failed to measure up to his abilities and ambitions. Asked to describe the jobs he has held over the last thirty years, Mr. Garrison laughed briefly and said, "You got all night I guess."

His early working years seesawed back and forth between government and industrial jobs. In 1940 he worked in a paper factory for thirty-six cents an hour, pushing bales of paper around from machine to machine. Then he joined a Civilian Conservation Corps camp, leaving a year later with "some very high recommendations. Out of 15,000 men, my educational advisor said that I would be way up in the top ten or fifteen men."

This high praise did not help him much. All he could find was menial work, first in a pickle factory and then in a naval ammunition dump.

He left the ammunition dump for the Navy, where he joined the Sea-Bees who trained him intensively as a surveyor. He did well in the Navy. High test scores made him a petty officer, and hard work made him "top man" in his unit by the time of his release.

But once out of the Navy, the old pattern of one menial job after another continued. "I would go to different places," he recalls, "and get excellent marks on their qualifying tests, and fill their qualifications easily and still end up with no job. This would go on not once or twice, but month after month after month, over a period of maybe eight years, maybe longer than that.

"I searched down here for a job, searched, searched, searched, got a little bit of shoe factory work, but nothing very good. Then I took a correspondence course in electronics and got one of the best marks they've seen . . ." But a depressing pattern haunted his working life. Mr. Garrison would start at the bottom of the line in a small company and gradually work himself up. Then the company would go broke, or move, or drop the line he was working on, and he would have to start over again from the beginning. Now he is making $3.00 an hour as an assistant engineer in the Allen Engineering lab, a job no more stable than any of the others.

Mr. Garrison says he thinks "being a Negro" probably resulted in his being passed over for jobs, but he mostly blames bad luck and a bad job market for his lot. He says that blacks should think of themselves as Americans before they think of themselves as Negroes, because "Well, this is their country, and even though they're not treated like, ah, they're supposed to be, there is hope that they will be some day. I think it works out better that way, being American first."

Mr. Garrison has never been able to do more than barely make ends meet. He works at Allen Engineering during the day and repairs televisions in the evenings. This combined effort barely keeps the family afloat. Mr. Garrison is the undisputed authority in his house, the decision-maker and distributor of resources, but nothing he can do in the outside world gives him control of enough economic resources to permit him to relax a little.

His only respite from unending work is a small, locked den, filled with old radios, country and western records of earlier decades, and packages of Twinkies, which he hides from his children so that he can have a chance of eating one himself. In this sanctuary, Mr. Garrison keeps his few valuables away from the tumult of the household.

In 1967, all nine Garrison children are based at home, although not all of them are there. Samuel Jr. (Sammy), at eighteen, is in Deer Island Prison on an auto theft conviction, but plans to return home at the end of his sentence to marry his fiancee, Paula. Catherine, sixteen, divides her time between looking after the youngest children and going to school. She is a good student— she earns the best grades of any Garrison—and deftly manages the combination of studying and caring for the children.

Fourteen-year-old James is waiting for his sixteenth birthday when he can drop out of school. In the meantime, he entertains himself with casual illegalities—driving around in stolen cars,

136

petty larceny, sniffing glue with Andy. He is in continuous trouble with his father, who threatens to put him in the Youth Service Board's reform school (he had already been there more than once) and with school authorities who have transferred him to the Godvin disciplinary school for excessive truancy.

The twins, Andy and Elaine, at thirteen, show more differences than similarities. Andy is shy, passive, self-contained; Elaine is active, aggressive, a non-stop talker. Of the two, Mrs. Garrison considers Elaine the more intelligent and more scholarly. It is true that Elaine reads constantly and writes poetry in school and out, but she is as likely as Andy to cut school and more likely to be in trouble. Barbara, a year younger than the twins, is Elaine's closest companion. They look for trouble together—jumping trucks, snatching purses, luring strangers into buying illegal wine from them. Both girls are full of exuberant energy. Andy is often swept along with them in their adventures.

Betty and Tina, at nine and six, are hardly noticed by the older children. Betty seems to be more like Catherine than Elaine and Barbara—she is quiet, shy, obedient, and helpful at home, docile and reliable at school. Andy says that she "yells all the time," but only when tormented by her older brothers and sisters. Tina is more lively. Andy says she's "always squealing," and Elaine comments loftily that Tina "likes to run around with her little friends." She is extremely pretty, the youngest girl, a little spoiled, and tends to get away with doing less in the house than Betty. She is a favorite with her teachers as well and brings home A's in conduct as well as good grades.

Bobby, the baby, is fourteen months old. Andy complains that he cries all the time and throws up on the floor—but he is attached to him and plays with him more than with anyone else.

The House

Even more than most families, the Garrisons seem reflected in their home. Samuel Garrison owns his house, purchased in 1960 in the best neighborhood he could afford—a rapidly changing lower-middle class area of Roxbury. When the Garrisons bought the house, the neighborhood was still pleasant. The houses were neat, the lawns and yards well cared for. But the house-proud homeowners have left and the street has been abandoned to junk, rats, stolen cars, and the rent collection man who comes through on Wednesday afternoons with his German shepherd guard dog. The Garrison's yard, which Mrs. Garrison remembers as fenced and green with flowers, is now trampled and littered, and the property "right out my kitchen door, which I thought went with the house, but it didn't . . . there's a parking lot there now and that's why it's in my yard."

The Garrisons consider their neighborhood one of the worst in Boston. Mr. Garrison describes it as "run-down, dirty, and a lot of whisky drinkers around." Thieves dump stolen cars there, he says, and prostitutes congregate on the corner. Parking lots and factories cut off the little residential enclave, making it more susceptible to crime and disintegration. Now Mrs. Garrison is afraid to go out at night; she says, "I wouldn't go out alone for anything," and the girls are not allowed out at night at all, except in the company of their father.

The house itself seems more part of the Garrisons than part of the neighborhood. It is a handsome Victorian, set back from the street, now suffering the effects of decay and disrepair, with peeling paint, boarded windows, and a collapsing porch. The porch was damaged, Andy says, when the family decided to cut down the tree in front of the house. A limb fell wrong, caving in the porch roof and breaking several windows. The inside walls are "all messed up" from various family activities. One wall is a mass of holes where a dart board once hung; the plaster is crumbling off another because baby Bobby picks off the pieces.

Major household repairs must be done by Mr. Garrison; there is no money for professional labor. But Mr. Garrison comes home from work to his television repairs and his desire to spend time with his family. Thus, a $125 plumbing problem becomes a six-month spare-time project, and it takes the family three years to save enough money for a stove. "The house is in pretty bad shape now," Mr. Garrison says. "I tried to do it myself with the kids, but just can't get to everything."

A major problem is too little space for too many people. In 1967, ten Garrisons live in six rooms on the first floor of the house so they can rent out the second floor. There is an unheated attic where Andy goes when he wants to be alone. Crowding means damage, especially when there are young children. Mr. Garrison says, "We play an awful lot in my house. We run the fire engine into the table, into the refrigerator, into the washing machine, or into anything else. We throw balls around and break the windows from the inside and from the outside. The cheap furniture we break up in three months, and expensive furniture wouldn't last more than a year." But the senior Garrisons continue to encourage their children to center their lives in the house, because they don't want them on the streets.

The Elusiveness of Andy

The Garrisons have strong family ties; they spend much of their time together. Elaine says, "I don't know, it might seem crazy to you, but like my mother and father, like we'll all be running around the yard, playing tag and all that or we'll sit on the porch, like 11 o'clock at night we'll sit on the porch when we can't sleep and sing songs. And when cars go by we'll all be sitting across the porch and the first car is mine and the second car is someone else's and we'll see who can get the prettiest car. We always hope for a car from Texas 'cause Texas got money and things . . . We just wish traffic would go by so we could say we have the one car. We go to the beach in the summer time; we go to shows in the winter time and we go skating."

Once a week the Garrisons go out to dinner, although sometimes the budget only allows half the children to go along. They take family trips to visit Maine relatives, and to other parts of New England as well. Andy's favorite memory is of an automobile trip with the entire family, "that summer when we

139

went to Connecticut and we almost got lost and we kept on going farther and farther, and then we stayed up there for about seven days . . . and we could see the Big Dipper, and you looked up and the sky seemed only about this far away." They play games together: ping pong, darts, Monopoly, cards. But there is also tension and anger. Mr. Garrison is quick with the strap; both parents turn to the courts and the juvenile reform institutions for aid when their children get out of hand and out of line with the law.

The children care about one another, although their loyalties sometimes shift and ebb. Mrs. Garrison says that Andy cries when Sammy writes him a letter from jail and adds, "they just miss him—all of them." Elaine and Barbara are the closest sisters, but Elaine goes to Catherine for advice. Andy spends hours in the attic sniffing glue with Jimmy, but it is Bobby that he takes with him when he goes out of the neighborhood. Elaine prefers to play with her more active siblings, but she looks after Andy with a kind of sympathetic contempt: "I'm always talking for the boy," she says.

Andy's place is unique in the noisy household. No one seems to quite see Andy; instead, one catches a glimpse of him, passing through. In the Garrison home movies there are parents, children, friends, some smiling expansively into the lens, hamming it up. But Andy rarely appears—we see his back, or catch sight of him turning the corner. Snapshots show him pushing himself back as if trying to blend into the wall or blurred because he has just managed to turn his head when the shutter snapped.

Andy will drink wine or sniff glue with Jimmy; he will go to the Supreme Market or to Cambridge with Elaine and Barbara; he will play cards with Cathy or tease Tina into screaming fits. But a part of him is always aloof, always poised for flight.

Mrs. Garrison says, "He's quiet, I mean really, very quiet. Where the others will dance and sing, like put on plays together, he is never in this. I don't believe I've ever heard him sing; I've

140

never seen him dance." Mr. Garrison says Andy is "no different from me," because he is "rather quiet, he could sit alone and work by himself, where the others usually get in a little group or at least two of them."

Both parents see Andy as similar to them in some ways, and both feel strongly connected to him. But Andy's feelings are not as strong. He loves his mother best of anyone, he says, "because I don't like nobody else," not even his father, who "loves me best of anybody." Elaine seems to understand this. She says she cares about him because he is her twin and she has to speak for him. But she does not expect her feelings to be returned. She says that Andy would "stick up for me if I got in trouble," but she does not expect a reciprocal level of warmth.

Only two people in the family expect warmth and responsiveness from Andy—his mother and baby Bobby. Mrs. Garrison says that Andy is always helpful, and especially solicitous when she is ill, and everyone comments on Andy's tireless play with Bobby the baby. But when Andy is asked what he likes best about his mother, his response is, "The way she cooks," and his only comment about the baby is that "he always starts crying and wants everything."

Andy is apparently detached from his family, but he wants them always near him. When he talks about his dream house, he describes a simple, uncluttered country place, big and white and straight, with varicolored rooms. His whole family is there, living with him. He doesn't like his real house, but wouldn't go anywhere else. He says he stays away from the cellar because there might be black widow spiders in it. His favorite place is his backyard, where he goes to "walk around; when the snow is there I just throw it, but now I guess I just walk around. When it's spring, when it gets warmer, I'm going to catch some mosquitoes." Andy sees his home as a refuge, a safe and private place where he can get away from his family while secure in their nearby presence on the next floor.

141

Andy's Inner Life

At 13, Andy feels constantly threatened, constantly fearful, tortured by doubts and nightmares. Much of this does not show to the outside world. He presents a shy and often charming face to his family and people at school. But his inner world seems dominated by his fears.

When the Garrisons describe Andy they venture few criticisms, although Elaine is a little contemptuous of his vulnerability and his unwillingness to lie. But when Andy describes his family, it is solely in terms of physical violence. "My father always hits us hard, like he's cruel to us, he always punches us. My mother always hits the wrong person." He portrays his brothers and sisters as a quarrelsome group, squealing, hitting, shouting, whining, always spoiling for a fight. Only gentle Catherine, the oldest girl, is excepted. Andy says she never bothers him and sometimes takes him places without the other children.

Andy's vision of his family stands in sharp contrast to the views of Elaine and of his parents. But it is consistent with his view of the world in general. Asked what animal he would choose to be if he were to turn into an animal, he says "a dog. They treat you better. You move around a lot and you go places and nobody can hardly beat you. And I guess people treat you better as a dog than they do as Andrew Garrison." Asked what aspect of himself he would fight hardest to protect, he says, first, the ability to hit back at his sisters when they hit him, and then, "oh, and not liking my family."

Linked to his fear of the family violence is Andy's constant fear of dying. He has never been unusually accident prone, but there was a time during his seventh grade year when he had three cuts on his left hand, each from a different accident with knives or razor blades. He cut his left index finger reaching into his back pocket, forgetting that he was carrying naked razor blades around. He sometimes wonders if he might stab himself accidentally with one of these razor blades while asleep, waking up to

142

find his wrists slit. He often wonders what it would be like to die in his sleep. And he adds, "if I keep thinking about it, it will happen." The dread of death is one of the things that keeps him close to home. He says, with a measure of truth, that he doesn't go to Blue Hill Avenue anymore because "people always get killed up there, mostly."

There have been a number of deaths in Andy's family—all but one of his uncles on his father's side are dead, at least one of them a suicide—but Andy seems to be the only child who feels the hand of fate pushing him toward an early death. Andy jokes about suicide occasionally, saying that he and his one friend, Jackson, would do it together, jumping off a building and changing their minds half-way down. The next day, he laughs, the headlines would read, "Two Idiots Commit Suicide." Or else, he adds, they might simultaneously murder each other.

Andy's preoccupation with death and danger spills over into his dreams. Most of his dreams—and he reports as many as ten a night—deal with spiders (one of his chief terrors) or with flying (his only positive desire). In one, a mammoth spider, 11 or 12 feet high and 6 or 8 feet wide, lurked in his house. In another, a much smaller spider, about 1-½ feet wide, hung in the doorway of the kitchen, spinning a huge web that could be opened like a curtain. One could pass through without danger, but always with a consciousness that if the spider bit you, the bite would be fatal. Andy's chief recurrent flying dream featured the whole Garrison family as able to fly, but once they started, they couldn't control it, and Andy would find himself flying when he didn't want to. Sometimes, in these dreams, the family all flew together, but most of the time Andy flew alone.

Another of Andy's continuing fears is unwarranted punishment for vague, sometimes unknown crimes. "You can't escape the law," he says darkly. "They always find you." In fact, Andy is almost preternaturally honest for an adolescent. He does not shoplift, will not participate in the ripping off of a newspaper. His teachers comment that he is unique among students in that he

143

always writes "back homework" on late papers, rather than trying to pass them off as current assignments.

But despite his honesty and caution in public, in Andy's private world there is always the fear of punishment. "You murder somebody," he says, "five years later, ten years later, they find you and you've forgotten about it." As with his fear of death and suicide, Andy is sometimes able to joke about his terror. Once, while playing Monopoly with his sisters and some family friends, he rolled the dice and landed in jail four times in a row. He smiled with the satisfaction of a successful prophet and said, "I think it's trying to tell me something."

Andy does various things to reduce his fears. He sticks close to home, because it is less fearsome than anywhere else. And, when he gets the opportunity, he escapes to the attic which seems to be the least scary place of all. In the attic, he turns to glue-sniffing, which effectively blurs his vision of the world, smothering thoughts and apprehensions, making his experience of life less painful.

Andy and Jimmy discovered glue-sniffing by accident. They were building model airplanes one afternoon and sniffed themselves into an unintentional high. Jimmy experimented further and enlisted Andy and Elaine in later sessions. Andy describes a typical glue-sniffing day. "I didn't know what anyone did until about noon, because I got up about one. Then when we got up, me and Jimmy started sniffing glue so we wouldn't know what happened." Even in the winter Jimmy and Andy would go to the attic to sniff; they were aware of the cold, but that didn't seem to bother them.

Glue-sniffing was one of the few things that got Andy into serious trouble with his parents. Mrs. Garrison discovered Andy and Jimmy one summer afternoon "in a little house that was built for trash barrels and I can see it from my livingroom window and I can see them in there and this glue-sniffing is going on all day long." She called the police and got them to take the boys to the station to scare them out of the habit. "A detective explained to them the damage this could do," she says, "and he gave them a little pamphlet about different kids that had sniffed glue, what they had done, and all the damage it could do to them. But he felt this would put an end to it . . . but it didn't; they still kept on."

Glue-sniffing was difficult in school. Andy says that the main reason he hates school is because "I can't sniff my glue there." So he and Jimmy worked out a way to hook school without getting caught. They would leave home in the morning, hang around someplace until around 9 o'clock, and then sneak in the back door and go up to the attic, where they would stay "in the bag" all day. Then, at about 3:00, they would sneak back downstairs and come in the front door as though returning from school. The only giveaway was the glue smell on their clothes.

No amount of parental punishment got the boys off glue. Finally, the senior Garrisons sent the boys to the Youth Service Board for a week, hoping that drastic punishment would root out the glue-sniffing and the truancy. That didn't work either. Shortly after Andy came back, he began sniffing again, less often and more covertly, under his father's threat to "send them away" if they didn't straighten up.

With or without glue, Andy only half communicates with the outside world. He speaks softly, in phrases rather than sentences, responds to questions with tantalizing half-answers. His memory, too, seems tenuous and weak. He forgets the names of relatives, teachers, schoolmates; he refers to people "vanishing"; he speaks of difficulty in remembering events and blames some school problems on his inability to pay attention. Many times when asked a question he will answer that he doesn't know, even if he does. Occasionally, he would forget something he had just said.

But for all his inarticulate manner, Andy will occasionally flash a smile, and will talk briefly and excitedly about the things that interest him—the models he builds, his animals, his chemistry set. Andy talks when he has something to say.

Andy As He Sees Himself

Andy doesn't have much good to say about himself. Comparing himself to other boys his age, he feels he is worse at "everything . . . except fly casting and collecting *TV Guides*." Others feels that he was competent at a variety of things—his art teacher praises his work, his teachers compliment the quality of the little academic work he did. His family reports that Andy makes exquisite small models of airplanes, and that he is a madman with a chemistry set. Elaine says, "We call him 'Destructo' 'cause he's always doing things like inkblots and vinegar. The last thing he did, he mixed vinegar and water and put a fly in there, then he took the fly and put him under his microscope and there was all kinds of germs floating around and everything."

But Andy does not take these accomplishments seriously. He is pleased that his art teacher likes his careful, meticulous drawings, but he has not convinced himself that his work was good enough to matter.

As for future work, Andy sees it as arduous and time-consuming, with few breaks, little free time. He dreams of becoming a chemist—and values his chemistry set more than anything in the world—but envisions the scientist's workday as long and hard, with perhaps ten minutes for lunch. Chemists, in Andy's view, are powerful. They "mix stuff and try to find cures for diseases." But there is danger, too. Chemists must learn "what not to mix together because it might explode or something," and Andy is not sure he could learn that. He says, "I'm too lazy to study," and adds that science is his worst subject in school.

Before wanting to be a chemist, Andy says he wanted to be a fireman, a job which had, in his view, similar characteristics. Firemen work endless hours, putting out fires and shining their engines. But the job would frighten Andy, because he would have to "climb ladders and I'm afraid of heights."

146

Andy doesn't worry much about race or how his blackness might affect his job aspirations. There is little discussion of race in the Garrison household. Andy says, "I don't want to be white . . . it seems to be the colored kids have it better, even though they don't get picked, like most white men get picked for a job." He "guesses" he is glad he is black. There is no race he would prefer to be, nor any he would despise. Other than the limited job opportunities, the only disadvantage he can see to being black is that he heard of somewhere in the world where blacks aren't supposed to kiss whites. He has little knowledge of black political activity in the mid-sixties and what he has is inaccurate. He identifies Martin Luther King as someone who "sings or something," and has heard only vaguely about some program which busses black children to white schools. Aside from Harriet Tubman and a few popular singers, he can name no celebrated blacks, living or dead.

Andy's concerns about interracial situations are strictly personal. He would avoid an all-white school because he would be conspicuous and might be beaten up. He would not got to a mainly white dance or party, "because I would probably have to dance or something." Andy has so many fears of people in general that the differences between white people and black people do not seem especially relevant to him.

Andy and Friends

At 13, Andy is a lonely child. His mother, comparing him to his brothers and sisters, says "All the others have one or two friends that come to the house, and they go to their houses, but Andrew doesn't have anybody that comes to the house . . . or he goes to their house that I know of. He doesn't have anybody." Andy, at this time, says that he does have a couple of friends, although it takes him a few minutes to think who they might be. His final hesitant answer is "I guess a boy named Jerry." Later he adds another neighborhood boy, Daniel Dever, of whom he says, "He's never hardly around, but I see him around when he is, and he works for an oil truck." And he adds that his brother Jimmy is

147

his friend. These boys are older than Andy, and it becomes clear as he discusses his relationship with them that they are really Jimmy's friends, who let a younger brother tag along and sniff a little glue.

This situation is typical of Andy. He has no evident friend of his own. The family sees him as a loner. In the relationships he calls friendships, he is always on the edges. He sniffs glue with Jimmy, Daniel, and Jerry, but when they go out stealing cars. Andy stays behind. Although he does not object to their stealing cars, he thinks he might get himself and them into trouble because of his inability to lie. And in any case he is reluctant to deal with the outside world. He'd just as soon stay home.

It is also typical of Andy that he acquires friends whose initial relationships were with others in the family. In the seventh grade, he relies on Jimmy's friends. In the eighth grade he makes the only long-term friend he has ever had—Jackson Davis, who is the younger brother of Diane's boyfriend, a neighbor, and a frequenter of the household. Andy's friendship with Jackson seems to have merely happened, because Jackson was there and because he was willing to take a good deal of neglect, teasing, and abuse from Andy.

Andy is passive in forming friendships. But he is the active one in his relationship with Jackson. Andy is the leader. He teases Jackson, telling him how fat he is, making fun of his ineptitude and his limited intelligence. Andy may or may not be physically stronger (although he certainly is quicker), but this does not seem to be important. Jackson says, "You know what's funny about us? We don't like to fight each other." And the two—one small and slight, the other larger, but younger, and fat—avoid fighting with others.

Andy at the Ryan

The Garrisons have been an inexplicable phenomenon at the Ryan school since Sammy entered the seventh grade. "The

Garrisons are famous for truancy," Andy's English teacher says, but every comment about the family's hooking tendency is tied to a testimonial on their brightness—"the whole clan seems to be very intelligent." Andy and Elaine (who was a year ahead of him, since Andy had been kept back in fourth grade) outclass the family reputation. They are considered the most brilliant and the most spectacularly truant of all the Garrison children. "He was truant I don't know how many days last year," says one despairing teacher. "And then this year, he didn't start coming in until the middle of November. Then he comes to school and volunteers to stay after school to help with things. To help with decorations for the dance. He was one of the three kids that volunteered; stayed after. A really capable boy; really intelligent. I don't know why he doesn't come to school. It's a great mystery."

Elaine is reputed to be "about the brightest girl in the whole school," according to one teacher, but Andy is quiet, shy, and steady, "a very intelligent boy, a good worker, a good writer, nice personality and all that. I never had any problems with him." Nevertheless, Andy will suddenly start hooking school, and once started, will stay out for days and weeks at a time. Then, equally inexplicably, he will start coming to school again steadily, doing his back homework (carefully marked as late), not volunteering much in class, but ready with an answer if called upon. "But Andrew was sort of funny," his English teacher says. "He was at school, but like his mind was someplace else, like he wished he was hooking." And after a few weeks of steady attendance, he will begin to hook again.

In the spring of his seventh-grade year, Andy stayed out of school for seven straight weeks. His parents and teachers collaborated in having him picked up and taken to court for truancy, and threatened him with the disciplinary facility of the Boston school system. According to Andy's homeroom teacher, Mrs. Garrison came to school for one of her rare teacher conferences, and said, 'Well, I don't want to sign any papers putting him under court supervision. But I do want to take him to court, you know, so he can see the seriousness of the situation."

Andy's appearance in court frightened him, and seemed to galvanize him into regular attendance for the rest of the term. He surprised everyone by pulling out a C+ average, after failing the previous marking periods and missing nearly a third of the time he was supposed to spend in school. His math teacher says that Andy got a perfect 100 on a test that most of the class failed—although Andy felt that math was one of his weakest subjects—and that alone raised his grade for the term.

This sequence of events is characteristic of Andy's school performance. He says that he began hooking school in fifth grade (the year after he was held back), when a friend suggested it one day and they "just walked around, stayed off the streets and then waited over by the school, watching them have recess." He felt "scared" that first time, and never lost his fear, even when truancy became his usual pattern. He never seemed to find hooking exciting. It was simply an escape from a less comfortable situation to a more comfortable one.

In junior high school, Andy usually heads for home when he leaves school. His mother will take him back in, rarely admonishing him (she doesn't think it does any good), but saying, "Well, you're home, so you can clean up your room or make up beds, or wash dishes. Just go along with me and help me doing things." And she adds, "It doesn't seem to make him unhappy, either."

Andy's description of school is moderately negative, although no more negative than his description of home. Asked to name his favorite teacher, he chooses one only because "I don't like the other teachers," not because he feels she is fair, or that she understands him. He has great difficulty remembering the names of many of his teachers, or of many of his schoolmates for that matter. He says the "kids are always starting trouble and take your money," they are "pests" who pick on teachers and on smaller kids.

Andy sees the Ryan as a battleground of hostile forces. On the one hand, students who pick on the white teachers, and on the other, teachers who "don't educate you . . . they are scared. They should sock you in the mouth, but they send you down to the principal's office and he suspends you and that's what the kids want so they don't have to come to school." Andy himself stays aloof from both groups—"I don't slander them much" he says of his teachers—and tries to avoid the conflict by keeping away.

Andy's dislike of his teachers is not reciprocated. The assistant principal calls him a "delightful little boy," and his math teacher speaks of his sense of humor. She says that he will leave little notes on her desk with funny drawings, appealing to her not to give homework that day. The notes were doubly amusing because Andy had been cutting school so much he never had a chance to find out that she hadn't given homework for a long time. Andy rarely has to be disciplined, his teachers say. Occasionally he would cut up like most of his classmates, but a simple "sit down and stop being silly," would bring him to his seat.

Andy says he doesn't like school, but he does report a few positive experiences. He enjoys art class, and has made some sculptures good enough to be submitted for exhibitions outside the school (although Andy does not know what became of them). He and his art teacher share a mutual respect for hard work and high standards. He also likes woodworking, math, and drafting— all skills relying on complex nonverbal creativity, visual acuity and a memory of detail. Andy has all of these to a high degree. They seem to be his counterpart to Elaine's quick tongue and facility in reading and writing.

Faced with Andy's evident intelligence and equally evident reluctance to go to school, the adults around him seem at a loss for explanation. Mrs. Garrison thinks that "one school is as good as another," and blames Andy's laziness for his truancy. But Mr. Garrison and Elaine both seem to feel that the school is somewhat to blame. Mr. Garrison says that the Ryan is an inferior school because the teachers come and go so quickly and because discipline is not stringent enough. And Elaine is even more specific. "Teachers don't talk to you like they do in fifth grade where there's only thirty but there's only one teacher, and they don't change classes. In the Ryan, you know—you're in and then you're out." Elaine feels that the Ryan has had a bad effect on the entire family, pointing out that Sammy was an A and B student until he went there, as were Jimmy, Andy, and herself. Only Catherine seems to have escaped the depressing pressures of the Ryan, and Elaine says that is because she was always "to scared to hook."

The Ryan staff have a variety of explanations for Andy's school problems. Many staff members see the children's school performance as a direct reflection of the home situation. Mr. James, an assistant principal, at a loss to reconcile the good qualities of the parents with the bad performance of the children, ultimately falls back on Mr. Garrison's job situation. "When he told me he was retraining, going to school at night, I didn't get an idea whether he was working in the daytime or not. And if he weren't working in the day, I wondered what they were using for income." And when the younger children turned out to be better students than Andy and Elaine, Mr. James said, "I think somewhere along the line the father's gained, and he keeps these other children better supervised."

Other teachers ascribe Andy's problems to an assumed rivalry between him and Elaine. One teacher says, "Somehow she is just so vivacious and talks, and is so active and aggressive that you know right off the bat that she is bright because she acts that way. And then you find out she has a twin and Andrew has been kept back. So you're expecting to meet this little boy who is perhaps a bit slow. Instead you find a nice, quiet youngster who is just as smart as his sister. But she takes the limelight."

And finally, some teachers feel that Andy's small size and slight build account for his reluctance to come to school. One teacher says, "I just hope he continues to get some encouragement to come to school. He's going to need periodic pushing until he feels he's big enough and strong enough to make it on his own. I think the fact that he's small has a lot to do with it. He doesn't need the tough boys and girls around him."

The guidance counselor, who spent perhaps the most time trying to figure out Andy's erratic performance, describes him this way: "He seems to function in waves; that is, now whether or not they're regular, I can't tell, because the waves for each subject are different. It seems to depend on how he feels. If he doesn't feel like doing something he's supposed to, he won't do it. The next time he might feel like it."

TRYING OUT LIFE—AT SIXTEEN

At sixteen, Andy seems less hassled by life. The Garrison family is more comfortable now. Sammy is out of jail, married, and working as an apprentice carpenter. Catherine has graduated from high school (a family first) and is working in an office. Sammy and Paula have fixed up Andy's attic and live up there now. Their contribution to the family income combined with Catherine's has allowed the Garrisons to take over the entire house, instead of renting out the second floor. For the first time, there seems to be a little elbow room.

Andy is still somewhat detached from his family, but he no longer feels assaulted and scared. He says he lives a quiet life, mainly sitting at home, "watching everybody make noise," rarely leaving except to go to an occasional dinner at a restaurant. He still "fades away when company comes" but he is more assertive with his family and takes a paternal interest in Bobby's behavior. "When he does something bad, say like if he says something back to my mother or father, I hit him," Andy says. "Or if he's playing ball in the house, I tell him to pick the ball up and take it outside and hit him a little—lightly." Andy keeps his room clean and helps with the housework. Although he drinks a little—not wine or rum because it's "too sweet"—he doesn't drink in front of his parents. He is generous with money and with clothes. "If they ask for, say 50 cents, I'd see if I had 50 cents and give it to them," and he recently gave his sister five of his sixteen shirts. He seems far more appreciative of himself and relatively content with his life. He says that his idea of a good time is "sitting around, maybe playing cards," daydreaming a bit, perhaps taking a ride in the country or going to a restaurant. And these relatively simple needs seem relatively simply filled.

Andy is far more positive about himself than he was in junior high school. At 13, he refused to accept much credit for his intelligence or artistic achievement. Now, looking back, he recalls with pleasure evidences of his superior intelligence and skill. "I got A in art just about every time, and printing—I went to school something like 40 times and stayed out 60 times, and I got all A's in printing. I'd miss it and everybody'd be just about finished and I'd come in and in two days I'd catch up with them and do it faster and pretty good, so he gave me A's."

Now art work has become amalgamated with his old hobby, model-building, which he has developed into an exquisite skill. He says that model-building is something he is far better at than most boys his age, and speaks with great enthusiasm about his technique. "I do it careful, and most of the boys who're my age try to do models, they splash it on and stick it together and mess it up. They're supposed to put a piece just a small piece on, and a little bit of glue and stick it, let it dry, and then start on something else. But they go on and try to do the whole thing in an hour."

He also thinks he now relates better to other people. He feels that he is especially considerate toward others, if somewhat quiet and shy. "Most of my friends that I know," he says, "when they meet somebody, they like to start some trouble with them to see who can beat who . . . a bunch of troublemakers, that's all." And, although he also says that he would like to be able to fight better, he no longer sees his reluctance to fight as a sign of failure or a source of shame.

Andy's view of himself as a considerate and unaggressive person is confirmed by Jackson, who remains his best friend, even though they have both graduated from junior high. Jackson is clearly still the junior partner in their relationship. He admires Andy, who tolerates his presence. Jackson says that Andy is his best friend because "most of the people, they don't want you to hang around with them and stuff" and adds that "some of them go out, you know, to do bad stuff." He and Andy do not fight, and their adventures are legal and inoffensive. One of the worst things that ever happened to them together was once when some bigger boys cornered them, shook them down for the few dollars they had on them, and then made them fight one another while they stood around and laughed. Both Jackson and Andy recall this incident with acute embarrassment and distaste. It went against the entire tenor of their relationship.

But the relationship between Andy and Jackson is not based entirely on tolerance and nonviolence. Jackson describes some of Andy's qualities which Andy himself has just begun to recognize. "I wouldn't like to go [bicycle] riding with him," Jackson says, "because some people don't like to wait 'cause if you're tired of pedaling, some will keep going. And what's best about him—he's not cheap like all the other kids [who] won't let you ride their bike, but he will."

Andy and Girls

Andy has come to realize some of his strengths as a person and as a friend over the last two years. He has also developed a successful technique with girls. He says that, unlike most of the boys he knows, he respects girls and "I don't jive around . . . I only like one girl friend and if I have a girl friend, I don't play around with other girls." He knows now that he is good looking and appealing, and augments his physical attractiveness with a courtesy unusual in boys his age. "Most boys I know," he says, "when they see a girl, they try to rap to her. They get nasty and everything. You're supposed to be polite . . . walking with her, always walk on the street side and let the girl go first through the door. Instead of asking, [most boys] don't even think . . . just stand near a girl and they'd snatch something from her instead of saying, 'May I have some?' or something like that. I can't stand it, not to be polite."

This approach has worked for Andy, and at sixteen he has a girl friend, Arlette. Arlette is twenty-one and has a six-month old child unrelated to any Garrison. She and Andy became involved in much the same way that Andy became friendly with Jackson—she was a friend of one of the older Garrison children and spent a lot of time around the Garrison house where casual visitors were always welcome. After a while, she and Andy starting holding hands under the table, and by Christmas she had moved in with Andy, even though they never seemed to have an especially intense relationship with one another.

Andy's primary relationship, in fact, seemed to be with Michael, Arlette's baby. Whenever he could put together a few dollars, Andy would spend it on the baby—on Pampers, on toys, on essential clothes that Arlette never seemed to get around to buying out of the $33 a week that she got from "the welfare." Andy soon became the central figure in Michael's life. It was Andy who held the baby on his lap and bounced him up and down on his knee. It was Andy who got up at night when Michael cried, and helped him learn to walk. Arlette spent most of her time playing cards or talking, listening only grudgingly while Andy explained to her that toys were necessary for babies to develop coordination, or that Michael needed someone to talk to him or he would never learn to talk.

Andy never seemed jealous of Arlette. He had not the least objection when she went off to parties or flirted with other boys. In fact, he happily stayed at home and sat with Michael. The relationship ultimately broke up, largely because of Andy's contempt for Arlette as a mother and her corresponding feeling that Andy was foolish and unsophisticated. Andy's strongest memory of that time remains Michael and his own involvement with Michael's development.

Now, he sometimes talks to Arlette on the telephone. Andy says, "I'll talk to her for a few minutes and I'll ask to speak to her son." But Andy has a new girl friend with whom he seems to have a much more typical teenage relationship. "She's nice," he says, "the one I got now. If she says something, like she'll say somebody's name and then she'll make a face and then come over and kiss me, and I'll say, 'yeah.' And she likes to bite me so I have

156

to smack her—not too hard and not too soft, and she'll try to grab my finger, but I manage to get two fingers around her whole hand and squeeze it and twist her arm a lot." Part of their "good times" consists of Andy's showing some bravado in front of his parents. "I'll swear at her in front of my mother and father. She'll say, 'I'm going over to my other boy friend's,' or something, and I'll say, 'You go and I'll break your ass,' right in front of my mother and father. But not too much—maybe five swears during the day, in front of my parents."

Despite the teasing and the sex play, Andy's relationship with his girl friends remains quite innocent. Andy says that he sleeps with his girls, but that he doesn't "do anything." He says that he isn't much interested in sex.

Dropping Out

One of the teachers at the Ryan described Andy as the "perfect drop out," and certainly a variety of forces seemed to channel him to that end. Despite his truancy, Andy managed to graduate from the Ryan and enroll in Boston Trade High School. Immediately, he got entangled in red tape. At Trade, they refused to believe that he had been promoted from the Ryan with 84 days of unexcused absence. Someone misplaced his white card, so he couldn't be assigned to a class, and he waited five hours while they organized the relevant materials. Finally he left because "there was nothing to do." The next day the school made him come back with his mother and his Uncle Fred to clarify the confusion. It was not a good start.

Trade was tougher than the Ryan. If you missed four days each marking period, you were held back. Andy tried to make an effort to get there, but he had to get up at 6:30 to do so and he was always exhausted, because he stayed up until midnight most nights watching television. Besides, he didn't like English class, which he thought he was going to fail anyway. "They had some special way they say you learn quick and I didn't even understand it." Nor did he care. "I'd say, 'What you gonna have to know where the noun is for?' They ain't gonna say, 'What's a noun?' when you go to work. You might have to know how to pronounce things but that's about all. You won't have to say, 'I want some Scotch; that's a noun.' Or whatever, you know."

Ultimately he was sent to the Godvin for truancy, and he remained there until he was sixteen. His description of the program of the Godvin is vague and spare. "You really didn't do nothing much there. It's just a disciplinary school. It have a cooking class, then eat it yourself, and a little bit of math and a little English and a little bit of shop. We didn't do nothing in shop. We didn't have homework. There'd be something like four classes a day and the kids would get out earlier than in a regular school."

At the Godvin, Andy developed a new method for getting out of going to school while carrying out the pretense of attending. He would get up and start to get ready to go, but then he would poke around, forget books or his comb or his bus fare, and thus would arrive at school more than one-half hour after the opening of school. At the Godvin, this meant they would refuse to admit him, and he, perfectly happily, would come home again. During that time he rarely spent more than a day a week at school and almost never brought home a book. His only observations about school were of peculiar physical features of fellow students and teachers—a very fat boy who sat next to him, a teacher with a 'beak nose.'

When he turned sixteen, the Godvin let Andy go. There was no legal reason to make him stay. They sent him back to Trade with a slip saying that he'd passed their courses and was eligible for entry into tenth grade. "I took it to the Trade," Andy says, "and they said that I didn't pass because I didn't have the shop there, no trade. They said I didn't have a trade and in order to go to the Boston Trade School you have to have a trade. So I called up the Godvin School and they said that I did pass and I did have a trade so they told me to tell them that." He told them that he had already said that, and the Godvin staff asked him to come back and get some more papers. So Andy trudged back to Godvin and then back to Trade. Trade said he had to bring a teacher from

Godvin or go into ninth grade. And at that point, Andy said, "Forget it."

Andy had begun to consider dropping out when he got to the Ryan and was barely dissuaded by his father. Everyone Andy knew had dropped out, except Catherine, who was the only one of his siblings to graduate from high school. Both parents expected that he would leave school as soon as he could, and Andy had no positive motivation to stay. He did, after his abortive experience with Trade, make a few desultory tries to enroll in another high school. But a neighborhood high school said it was too late to enter, and Boston English wanted more papers. Andy was not going to go that route again. So he gave up and began to think about getting a job.

Andy at Work

Andy had worked while still in junior high school, renovating and repairing the insides of houses with his Uncle Fred's crew, preparing walls for painting, spackling, manning a roller. He was quietly proud of his facility at this work, and even admitted that he was able to paint a wall faster than his older cousin, a veteran of four hitches in the service. He had thought that he would earn more than $1.25 an hour for this work if he weren't a relative, but he seemed more amused than resentful about his low pay. Money is not important to Andy, and he sometimes would work for his uncle for free when he was hooking school. He always gave some part of his small earnings to his father to ease the strain on family finances.

Now, as a dropout from Trade, he was ready to begin a serious job search. He went to the local community action office, which referred him to the Urban League, which sent him to a company willing to sign him on as a full time apprentice construction worker with Saturday morning classes. Andy was still a year and a half underage, but his shy charm convinced the appropriate officials to age him fast enough to complete the application.

The construction site was a large building complex, and jobs there were at a premium because it was a long project and the pay was high. Andy earned $3.08 an hour; Mr. Garrison comments wryly that it took him nineteen years to earn $125 a week. At first, Andy like the work, but as the weather grew colder, his pleasure began to wane.

Andy thinks he is a good worker. "When I work, I'm serious," he says, "But when it's cold, I'm not going to work that much unless it's inside. And when it's warm, I'll work, and everybody else I know, they get a job, some little job, and they don't work as good as I work." Unfortunately, it was winter and the work was outside. Further, Andy did not like the low standards of the job. He did rough carpentry, "just nailing up wood any kind of way just to hold it, and then they pour cement in it and they build supports. But it wasn't too good, because we didn't do that much and it was always cold there."

The Saturday classes also wore Andy down—he had to travel in the early morning to South Boston and he didn't want to go that far or into the traditionally hostile area. But the job was tied to school attendance, so he kept going for several weeks. Then he couldn't stand it any longer and stopped going to school. The job went when the classes did.

From the end of that job, Andy has worked only occasionally. He briefly held jobs at construction sites, apprenticing and doing ceiling carpentry. He worked from time to time for Uncle Fred, but a torn knee ligament sent him to the hospital for a week, healed slowly, and still often hurts too much for strenuous work. Now, nearly seventeen, he says he spends most of the time, "just hanging around. Haven't been doing too much of anything."

He has some regrets about the way things have gone. He is sorry he left his original, well-paid construction job, although his hatred for working in the cold has not abated. And he has his moments of deep regret about dropping out of school. "I wish I had stayed, had finished, and maybe I would of had a good job or something." But he feels his bad memory would have plagued any further efforts. "I wasn't learning too much anyway because, like if I learned something, I'd forget it the next week. I learned all that stuff and two weeks later I had forgot all of it. I would need a refresher course for the week back." He imagines what it would be like to have a good job, which would allow him to save money. "I'll be saving money in the bank. If I bring home, say, eighty dollars a week, I'll put fifty of it in the bank, and give my mother twenty, and ten dollars I'll buy some clothes, maybe a pair of pants or something."

Unlike most of his contemporaries, Andy's concept of the "good life" does not involve "making it big." But it does require a drastic change from the homebound existence he has chosen. Andy's ideal job would be skilled carpentry. He says he would work daily until "five-thirty, come home, eat, rest for about an hour, take a ride." He sees himself in this life as "active, working a lot, moving around a lot. When you get out from work, take a quick ride someplace, and on the weekend go to Canada or the Cape."

Andy and His Family

At sixteen, Andy is more comfortable with his family than he was earlier. He now returns his father's long standing admiration and says that he feels closer to his father than to anyone else, although he would turn to Sammy or Jimmy in a real jam, because they wouldn't tell on him. But he has learned to respect his father's intelligence and his ability to rise to the top in every job he has held. He tells of his father's stint in night school when he got virtually all 100's and knew enough to correct the teacher about technical points. He knows that his parents are concerned about him—that they are sorry he dropped out of school and that they would feel better now if he "got a job and helped clean up the house more." But the discomfort at home combined with the urgency to avoid the world during his junior high school years has diminished. Andy seems able to live reasonably comfortably, even with his parents' disapproval.

161

Part of the increased peace of the Garrison household may have occurred because Andy and Jimmy have given up glue-sniffing. Andy stopped first and teased Jimmy about "messing up" his mind until he stopped too. And Andy never went to any harder drugs. He sampled perhaps "2-½ tabs [of acid] in my whole life. I don't take it that much. Reefer, that's not really mine. My whole life, maybe I had two bombers. My whole life, I had three snorts of coke. And that's about it." He says he never went near heroin—"I don't like them needles. I don't even like the doctor to do, even less sticking myself."

The only drug experience he thought worth describing was cocaine, and it did not seem profound. "I just talked a lot, you know. I didn't mind that because I really like to talk when I can, even if I don't talk about too much. I was just laying up here. I looked up into the air and I could see a light flashing. So I looked out the window, you know what it was? The top of the Prudential building. I just stayed awake all night feeling queasy." He took coke twice more, but then his parents got the idea he was into something and told the girl who had given it to him not to do it anymore. Andy says that was okay with him.

He also tried drinking, which his Uncle Fred suggested as a way of getting off the glue. He and a friend who worked with him on a construction job would polish off a couple of pints a day after work, then they would go to sleep, waking up in the morning "feeling good and we wouldn't get sick or nothing." But he stopped hanging with this friend because he thought they were drinking too much, and the rest of the family began to cut down as well, "and then everybody around here, like my cousin and my sister's boy friend, stopped drinking." Now Andy drinks a little—perhaps a pint a week—and his pleasure even in that has been blunted by the death of Uncle Fred, his favorite relative outside the immediate family. Andy says, "Liquor killed him in the end."

Andy and Elaine in Trouble

If truancy and glue are no longer a source of trouble for Andy, trouble has not stopped. Shortly after his sixteenth birthday,

162

Elaine was caught shoplifting and Andy was with her; both were charged with larceny. "When I go to court," Andy says, "I stand up straight and try to look my best." Elaine, on the other hand, looks sullenly out the window, paying no attention. They asked him a couple of questions, he says, and he answered politely, "Yes, sir. No sir." The judge let him off with an admonition that he stay out of the store, but Elaine swore at the policeman and was given a week of detention. Andy was on probation for three months, largely because of the intervention of his probation officer (assigned to him during his truancy troubles). Afterwards, he recalls, "I had a much worser time when I went up there for the truancy charge."

The senior Garrisons did not seem to react very violently to this incident. Sammy, after all, had been in much worse trouble and he had straightened out. But Elaine escalated. Instead of "learning her lesson" from her week in the Youth Board detention center, she got angry at her parents for requesting that she be sent there and ran away from home. She was gone nearly two weeks, and the police and juvenile authorities were looking for her. Then one night she appeared around dinner time. Mr. Garrison, furious, handcuffed her to his bed and then returned to the table, insisting that the family proceed normally with dinner. In the meantime, Elaine set fire to the bed, whether on purpose or by accident, no one is sure. The Garrisons called the police and had her sent back to the Youth Service Board, this time for several months, while beginning legal proceedings to make her a ward of the state. After two or three months at the Youth Board, she was sent away to a Catholic girls' school in western Massachusetts, where she seemed happier than she had ever been in school before. The tenuous balance of the Garrison household returned to its delicate equilibrium.

ANDY AT TWENTY—IN THE ATTIC

At twenty, Andy is more reclusive than he was at sixteen. When Sammy and Paula moved out of the attic room, Andy claimed it for his own, and he has built his world within its walls. The attic room reflects Andy's private life. He has a fish tank, a closet full of clothes given him by his brothers and by his girl friends. And, mainly, he has models, dozens of them, mostly cars, intricately constructed, beautifully finished. Andy is very proud of these models. He begins with kits, he says, but then combines parts of different models or "customizes" them by improvising new parts, or by experimenting with new techniques of painting, using his mother's nail polish and bits of junk he finds around the house.

Andy is content in the attic. He still occasionally dreams of a life in which he has a job, goes for trips to Canada or the Cape, but essentially, he says, "I like just being here. Half the time nobody's even home and half the time you don't know anybody's home, so I can't say it's the people being here." Staying in the attic allows a detachment from life that any venture out precludes. "I want to go out, but then I don't want to go to no parties where there's a lot of excitement and everything. It's not too bad, but I like to watch. Most of the time a girl'll come up to me and say, 'Let's dance' or something. You say, 'No, thank you,' or something and they say, 'That's a stuck-up brother.' I really don't like that, so I just don't go no more too much." He restricts his outside fun to an occasional ride in the car with a brother or a friend and stays mainly in his room.

Andy says that if he had some money, he "wouldn't mind staying in his room forever." He would buy a good pump for his fish tank and build a reel-to-reel tape deck into his closet, get a television set, panel the walls, and settle in. Evidently, he has thought a good deal about improving his sanctuary, because he describes intricate plans for renovating his closet as a model showcase and entertainment center.

Although Andy does not seem as depressed as he was at thirteen, his self-description is much the same. He sees himself as "quiet, not much of a conversationalist, . . . that's about it. Once in awhile I get in a good mood and I might talk to some girls and that's about it." Pushed to give more details, he adds that if people "look at my models, they might say, 'He may be creative.' My father might say I like to work if the work is right. That's about all." Andy no longer speaks of terror, nor of early death or suicide. He does have fears—of being thirty, unemployed, homeless—but he seems to have come to terms with himself and with life—to have settled his limits and his possibilities.

Andy and the Family

The Garrison family is smaller now and less hard pressed. Sammy has separated from Paula, but lives in an apartment three blocks from the family home and visits often. Catherine, her boyfriend, Donald, and their baby live on the second floor, and contribute to the family income. Elaine and Andy Davis (Jackson's older brother) live a few blocks away. Only Tina, Betty, and Bobby are still in school. For the first time the family finances are sufficient, if not ample.

This sense of security is tenuous, however. Mr. Garrison still works for Allen Engineering, and his salary, while higher than it was in 1967, is not high enough to keep up with inflation. Further, there is talk that he might be laid off—an unfortunate prospect for a 56-year-old head of a family. This hangs over their heads, but it has not stopped them from enjoying every scrap of good fortune. Mrs. Garrison has learned to drive; the family took a trip to Nova Scotia. No one is confident that good times will last.

But the family sticks together—to a surprising extent. Looking back over the past seven years, it is clear that Andy isn't the only Garrison child unable to stray from home. Catherine and Donald live in the house now. Sammy and Elaine are no more than a few blocks away, and Elaine, reconciled with her parents, spends most of her time with her mother. All this proximity is not coincidental. Elaine, who always seemed more independent that Andy, who always talked about leaving home and living far away, was sent once, in 1968, to a special summer program at Smith College, designed to prepare talented youngsters for college preparation programs. Elaine returned home after only a few weeks, saying she was terribly homesick. "One day we had a bad storm and I kept calling my mother up and all that, 'cause I didn't

165

know what was happening over there . . . so I called up and said, 'Is it raining?' and she said, 'No, it's just drizzling,' and all that, but I didn't believe her, so I went home the next day."

Few of the Garrison children see the intensity of their ties to home, but Andy see them clearly. "I just like the house. I don't know. Everybody stays here. Everyone's always saying, 'I wish there was someplace to go,' or 'I'm going out. I'm not staying in the house.' But they're always here. And everybody comes—you see all the people down there, everybody comes over here."

With everyone around the house—children, neighbors, friends, boyfriends, animals, Andy is hardly noticed—almost forgotten. If someone calls on the telephone and asks for "Andy," he will automatically be referred to Andy Davis, Elaine's husband, who does not even live in the house. Andy Garrison tries to think of ways to ensure reaching him, and is hard pressed to find one. Finally, he says, "Say, 'is your son, Andy, there?' If it's my mother, she'll say 'yes' . . . if it's one of my sister's they'll call me. But they don't know whether I'm home anyways." Andy seems amused rather than resentful that his family forgets his existence.

Andy and Other People

Andy's retreat from the eyes of his family is matched by a general retreat from the outside world. He no longer sees Jackson. Another friend, his drinking buddy, Greg, has drifted, almost unnoticed, out of his life. He spends some time with Catherine's boyfriend, Donald, who lives in the house, and with the husband of one of the neighborhood cousins. But he says he has no best friend anymore. "Really, not nobody. I mean, like, one day they're all right, then the next day they're talking junk."

But he is not entirely alone. Sharing the attic room with him is Ritabeth, a white girl who grew up next door to the Garrisons, and her baby Carey. Like Arlette, Ritabeth wandered into Andy's life haphazardly. She was being abused where she was living, and Andy said she and the baby could move in with him if she wanted to. Now, several months later, she and Carey are still living with Andy, who can be heard explaining to Ritabeth, as he did to Arlette, that the baby will never be able to walk unless she stops carrying her all the time, and that she'll never be talking if Ritabeth watches soap operas all day instead of spending some time with that child.

Once again, he seems to care more for the child than for the mother. Asked if he has any problems going out on the street with a white girl, Andy says, "Maybe once in a while. I mean, nobody would say nothing directly to us, but we can hear somebody saying, 'Oh, look at that stupid-ass white bitch' or something. She knows if something happens or somebody says something to her and she don't keep walking like she should, I'm just going to keep going about my business. She can stand there and get her ass whipped or beat somebody's ass. I ain't gonna get involved. Shit!"

Much of the time, Andy seems barely to tolerate Ritabeth. He says that the only way he is ever going to get rid of her is to go off to the corner store one day and not come back. He is willing to let her live with him, and he is very tender toward Carey, but he is not going to get "stuck in the middle," defending her against the outside world.

Andy and Work

Andy can't work in his attic and so he has, for the most part, stopped working during the last six months. Before that, he did construction work on and off, but never found it satisfactory. "I wasn't working too much and if there was something that I couldn't do, they'd tell me, 'Well, stand behind the wall.' I'd stand behind the wall for about an hour, just not doing anything or maybe I might be hammering a little or something. I always did like carpentry, but that made me change my mind a little bit, because they wasn't doing too much and I was always behind the wall." He never felt he was being taught the skills a carpentry apprentice was supposed to learn. Eventually the futility, the cold, or both, overcame him, and he quit.

167

Between construction job stints he had a few other brief periods of employment. He worked, on a stand-by basis, for a garbage disposal company, but hated it. "The garbage was sometimes too heavy and that was in the winter time and it was cold and rats were all over the place."

Between 1970 and 1973, Andy's longest job was with his father's engineering company, a job that lasted nearly a year. It seemed an ideal job for Andy. His father brought him in and taught him how to do product testing and wiring, not allowing him to be shoved "behind the wall" by more assertive workers. Andy was good at the fine motor skills involved in wiring, and was even able to use some of his school printing experience to make up labels for company products. He speaks more enthusiastically about this job than of any other. "Everything was beautiful. It was nice there. I like printing and I liked everything."

But after nearly a year of evidently happy and productive work, Andy got sick, stayed out for a week, and never went back. He says, "I got lazy, really. I was staying over at a friend's house, and I was sick maybe one or two days, and I just stayed out. I'd wake up in the morning and I'd say, 'Oh, I don't have to go to work,' and I just lay back down in the bed." He says he didn't need to work, because "my friend's wife and my girlfriend were cooking and they'd clean up," but he felt uncomfortable there, eating their food and not paying anything so finally he returned, out of work, to his attic room.

Andy doesn't need much money for the few things he wants in life, and there always seem to be people willing to provide him with the little he needs. At sixteen, he said that he never spent more than a quarter a week, and he got that from a friend who would give him a couple of dollars once in a while. When he left the job with Allen Engineering, he used money his girlfriend gave him to supplement unemployment funds to buy himself a gold birthstone ring. He doesn't beg, doesn't feel that he demeans himself in any way. He just needs things and other people seem to provide them.

On the other hand, he is very generous with money when he has it. His parents never asked him to contribute any part of his pay

168

when he was working. But he gave his father $25 or $30 a week when he was working at Allen. Sometimes he would give his mother an additional $20, not telling his father, so that his father would not cut back on the housekeeping money.

Now that he is out of work, he says that work is unnecessary for him because "I was staying with my mother and father and I didn't need no money." But, on the other hand, now that he is not contributing anything to the household, he doesn't feel entitled to eat his parents' food. Normally painfully slender, he is now emaciated, because "I don't eat that much because I don't want to eat downstairs with my mother and father. I'm not paying any rent or nothing. Once in awhile I eat next door. I haven't ate anything today. Yesterday, I was lucky. I had a piece of steak with my cousin. He offered me a piece of steak. And the day before, I went downstairs late at night and had a couple of peanut butter and jelly sandwiches. But I don't eat nothing."

His parents do not like his behavior, although it does not seem to upset them greatly. "My mother might mind a little," Andy says, "like if she asks me to mop the floor or something and I don't do that, she'll say, 'You lazy ass! You better get a job!'" He says his father "don't mind none of us not working" as long as they don't bother him. Andy has a mild interest in going back to work for Allen Engineering, but says with a sign that his father doesn't seem to want him to.

At sixteen, Andy had an image of the kind of life he'd like to lead—active, full of travel, hard-working. But at twenty, his fantasies of the future have faded. It seems that his abstinence increases yearly—less food, less work, fewer fantasies. He is more vague about what he wants, and his thoughts about the future are bleak, although he doesn't sound depressed as he describes them. "I just was thinking—was it yesterday, or maybe it was ten minutes before you got here today?—I was thinking about what I was going to do. I was looking at somebody and I was saying 'ten years from now, what am I going to be doing?' I might have been looking at some man out in the street. It was down the unemployment office today. There was two guys standing there talking and I was saying, 'Look at that. I might be like them guys out there, just doing nothing or I might . . . I don't know.' " How does Andy feel about these prospects? He laughs, "I don't know. I just kept wondering, you know, but what's going to become of me? I can't stay up in this room forever."

FOCUS: ANDY GARRISON—
THE GARRISON CONDITION

Andy's father is a hard-working man and a loyal and dedicated father who is loved and respected by his children. Andy seems fortunate to have a father who provides a positive male model for him to emulate. Paradoxically, however, the lessons learned from Mr. Garrison's example may have caused Andy to reject his father's way.

The Garrisons are Yankees with dark skins, proud, independent, family-oriented, industrious. But the system which rewards these virtues in whites, often ignores them in blacks. Had Mr. Garrison been white, his extensive navy training would have made it possible for him to get a job as a surveyor, and his family would be living a comfortable life. Mrs. Garrison, as the wife of a man in comfortable circumstances, would be rewarded for her sensitivity and her love of family fun. She would be considered a good mother—loving, but not pushy; interested in her children's lives, but not intrusive. Andy and the other Garrison children would see traditional virtues rewarded and might be more tempted to emulate them.

But it has not worked that way. Mr. Garrison is black, not white, and the doors to higher pay and advancement in the blue-collar world have been repeatedly slammed in his face. At fifty-six, his pay remains meager and his job insecure, even after more than ten years with the same company and an exemplary work record. His successful efforts to obtain job training have not helped him to improve his precarious financial position.

The elder Garrisons illustrate for their children in every possible way how our society often makes disadvantages of honesty, diligence, and perseverance for black Americans. We cannot say how much their parents' experiences have influenced these children to avoid conventional work, but it would seem inevitable that the children have learned something from watching their parents. The younger Garrisons cannot help but compare their parents' fate with that of some of their neighbors and the parents of some of their classmates. The children see people rewarded equally for hard work and family loyalty and for idleness, lack of initiative, and desertion. As Andy notes at more than one point, the fatherless families often seem able to do better on welfare—which his parents have taught him not to accept— than his family is doing on a working man's salary.

Andy is aware that his father is bitter about the meager results of years of hard work and is resentful of the society that has put him in this position despite his unrelenting efforts. Andy sees how his father overlooks a job record which is full of the most blatant discrimination and how he goes on to blame himself, bad luck, and poor planning for the failure of his steadfast efforts to better his income.

The Garrisons live in a racial limbo—psychologically and socially removed from the black community and culture; ignored and abused by the whites with whom they identify. As the victims of over-assimilation, they think of themselves as Americans first and blacks second, while America perceives them the other way around.

Chapter
6
Anthony Dobson—
Staying Clean

ANTHONY AT SEVENTEEN—THE HUSTLER

Lounging gracefully in front of the battered, massive facade of the Ryan, Anthony Dobson at seventeen is the epitome of teenage, street-wise, hustler cool. Taller (although at 5' 10" he will not remain taller long), older than his classmates, Anthony is proud and "clean"—well-manicured, neat, with a keen sense for the multiple elegances of the contemporary scene. He is an important figure at the Ryan: president of the student council, "most popular boy," handy with a basketball or a pocket full of reefers, respected, if not always liked, by his teachers. Anthony's facade, unlike the Ryan's, is flawless. Behind the facade, though, are insecurities and uncertainties that few people suspect.

Anthony believes in his strength, his toughness, his ability to take care of himself. This is not a pose, although he may exaggerate details of fights and confrontations. He is tough and has proved himself in scores of conflicts, even at seventeen. At the same time, however, he sees himself as fragile, small. "At seventeen, 103-4 pounds, that ain't too sporty, you know. That's a lightweight. As much as I am tough, I should have some back-up . . . should be bigger."

Similarly, Anthony is proud of his agile tongue and knows that he is naturally attuned to people's strengths and weaknesses. But, while recognizing his own glibness and the power it gives him over

173

other people, he needs to test it constantly in a variety of situations to continue to believe in it. At seventeen, this requires that he "hangs with, like say, an older crowd. Crowds like comes from college and so forth, whities." This group frequents the "Big M" and the "Improper Bostonian," fashionable bars where a slick black youth is not only acceptable, but chic.

From these friends, from his family, occasionally even from himself, Anthony hides the source of his greatest insecurity—the fact that he can barely read. This would hardly seem a likely source of shame to a street-wise boy who knows he is intelligent, but his whole tone and bearing change when he discusses the subject. In the ninth grade he becomes defensive when the subject of reading is broached, saying he doesn't read much because "I don't get the time." Besides, he adds with characteristic bravado, "every time I read something, it's the same thing—I already know about it."

There are reasons for Anthony's mixed feelings about himself underneath the smooth and polished shell. His mother describes him as "kind of puny as a little one," a child who could not walk until he was four years old, talked late, tended to be sickly. He missed a lot of school in the primary years, and was kept back in the first grade, and then again in another early grade, partly because of illness, partly because of his difficulty with reading. At thirteen, Anthony recalls, he spent a lot of time in the hospital, being tested for "a little bit of everything. They tested me for my heart, and my hand was paralyzed." The paralysis turned out to be temporary, the result of a bad cut, but Anthony says that accident caused him to lose a year of schooling.

Anthony's physical disabilities and his trouble with school may have been exacerbated by his family circumstances. Anthony's family came from the rural South. His mother, married at fifteen, had nine children and little comfort. Looking back, she says she thought getting married would solve some of her problems, but "it didn't do nothing . . . just created more trouble." Anthony's father worked in a mill, and on payday, his mother says, "he was always fighting. Once he hit me with an axe. I said, 'Oh, God!'

174

And one time he beat me so until I had to call the doctor. And I wouldn't tell the doctor what happened. The doctor said, 'You just keep right on keeping this to yourself and you'll find yourself dead.' That's all he said to me." But she felt trapped by the helplessness and number of her children and stayed with her husband until Donna, the oldest, was eighteen. The pain of those years still lingers. "Gee, it was awful," she says. "I hate to think of the things that he had done to me in the matter of that time. He wrecked me. I never will forget that."

Despite her bitter memories, Anthony's mother says she does not hate her former husband. "I can't hold it against him, because I had a side, too. I should have learned to keep my mouth shut." She attributes much of his brutality to his lack of education. "If he had some education he wouldn't been like that. He would of consider himself, 'Well, this is ignorant.' Now I have talked to people that have husbands. They are all alike when they can't read and write. They think you're reading something against them. I did have him almost to the place that he could write his name. And then he would tell me, 'I can write. I don't need you to tell me.' "

When Donna was old enough to help manage the family, Anthony's mother made her break. She left North Carolina and moved to Boston where she had family. The first years in Boston were wretched. The court had ordered Mr. Dobson to pay five dollars a week to support his wife and children, not enough to pay for food, to say nothing of rent, fuel bills, clothing. "Those were awful times," Anthony's mother recalls. "Times when I remember that there was no food and one snowstorm right after another. Didn't have money to get coal."

Finally, hard times forced her to go "on the welfare." "That was sickening, disgusting. If I had it to do over again I wouldn't. I didn't like the idea of them knowing all my personal affairs. I said if I ever get off of there I never get back on that thing again. And the lady asked me why did I want to get off it. I said, 'Because I don't want you to know my business anymore.' So she says, 'Do you think you will ever need it again?' I said, 'I hope I would never have to need you to help me again.' I still didn't tell her I got married. Ain't none of her business, you know."

The marriage that liberated the Dobsons from the welfare rolls reinforced Anthony's mother's belief that the Lord will provide. She was always an ardent churchgoer and participant in church activities. Nevertheless, when her minister proposed marriage, she was taken by surprise. "One night he said to me, 'You want to talk to me?' Oh, gee, I thought I had did something and didn't know what had happened. What have I done this pastor want to straighten me out about? So then he said to me that he wanted to marry me and take care of my children. I said, 'Gee, this is something new.' If he'da kinda half way made a pass at me or something, it wouldn't have shocked me. Then we plan when we was gonna get married and we were gonna let the church know. Then we decided that we were not gonna let them know because they would only get mad, because practically all the women was single. So then we married in Baltimore."

Four years later, Rev. and Mrs. Brown and five of her nine children live in their own home in North Dorchester. Three others live with them, children of Mrs. Brown's dead sister. The Brown's house is a three-decker in a rapidly changing neighborhood. The family occupies the entire house; Rev. and Mrs. Brown live in the second and third floor apartments with Anthony, his older brother, Daniel, his younger siblings, Bruce and Conny, and his three cousins. The ground-floor flat belongs to Rev. Brown's daughter, Joan, and her small children.

Anthony's oldest sister, Donna, now lives with her husband in Boston. William, the oldest Dobson brother, has an apartment near the family home. Another older sister lives close by. In 1967, the Brown/Dobson family has settled into a comfortable routine. Enough money is coming in to meet its basic needs, and the rest of the family is living close enough to be supportive. But in the background, still much in the minds of the older children, is a time when things came very close to falling apart.

Anthony, at seventeen, feels good about his family. His mother, he says, "provides for us, helps us out. Like my brother William, if he gets in trouble or anything, she'll go help him out . . . get him out of trouble, get him out of town." Anthony describes his younger siblings and cousins with admiration, Vicky Franklin because she's "a smart little girl," and his brother Bruce Dobson as "plenty smart," because he got a double promotion in school last year. Anthony admires intellectual competence as shown through school success. Like his mother, he believes education is the way out of "ignorant" behavior.

Anthony gets along with the older members of the family as well as the younger ones. His mother says he likes his sister Donna best of all his siblings, because she is "like a mother," and helps him with his homework. Anthony himself claims Donna's husband, Marvin, is his favorite relative, because "he talks to me. He tells me I should go to school. He's nice to me and tells me what to do when I get in trouble. When I need money, he helps me out. I want to borrow his car for anything, no sweat." Anthony says also that he is very close to his older brother Daniel, who, at nineteen, still lives at home. Anthony reminisces happily about the trouble he and Daniel used to get into as children in the South, and says that he still likes to do things with Daniel, that he feels closer to his older brother than to any other man he knows.

Another older brother, William, has had a strong impact on Anthony's life. William is a pimp. Anthony loves to go to William's apartment, which he describes as a sumptuous haven: "Big round bed, turn it anyway you want. Color TV in every room, telephone in every room. Steady money, steady clothes." But as much as he envies his brother's worldly goods, he thinks he lacks adequate moral standards. "Things turn me away from him. Some of his ways I don't dig. Like he sniff coke. I don't dig that. If he gets low on money, he'll do anything for money. Which I won't." Anthony says his brother would rob people making supermarket deposits or beat dope pushers out of their dope. He does not object to his brother living off the earnings of prostitutes, but he finds robbery and dope morally unacceptable.

177

Many people, according to Anthony, see him as like his brother—
"They see me Sunday when I'm dressed up, and they say, 'There
goes the little pimp' "—and he's partly pleased, partly turned off
by their teasing. He prefers the quasi-legitimacy of his stepfather,
whom he describes as a "legal pimp," a man whose exploitation of
his followers (in his case, his congregation) is sanctioned by the
law.

Anthony admires his stepfather, who "has it made—he's got
him a '67 Cadillac, he has a '67 Oldsmobile station wagon—big
man, big money." Anthony says, "My stepfather, he is a nice guy.
Nice, quiet. But he gets in my way sometimes." They have had
serious fights, including occasional physical battles. "One time he
grabbed me. I said, 'Look, old man, take your hands off of me. So
he got mad and hit me. I walked away, so he hit me again. So he
ran on me and I took him in the groin, hit him in his forehead,
knocked him out. But he learned his lesson. We understood each
other, and we get along together." At seventeen, Anthony is very
concerned about his ability to defend himself against older and
stronger men. He says that he has a pistol and will shoot anyone
who "messes with me."

Anthony says he is more like his real father than anyone else in
the family, but he remembers him with a combination of
admiration and bitterness. He says he shares with his father a love
of money—"except he likes to work for it, which I wouldn't"—
and, like his father, he's fond of whiskey, women, and fun. But he
says, "If I were a father, I wouldn't mess with the lives of my kids
that way. He messed up my life, but I would keep my kids
together. So that's the way I am different." He remembers vividly
the parental battles of his childhood and recalls with relish the
time he and Daniel put sugar in the carburetor of the family car to
avenge their mother after a family argument.

In contrast, Anthony talks about his mother with nearly
undiluted warmth, and sees himself as unlike her. "She do for her
kids. Like my father, he wouldn't come home, and she'd make
sure we had clothes and food and so forth. Nice Christmas and all

that, as far back as I can remember. She's soft-hearted, which I am not. She's like religious, which I'm not. That's why she have so much trouble with me. I don't give nothing to nobody."

Mrs. Brown, on the other hand, sees Daniel as his father's son and Anthony as much more like herself. She agrees that he causes her heartache, when he "talks rough to me," and says, sadly, that he "isn't the nicest boy that I know of." She says, "I always make him know that I'm mother and he has to respect me," but she sets few rules for Anthony and treats him more or less as an adult. "I know he's slick," she says. "He's a big boy and he can go into clubs. I don't prefer him to do that. I don't want him to get involved with dope. That's one of the things. But how can I help it? He's out on the street and not at home."

Anthony's mother has felt increasingly helpless to control his behavior over the last few years. Several heart attacks have made her less mobile and more dependent on her children for help in the house. She says that Anthony does do things in the house. "He will cook if he has to. He'll help me clean the house and he'll put up a table. Most anything, if I can get him there and get him to do it. And Anthony will do the clothes, his shirts, and wash them. He needs something clean, he'll wash it if I don't get around to doing it, and he will iron his clothes."

Anthony sees things somewhat differently. He agrees that he makes things rough for his mother sometimes, but perceives himself in a special position, as *de facto* head of the household. Anthony says that he runs the house because his stepfather is "old, don't have too much to say, he let me do it." He says that he organizes the cooking and cleaning, manages the money, gives opinions on potential purchases. Mrs. Brown may well turn to Anthony for advice now that Donna is gone (and sorely missed), but she sees herself as the one who "do decisions about clothing and food. I guess I'm the boss," she says, "as far as bills and all." If she discusses issues with her husband, he always tells her to do what she wants.

Anthony sees his world pretty much as it is, except that he exaggerates his own power to control what happens in it. He

179

claims, for example, that he gets a $25 a week "cut" of the family money as repayment for running the household. His mother says she used to give the children small allowances, but that she had to eliminate them when her brother's children came to live with her, because she could not afford to treat them all equally. Similarly, he claims that he and Daniel once "knocked out" their father when he mistreated their mother, a story which seems unlikely, since their separation occurred when Anthony was six and Daniel eight years old.

Anthony spends his street time with several distinct groups of young people. Besides the nightclub college crowd, he "hangs around with kids that play basketball and go to parties," and another group that swims at the local pool. Girls are an important part of Anthony's life, and he is proud of his prowess with "older girls—women. "I had this one who thought she was real slick. Her name was Judy. She ran this game down. Well, she knows she's fine. So she always getting down how slick she is. Like she's going to turn me on to something. All I know is she wanted to be a whore . . . but not for long." He says there is also the "regular crowd—a couple of white girls I mess around with down at the club. You know, give me money and so forth, stay over at their house and all that junk." But the only girl Anthony takes seriously is Barbara Morris, the younger sister of his best friend. "I don't mess around with her," Anthony says. "She's the only one I have any feelings for."

Barbara is special in a number of ways. Anthony speaks of her with some tenderness, interlaced with his customary cynicism. "She's all right. Got a high school diploma, college education, just in case I don't decide to work. That's why I don't mess with these young girls on the street. She's working now. She's earning $110 a week." Anthony thinks more about marriage than most of his classmates—perhaps because of Barbara, perhaps because he is older than most—and he has very clear ideas about what he wants. Two children, "one of each . . . she'll want a girl, so they can dress up, and a man would want a boy so he can ride along, you know, 'This is my son.' I would like a boy. When he gets older, I'd keep him just as clean as he could be."

Being "clean," and "fast," with no hard physical labor and plenty of money is important to Anthony. An educated wife, who can work if need be, and who will leave him free to hustle as he pleases, is an insurance policy on the clean life. Anthony has his plans well made.

According to Anthony, the cleanest, fastest guys in the crowds he deals with are "the pimps and myself." Pimps and Anthony stay loose, act cool, prefer pot smoking to drinking, avoid fights and unnecessary difficulty. Anthony speaks of "Steady" Austin, a pimp friend, as living the kind of life he wants. "I'd want to be like him—he got a helicopter and a Cadillac, big farm house in the country. He has money." But, while Anthony is clear about what he wants in both material goods and life style, he doesn't like what the pimp label connotes. He describes an acquaintance, Jim. "He's a pimp. He knocks people in the head. I don't want to be like him. He just knocks people in the head, getting drunks and taking rolls and things. And then he calls himself a pimp."

Anthony gets around the label problem by saying that he is more a "hustler" than a pimp, and differentiates the two labels at some length. He says he has one whore working for him, but unlike a straight pimp, "I get money anyway I can. A pimp only gets money one way. That's the difference. I sell narcotics and stuff—pills, reefers." Later, he makes the distinction on the grounds of physical violence. Pimps will roll drunks and rob them, while hustlers simply use a variety of ways to earn their money.

Anthony has a high opinion of his own cool. If someone was going to try to take his place, he says, he would have to "have a hippy walk and . . . the way I hold my head up. And wear the things I wear. And when he goes into clubs, to be cool—just sit in a corner, so nobody notices you, don't bother nobody." He sees his "cool" as the basis of his ability at "pulling girls," and his capacity to stand back and analyze situations as the basis of his skill in sports. "Me, I analyze what they do," he says, "how they work out things. I think about it. Other kids, they don't think.

They just play." And on the foundation of these skills, Anthony claims, "I can do anything I want to."

Anthony in School

Anthony has always found schoolwork difficult. When his mother moved the family North, he was made to repeat first grade, and a combination of reading problems and illness forced him to spend two years in the third grade as well. His memories of elementary school are unpleasant. He recalls hating to read "because to me it seemed silly. You seen the pictures. You know, that's Jack. And you knew that was Jack and that was Dick and that was Sally. And you seen the pictures and then they want you to read it." Now, Anthony says, "All I read is dollar bill signs." He manages at school with a combination of charm and intelligence. "On the tests, I just use my imagination. I come out all right."

His mother knows that Anthony has trouble reading, but she does not know how severe his problem is, nor can she readily account for it. "He's behind in school," she says, "and doesn't read too well, as far as reading out loud, he doesn't. He might do silent reading very good." None of her other children have had reading difficulties. Mrs. Brown thinks that perhaps Anthony's troubles stem from his classic poor eating habits, or perhaps from poor eyesight. But his reading problems do not concern her greatly now, because Anthony's grades at the Ryan are excellent. He gets "B-minus, A, and B. I don't think he had any D's or E's . . . he isn't one to stay out all the time. He studies and he does a lot of projects, you know, ah, book reports." And she thinks that probably, if Anthony would only work harder, he could go to college.

None of the older Dobson children has finished high school, and Mrs. Brown has staked her hopes on Anthony. "I want him to be in college. I'm hoping. I don't know if he's going, but I'm going to push him and try to make him go. The main thing I want him to do, just finish school. Just one of them finish school, I'll really be proud. Just one, if he be the one . . . I'll be a proud mother."

In Mrs. Brown's mind, education is the route to a good occupation. "I would like for him to get a decent job. And to get a decent job he needs to get his education. That would be one way that he would be able to get one. I don't want him to have to go and work in a factory and do some of the things that I had to do. And to do that then he has to get a high school education." She sees education as especially critical for a black man, "because the white man, even though he's not even qualified for a job, but if you be white then you get the job."

Anthony is very much aware of his mother's anxiety that he do well in school, and he delights in being able to please her. "My mother, you know, she's proud seeing her kid getting awards and all this shit. So it comes the time they're giving out awards. I got basketball—two basketball awards, and I got a Most Popular Boy award, and then president of the student council . . . so that makes her happy." But he is also aware that being president of the student council does not necessarily enable one to complete an education. Sometimes he has fantasies in which he'd "get me all kinds of degrees. Oh, they do things for you . . . you got a degree. Get a Master's degree, you can get a job where you come in and you can say, 'Anyone call, I am at the so-and-so country club! . . . something like that." But when he realistically assesses his own prospects, he has no illusions about completing college and says he has no definite plans. And, although he sometimes declares that he can go as far as he wants in school, ultimately he views his parents' hopes and dreams for him as unrealistic. "They're thinking I can go far. They're wrong. See, they don't know."

Despite his academic problems Anthony does not hate school. He sees school as an exciting and stimulating arena in which all his skills—conning, intimidating, bluffing, maneuvering—are tested and refined. Asked what he likes about school, he replies, "All of it. Everything—subjects, lunches, all of it." His teachers, he says, think he is best at "talking a lot." In his own estimation, he declares he is best at "everything, everything, anything."

He talks extensively about his adventures at the Ryan, boasting about his skill at managing the teachers, his prowess at winning confrontations with other boys. "If you're good with the teachers," he says, "you can make it . . . be a pet like me. I think I leave the school more than anybody! I come in late more than anybody. But I don't get in trouble for it." Maintaining his control over other boys he finds more difficult, although he speaks of the time when another boy "told everybody Anthony Dobson is getting too big. So the cat carried a knife. So I was ready. So he approached me with his knife and I had a little .22 in my pocket. And I said, 'Pull it out,' and he quit. So we were suspended." Whether or not these stories are true, they indicate the level of excitement and challenge with which Anthony perceived his Ryan days.

Anthony can be critical of his friends at the Ryan. One friend, Randy Walker, is much like Anthony—a basketball player, a cool and popular boy. "He thinks basketball is going to get him through school this year; he didn't graduate," Anthony says critically. "He got a complex. He always makes people look up to him, so he does things, tries to be amusing and so forth. Trying to make them say, 'Oh, Walker did that.' "

Anthony says that he likes Walker. He saves his full wrath for Brian Henry, the "good student," whom Anthony condemns with a remarkable lack of cool. "He's hell. That no-good fellow makes all kinds of shit. Tie-choked up to the collar. He looks smart carrying all his books and shit and all that . . . reads his ass off." Teachers, says Anthony, say Brian is a "lovely young man." But Anthony declares that his crowd "don't think he's too slick."

Anthony is also critical of the Ryan and of many of his teachers, although he says he will respect any teacher who shows respect for him. "I respect every colored teacher there," he says. "Some of the white ones I wouldn't give two cents for." If he could reform the school, he would get rid of all the "old teachers out of there," replacing them with a younger, integrated group. He says he would have "a colored principal; he understands the hardships that kids take, at home . . . same thing carries with the guidance counselor, too. All them guidance counselors over there—they got about ten—there's not one colored. So I'd get rid of all that."

Anthony doesn't consider the Ryan pupils as troublemakers. Instead, he sees them as victors in the ongoing battle with teachers, adept at outfoxing authority, competent at getting around strict disciplinary measures erratically enforced. He sees himself as the "top gun" in this group—the cleverest, toughest, most adept of all—and backs up his quick tongue with a wide assortment of conventional and unconventional weapons. "I used to carry sulfuric acid to school," Anthony says . . . "First off, I used to carry two pepper shakers. Got in a fight, threw pepper in their eyes." He says he carries a gun—"A little .22"—but "don't shoot nobody."

Not all teachers (or students for that matter) are dazzled by Anthony's style. One teacher, he says, refers to him as "Anthony Dobson the Great Leader, and so he thinks I should be a leader. Every time something goes wrong in the school that teacher says, 'Well, that's the Great Leader there.' " Anthony resents this teasing and calls the teacher a "joker" who "expects too much of me."

But Anthony's relationships with teachers are not all hostile. He is especially fond of Mr. Donner, his eighth grade math teacher. If you answered a question wrong, Anthony says, "He'd make a joke out of it. If you said you didn't know, he'd say, 'What do you mean, you don't know?' And they he'd find out why you didn't know, and so forth. Then he'd help." Anthony says Mr. Donner is fair to "everybody except me." From Anthony he evidently expected higher standards of behavior. But teacher and pupil spent a lot of time together outside of school, talking and eating out. Once, Anthony says, Mr. Donner gave him a dollar as a birthday present.

Mr. Donner is equally attached to Anthony and impressed by his sensitivity and insight. "He was the most incredible guy that I met, with respect to what he could see about other people," Donner said after Anthony graduated. He went on to point out that, "Anthony was perceptive about sociology, anything political—things that were going on around him. He had an incredible amount of experience. He had been on civil rights things. He understood how the school ran, he understood the adults who ran the school."

Mr. Donner understands Anthony's style, but has only a partial understanding of his limitations. He says that Anthony is a "B-C student who couldn't read very well," but ascribes most of his school problems to Anthony's unwillingness to prepare for classes. "Knowing all those things," Mr. Donner says, "he was able to use them, able to get by really well. The guy was kind of quick. He wasn't as quick in thinking, but he was good enough to get by in doing things without a whole lot of preparation."

Mr. Donner feels that Anthony is a person with insight and talent who is not going to be able to use his skills to their full extent. "He doesn't have a chance to use any of what he's got," the teacher says. "He might find a chance—he's got a way of finding himself, of getting what he wants. But, like right now, he's looking for a job, and where is a guy going to find a job? He doesn't want a $1.50 an hour car wash job, he wants a decent job. He thinks he deserves $2.50 an hour and interesting work. But he can't find a job. He can't fight the thing."

But Mr. Donner sees only the Anthony that Anthony wants to reveal. The black physical education teacher, Mr. Taylor, takes a more hard-headed view. Mr. Taylor says that Anthony is a "boy of the street . . . worldly wise," more successful in the street scene than in school. He explains his apparent determination to finish ninth grade in terms which could have come directly from Anthony. "He liked it at the Ryan. And there were still girls there. He was going to be top dog on the campus and all."

While Mr. Donner sometimes saw Anthony as a little slow, Mr. Taylor says he has a "good mind. Good tongue. And he knew how to work them both." Anthony, he said, was greatly admired by the other kids. "He could get around people, beat his way in and out of anything. He wasn't any problem in school. He never gave anybody a hard time. He was too smooth for that."

Anthony and Mr. Taylor had a solid, honest relationship at the Ryan according to the descriptions both of them give. Mr. Taylor recalls with amusement some of Anthony's early hustles. "One time, he was walking around school with this satchel-case. I said to myself, 'He can't be carrying books.' So one day I called him in my office and I said, 'Open that thing up.' " Anthony argued, claiming he was only carrying his gym uniform, but Mr. Taylor was not taken in. "So he opened it up, and he had that thing loaded with cigarettes. And this kid, he'd been coming to school for two weeks, hustling cigarettes. So I finally said, 'Well, leave me a pack there—a carton.' So he said, 'Where's the money?' So I said, 'You don't trust me?' 'No, I don't trust you,' he told me. I didn't want to buy them anyhow—I don't smoke cigarettes anyway. I knew what he was doing around the school."

Mr. Taylor told Anthony that the president of the student council shouldn't be hustling cigarettes in the school corridors. "Oh man, you're dogging me now. You're trying to make me feel bad," Anthony responded. Mr. Taylor denied that, saying only that "if he wanted to be the president, then he had certain obligations that go with the office. It clicked in his head. O.K. So he stopped. We went on a no-smoking campaign with the student council. They cut out the kids from smoking and what-not. He was the one who was leading it, you know. The kids didn't give him any hard time. They cut out smoking. No problems . . . no squabbles . . . no fights. It was successful. And he was the one who was doing it."

Mr. Taylor is the only one of the several teachers who took a special interest in Anthony who understands the full extent of his reading problem. "If Anthony could bullshit his way to a Ph.D., damn it, he'd do it. Let me put it that way. Whether he's going to make it [through school] or whether someone's going to catch up to him by that time—I don't know. His only hope for salvation is the military service. Maybe by getting him away from this sort of life . . . He may be able to find himself in it. Make him realize that maybe he can do something. That he is capable of doing something."

But the teacher sees this as only a remote possibility. "I always got the impression that Anthony was just going to be a hustler, I guess. With his smooth ways, his tongue and lying and his bullshit, he'll make it." He expects that Anthony, like his brother William, will be a pimp, because he "sees this kind of a life and the glamour and everything." And Mr. Taylor sees no way the school can turn him away from that course.

Throughout conversations with Anthony, one never learns a critical fact mentioned by all his teachers: by the ninth grade Anthony is enrolled in a "special class" called "Operation Second Chance." According to Mr. Taylor, this class seems "more happy-go-lucky than anything else . . . more like a social promotion unit that worked with kids who had repeated a grade." It is not clear what was done in this class. Evidently it was not enough to discover that a clever, determined boy like Anthony could not read.

Although Anthony says that he wants to finish high school, by the ninth grade he is already saying things which mean "drop-out" to the experienced ear. His high school plans are very vague—no one, including Anthony, can repeat the same ones twice. He says, "I had a chance to go to Hyde Park High. I got accepted there. I was supposed to go out there and take a test, but I was sick the day I was supposed to go take the test. So they took my records to Dorchester High. 'Cause to me, I just don't really care."

Despite his defiant noises, it is clear he does care. But the prospect of trying to complete high school without relying on his nonacademic strong suit, basketball, is frightening. He worries that he is overage, worries that he will be penalized two-fold because he is older than his classmates. "They'll be hard on me," he says, "because I'm behind, I'm older." He vaguely considers finishing school in Greensboro, North Carolina, the family hometown—"Down there you play the class. As long as you graduate with your class that you came in with, then you can play on the team. If I go down there now, there's a chance that I'll go another year and play."

When he is being straightforward, Anthony admits he sees no scholastic future for himself in Boston. And he feels that his teachers, if not his parents, agree. He says of the teachers, "Oh, they're rough. They don't even say high school. They say until I'm 17 . . . I'll be drafted. They think of every excuse—they figure the teachers in high school will not take the shit they took. But soon as I get in high school—I don't figure the teachers take no shit." Nevertheless, he says he and his friends plan to stay in school. Speaking of dropping out, he says, "We joke about it, but that's about as far as we go. But they know that they got to make it through high school, or they won't make it at all."

Anthony on Race and Work

Anthony stands out from other boys in his group in his strong antipathy for whites. Life, he says, is generally more unpleasant and more difficult for blacks than for whites, systematic racism deprives him of his natural rights. "You work for a white man. Okay, so you buy food. Who gets the money back? The white man. So that's a disadvantage. You don't get nothing from him. Everything you do goes back to the white man. So everything is a disadvantage."

Despite his anger at the white world, Anthony spends a lot of time with whites, especially those who "hang out" in the integrated Back Bay bars. He says he can't stand the whites who try to act like blacks. "Oh, the white guys, they try to be—when they're around us, they try to make believe they're colored. All cool and buddy-buddy. I hate that shit."

Anthony says that he hates to see a black woman with a white man, although he likes "to see a Negro guy messing with a white girl." He says that he "messes with white girls," himself, but doesn't really care about them. "I stay at their place. They only mess with me because their own group throw them out and so they come to me. And when they get tired of me, they'll go back to their own people. So that's why I can't stand the whites."

Despite his strong feelings about whites, Anthony is not reluctant to go into white situations. "Anything I can use, I'll go ahead and do it," he declares, saying that he would not mind going to an integrated school because "say I was the top student in the school. That would be something." In fact, he says, he prefers an integrated school faculty—white teachers for subject matter courses, black guidance counselors. A black principal would be nice, Anthony adds, "because you want to have a cat you can talk to. But at the same time, a whitey principal would be better."

In his various encounters with whites, Anthony prefers to rely on his own personal skills. He does not see contemporary civil rights leaders as helpful to him. "It's odd, you know, all of them are speaking for you. Why can't you speak for yourself? They don't know what you want. They know what *they* want. See, I might go to a march, but I don't have all the dough in my pocket that Stokeley Carmichael, Martin Luther King and all have. Therefore we are not equal." Anthony likes the Black Muslims and feels that they command respect from black and white alike, but he does not feel that he could handle their religious laws. "They're out to educate you, to let you know what you are. You got to have some respect for them . . . and the white man, they do respect them. But—if you are straight, just plain old Negro, or black man, as they call themselves, you don't get no respect from the white man."

Anthony hustles the work world as he has hustled the school. He has had a few menial jobs—washing walls at Technical High School, working for the same catering firm as his mother "polishing silver and loading the dishwasher." But he doesn't like those jobs because the work is too hard. The only job he remembers with relish is day camp work, for reasons related more to work conditions than to the intrinsic merits of the job. "Whitey's the one now . . . he's a pretty good boss; you come in late in the morning and he still give you the time. He's a pretty good boss."

He judges jobs by their benefits and their hustle potential. "How people act on the job, how much I get paid . . . or find out how much sick pay and all that. If I get laid off, do I get paid and all that." Anthony says he has never been fired from a job, but that "I didn't stay long at any of them . . . 'cause I don't like to work." What he would really like is to be rich and powerful—"a banker or president of the United States."

Anthony says he would like to be a lawyer—that he is well-equipped for the profession by his talent for "running off at the mouth." His second choice is professional basketball; he envisions the cheering (and paying) throngs. But asked about a third choice, he comes down to earth and says that he would probably be a welder, "pick up some kind of trade." The prospect does not interest him at all, because, he says, he is "too lazy" for strenuous work.

ANTHONY AT TWENTY—ON THE STREET

Three years later, Anthony's life has changed completely. He has dropped out of school, left home, married Barbara. At twenty, he is head of a household, father of two, a full-time hustler, piecing together a high but insecure income by running a variety of hustles.

He left home before his marriage, after a fight with his stepfather—the last in a long series. "He put me out of the house," Anthony says. "His daughter was staying there and me and her got into an argument, so I knocked her down and he jumped up and told me he's going to put me out and shoot me with his gun. So I knocked him out and left."

He went to live with Marvin, his brother-in-law and close friend. He chose Marvin partly because he knew his brother-in-law really wanted him to finish school and would do anything he could to help. Anthony says that Marvin bought an encyclopedia for him, taught him to read square roots and introduced him to the dictionary. But it was too late for Anthony and school. He finished at the Ryan and bounced from high school to high school for a while, landing finally at Boston English. He left English High (the last in the series) after a spectacular fight on the school bus. Anthony says that the white boys started it, but that he then

191

"advocated the whole thing. I told the bus driver to get off. I made all the white boys get off. I was throwing them off and taking their money, and the cats that didn't do it, I said, 'Hey, come on,' they had to go too. Teachers told me—they put this in my mind—I was a leader and so to follow me." Seven students were suspended after the battle—Anthony for the last time.

He wanted to stay in school, to find someplace where he could finish. But he had been suspended from too many places, and Barbara was pregnant and pressuring him to marry her. These factors combined with his fears of being "found out," channeled him into full-time street life. "I got a hang-up," Anthony says of the situation. "I got my wife pregnant so I had to quit school and get a job."

Anthony and Barbara and their two girls live in a four-room apartment on Blue Hill Avenue, part of a housing complex of low-rise brick buildings surrounding a paved inner courtyard. Anthony plays basketball with the neighborhood boys in that yard, teaching them his old plays, letting them confide in him. He likes his apartment, delights in describing it. "Well, as you walk in the front door, there's a little hallway with a piece of carpet, and then . . . I had my other floors covered, but I took it up because I have hardwood floors. The whole apartment is painted one color. Then I have a love seat, my record player and knick-knacks and pictures that I have drawn. Then I have a TV and wall lamps, then other pictures and a couch. That's the front room."

Anthony says he would need to earn $600-$700 a week to support this establishment. Clearing that amount, or anything near it, is a weekly hassle. When he first married, he had a job in a hospital, but augmented his income with a number of confidence games. He is particularly adept at phony accident cases. "Say I see a whitey driving slow in town. I jump on the car—this year alone I had $9,000 for accidents." He also makes money pimping, but says, "I got four rents to pay and all I get outside of that I give to my wife and it goes in the bank." "All I do is con: through school, jobs, women, everybody and any way I can see I can really get something out of it. It's like a junkie—if he can get money, he'll go get his narcotics. If he can't he go steal it."

Barbara wants him to get a regular job, Anthony says, mainly to satisfy her family. But he says she is a "pretty smart girl, except she lacks common sense. She's all right, except she wants to be the boss." Anthony admires Barbara's brains, and speaks proudly of her year in college. But he is king of his castle. He comes home, he says, "kick my shoes off, wait for her to pick them up, bring my supper. That's the way I portrait myself. 'Don't have no kids to wait on me, 'cause I'm not going to bed with them. I'm going to bed with you.' " Anthony is not about to let himself "get beat by a woman."

Anthony is proud of his daughters. Like their mother, he says, they are "very smart—they have their mother's smartness as far as schooling and then they have my common sense. They observe everything." He describes them both as exceptionally verbal and loving—"every morning, each is on one side of the bed to wake me up . . . that's why I never left home. Two beautiful kids."

Anthony worries about his girls in the context of his hustling, pimping life. "I couldn't tell them not to be whores or associate with pimps," he says. "All I could tell them is go and get their education, and after their education, I have nothing to do with them." He says that he wouldn't want his daughters to feel bad because their father was a pimp, so "I'd say when about thirty, I'd tell them that I'd retired and get a business or something." But "if they want to be in this fast life, I couldn't say no, because, like, I did it."

Anthony's life on the street is uncertain, fast-paced. His closest friend is still his brother-in-law Marvin—"We have a father-son relationship . . . I could talk to Marvin about anything." He visits Marvin on his day off and borrows his car, shoots pool, or just sits and talks over a couple of beers. He sometimes feels uncomfortable with Marvin's brothers, one of whom is in Boston College, the other at Harvard. "When we sit down and talk, they'd be up on this level, and I'm still down on this level. I play chess with them. I beat them every time, but the first thing they say, 'I go to Harvard,' 'I go to B.C.' and that shit . . . I don't like to hear it." But Marvin, "He don't talk on that high level which he

193

has the education to—that I don't have. He don't make me feel like I am somebody who stands before you like a dog."

In the hustling life Anthony most admires Louis. "This cat," Anthony says, "is my idol. Like I go to his house . . . you would think, like, you see pictures like you're in Hong Kong. The whities wait on me hand and foot, take off my shoes, that sort of thing. This cat really got it; makes money, nine whores." Compared to Louis, Anthony says, he is a small time pimp, who rarely clears more than $400-$500 a week, even when he augments his income by picking the pockets of big pimps' girls.

Anthony spends most of his time with this street crowd, going to nightclubs "where whities are." They drink, exchange advice "about different broads and how to cop them, about saving money; not getting into the pimp game and how much trouble it is." The group will "go over different broad's house and rest, or they come to my house when my wife ain't home and rest."

Some of the "resting" involves drugs. Since he left school, hard drugs have become more and more a part of his street-life style. At one point, several months ago, he says, he had a heavy habit. "I didn't shoot it so that I got strung out or I took money out of my family's mouth or my kids' mouth and sold things. It wasn't that type of thing. It was like shooting it to have something to do. Better than that, I just glamorized over it; like, say, 'Well, I'm shooting dope now, digging it with the crowd'—it was that type of thing, like letting everybody know that I'm shooting dope." One day, he recalls, someone commented, " 'Hey, here's a young nigger; you're always suppose to have money; but you can't have money if you give it to that boy [who sold heroin].' And I really dug; I said, 'Hey, what the hell am I doing?' and stopped shooting." Now he sniffs cocaine, which he does not consider addictive.

Anthony and some friends joined a riot and were arrested on "twenty-five charges—breaking-and-entering, assaulting an officer, receiving stolen goods, assault and battery with a dangerous weapon—oh, I had them all." He was arraigned and sent to

Charles Street Jail for two months pending trial. It was an experience he says he will never forget. "I wouldn't wish that on nobody. Like, I never used to like anyone watching me take a shit. Here you are, you got to take a shit in this little fucking thing and they take that mother-fuck out when they get ready. They had me eating breakfast, and fucking pigeons and shit flying over you. They'll eat the food then shit in it, and it's just nasty." He shared his cell with a man whom he said he had to beat up every night for three weeks to stop him from making homosexual advances, and had to deal constantly with abusive jail personnel. "That nigger thing—the first thing that come out of their mouth . . . 'you black mother-fucking nigger,' that type of thing."

When he finally went back to court, the judge threw out his case, leaving him feel that "I spent two months for nothing." He sees criminal justice in strictly economic terms—"If you got the money and you're black you don't even have to see the court house. You go into the judges' chamber and, boom! Like I had a few cases I should have done five to ten, but it cost me $300 and I went nowhere. White or black . . . if you got the money you can beat it."

Over the last two years, with his developing experience with marriage, money-earning, and trouble, Anthony has become more sympathetic toward his own father. "I don't knock the things he's doing," Anthony says of his father, "because, like in a sense, I doing the same thing. Like people tell me I'm like him now. I've learned my mouth; I talk a lot and he talks a lot. He's always scheming or thinking, like his undeveloped mind is always on money. If his mind was more developed . . . he'd really be something." He says he would like to be different from his father in only one way—"What he doesn't have is an education—I would love to have a better education. That's about all."

Anthony is obsessed by education—its intrinsic value, his limitations because of his dropout status. He returns to the subject over and over. Virtually any topic is set in its magical context. He says, "I'm not lost like the ordinary cat that really quit school; like they jump to drugs and that type of thing. I always been a fast-learning kid, anyway." But when he talks about his reading problems, his voice changes, and he says, "That's my gap; that's my only hang-up. Like I got a complex ... some things ... I can't read, or like if I go somewhere and people say read this and I feel in my mind that I can't do it ... I won't do it, 'cause like I don't have the education. But if I knew I had the education, I'd be really something."

In his better moods, Anthony sees himself as a nice guy who can "gigolo" a job, a woman, a street situation to give him maximum benefit with minimum output. "I have a smooth style, say with the women," he says, "I fit into any kind of conversation and any kind of people." He says that when he left school, he thought he could "get big cash right now—from women and things and anything to do with hustling—Mastercharge, writing checks—everything without really jeopardizing myself; picking pockets—anything with skill behind it—skill or in the mind. I wouldn't go and stick up nobody. They say as a pimp or player you have to learn how to beg; and like you know the right way to beg.

"You have a rat in a cage and like he don't want to go to the right. But there is an electricity wire and every once a while someone pushes it and it shocks him, but it makes him go to the right. He knows the right's the wrong way, but it's a way. And with me, I know pimping is the wrong way, but it's a way. And all I'm asking, and as rich as this country is, that somebody give me an education. That's all I want."

He sees himself presently at a crossroad in his life and says, "I'm squared up for a while. Look to see if I can find myself a little better ... see if I can find myself a job. Whatever I do in the next few weeks will determine what I do for the rest of my life: pimp or get a job." But without an education, Anthony does not believe that he will be able to get the job he wants, a job in data processing where "I could keep my fingernails clean ... any clean job.

"Computers was always my goal—really dig the place. Nice, cool atmosphere, guys in suits; big money, nice cars ... it's not hard work. Something like a staff thing where I can run my mouth—a thing I do best."

Anthony has in fact looked into a variety of programs intended for motivated black young men. He has found his investigations frustrating, especially when they involved community-based, predominately black social service organizations. "Like they advertise all this stuff on TV. I sign up for it and, boom, they go ask me what kind of background I have. Now, like, bullshit—I tell them what I want and they ask me all this old . . . 'We don't have room for you right now,' or 'Why don't you go into the service?' I don't know what to do. I'm sick of all this bullshit. I've told them all I want—I want a motherfuckin' education—boom, point blank."

Looking back on the school experiences he had, Anthony feels that the system prepares a black youth poorly to deal with adult life. His own preparation, he says, was "very raggedy. I'll explain. Like the contact I had about the airplane pilot. I didn't know you had to have a college education to be that, or to be an officer in the service. And like they do not prepare black kids—have them run around as athletes until they get out of school. Like now, you talk about needing a high school diploma; a high school diploma isn't worth shit."

Anthony says that being black in this society means that "everything, all things, life itself," puts him behind. "I'm just a poor black boy. Money can't change it. I was born that way, so that's the way I live. No matter how much money I have, I'll still be a poor black boy. It's not so much money, because a black man can get a million dollars and a white person can get a million dollars, but the white person be on a higher pedestal than a black person, so it's not so much just dollars."

Anthony has been active in civil rights activities, working with a number of Roxbury organizations, including a group called the First Freedom Choir, which was "chased by whities" in Alabama where they went on tour. He was a Black Panther briefly, quitting after an altercation with the leadership, who wanted him to cut his processed hair and grow an Afro. Anthony does not allow his political life to encroach on his sense of personal style. "Somebody can get what they want. That's the way I feel. 'Cause I'd get a Do if I wanted it, or like my hair is now, dyed red. Whatever I want to do, I'm going to do it, regardless of what anybody says."

Anthony says he has no close white friends because he really doesn't like white people and doesn't trust them. He views them in the same way he sees women—easily manipulated by flash and charm, but always to be watched, to be used. "I use a white person the same way a white person use a black person. If I don't like them as a friend . . . really I'm going to misuse them, anyway, 'cause the whitey got it; he's born with it. He's white, he's got the silver spoon. So all I know is, misuse them."

ANTHONY AT TWENTY-THREE—THE PLAYER

When he was nineteen, Anthony talked about altering his life— to get his long-sought education or to give up that dream and become a big-time pimp like his friend Louis. Over the last four years he has tried both. For several months, he stuck to street hustling, spending much of his time in a restaurant owned by some of his pimp friends, where Anthony's mother worked. "I was selling stuff, not like in robbing or none of that. Anything I was doing had finesse to it. You know, something where you had to think." The restaurant was the center of his life for a while, a place where he could retreat when he was tired of his street life and have "fun hanging out doing things I like to do . . . like a broad might come in and she might see and like you and that sort of thing."

Anthony describes that period as an unsatisfactory time, when he was doing things that "niggers do . . . you know how niggers do in the city, that ain't going to school." So when his brother Daniel told him about a training program in health careers, Anthony approached the black director with somewhat suspicious interest, never losing sight of the bad experiences he has had with community based programs. But he and the black program director got along well. "This was the first time that someone talked about doing something and could do it, and that's why I said, 'Hey, you know, he's cool.' "

Anthony was enthusiastic about the program and went to class at Northeastern University every day from noon until two in the afternoon. The program combined limited classroom instruction with a lot of self-paced independent study materials. "You taught yourself," Anthony says, "and if you didn't read, there was no one else, there was just you. So you didn't hurt no one and there was no one to say, 'Hey, you got to do this.' It was all self, self-ambition. If you didn't have the ambition to do it, you didn't do it."

Staff members were available to provide students with assistance, supplies, and tests of their progress, but Anthony felt isolated and increasingly frustrated with his own progress. He talked to the staff about going into formal courses at the university, but they said that he had to wait until his skills were better. After three months, disillusioned and depressed, Anthony dropped out of the program.

After he left the program, Anthony says he went into a "slump." "I just hung in," he says, "I stayed in the house, took money I had, bought a lot of dope, sold dope for a while. And snorted it for a while." But, with the help of some pimp friends, he pulled himself together and decided to go back to the Health Careers program in the summer of 1972. "They told me, 'Hey, man, what we doing is cool, but what you trying to do and want to do—that's where it's at.' "

Bolstered by the encouragement of his friends, Anthony tried again. But "then things got like kind of rough," he says. "I wasn't doing too good. And I stopped working in the restaurant. So I went into a slump. I lost faith in myself. And now I'm just coming out of it."

The second depression was a bad one. Anthony started on drugs again, "doing things I knew I shouldn't be doing—I'm not that type of person, you know what I mean?" But at the time, he says, "I just didn't care enough. I wouldn't get my hair done or my fingernails manicured or nothing. Wouldn't even dress." He tried a methadone clinic, but got higher off the methadone than he did from drugs. Then he tried to go back to the group of pimps who had given him support in his first "slump." But they didn't really want him this time. "I was too much in the slump," he says. "It was like spoiling their thing."

Finally, Anthony again got himself off drugs and is now making new plans. But it is becoming harder and harder for him to regroup. "They tell me I've got lots of talents, but I don't use them," he says. And, despite some talk of trying the Health Careers program for a third time, Anthony did not reenroll in time for the 1973 term.

But he will not give up. "I know what I want to do, and I want to do, truthfully, everything I possibly can. I want to pimp; I want to go to school; I want an education." He says he wants to "really greater myself," into playing a pimp on a different level. "'Cause, like they have whities like politicians, they're pimping, but it's on a great level. It's for big money. And I want to get myself to the most highest I can go. Like they say, you can't free yourself, free your mind. Well, I'm trying to free my mind."

Anthony has many explanations for his failure in the Health Careers program. He blames it on their failure to put him in regular college classes soon enough. He blames it on the university not permitting him to play on the basketball team. "This was taking too long, like they was running me 'cause I didn't graduate through high school, right? And I wanted to play *now* and like, I know there's some way, man, they could have—they could've speeded this course up. Here I am, willing to learn and, hey, you know, I'm not dumb. Got very good common sense."

Anthony recognizes his reading problem as a contributing factor to his academic failure, and, for the first time, is able to discuss it freely. The Health Careers program, he says, dealt with reading problems badly, "because reading is something that—is about the only thing that you really have to be—that you can't be self-taught, because how can I teach myself something I can't pronounce."

Looking back on his schooling, Anthony now perceives his ability to "gigolo" his way through as a source of present problems. "I like to lay around. Even when I was in school, I went to school when I wanted to. I was never behind . . . and I was never pressed. I was always up with my class . . . I was an Honor Roll student. So I know that was bullshit. In school, I was so cool—everybody would be suspended for something I would do, but I wouldn't get suspended because I had like a game and I could talk to someone . . . I had more bullshit teachers in school—it was a shame. Every white teacher I had was bullshit. I used to go to algebra, he was a bullshit, he didn't teach me nothing in algebra. But I passed. I'd be in reading classes and I *know* that my reading was slow. That's the only slow thing I have about me is reading, but they passed me. I was passable for them."

Only two teachers, both black, stand out in Anthony's memory for having seen through his "bullshit." His civics teacher, whom he did not love at the time, he now remembers with respect because "he seen the bullshit in me. Like I used to go in the class before a test, right? And I would be the one. It was my thing to bullshit him for these 45 minutes of talking and boom! bang! bang! you know, before a test. And he would say, 'Now, tomorrow, Mr. Dobson, we hope you have the right attitude and we're going to still have this test.' " The other teacher was the basketball coach, who understood Anthony's reading problem when he was still at the Ryan. "Mr. Taylor told me I had a very lot of talents and things. These people here, I had to be truthful with, because they seen the bullshit in me and they seen the things that I had in me, you know, just waiting to come out."

Anthony and His Friends

As always, Anthony has a variety of acquaintances, but few friends. He spends most of his time with the pimping crowd, who, he says, are the only people he trusts. He has become secretive and protective of his hustling friends, and will not refer to them by name. But he does single out one man—calling him "The Player" and later "The Gentleman"—as his closest friend. The Player, according to Anthony, is a "real man. Even people who know him, they'll say, 'That's a gentleman.' " Anthony says that the "Gentleman is like more of a father, because we came from down South, and without my father, and I've been up here for fifteen years and really without my father for fifteen." When he met "The Gentleman" he felt he had found the person to give him the advice and support he needed. "Like I'd go by his house, you know what I mean? Watch his color TV, and do this and that, and things I didn't really know about, or even thought that you could get, he showed me. 'Hey, man, you can do anything you want to get. But you gotta want it.' "

When Anthony hit his bad "slumps," it was the "Gentleman" who helped him find his feet again. "Like once I went to him and he said, 'Hey, and, you know you've gotta leave that dope alone. Man, and the people you mess around with . . . even my woman, she was messing with it too. 'Hey, you know,' he say, 'You have to leave your woman alone, leave her alone.' And so I stopped. I went hanging back around with him. He helped me get myself together, my wardrobe together—he made me see more than this, he was hoping that I could see more to me than what was showing there, you know."

During Anthony's severe depression—after his second failure in the Health Careers program—it was the "Gentleman" who intervened again. "I started messing around again, and I was, you know, getting money, but I was going back into the same bullshit. And, like, he always said—'Go forward'—you know. And when I was in school, the teachers always told me, 'Go, forward,' even playing ball. So I understand this cat can't be bad, because he never tell me, 'Go back this way.' Like they say you reach a goal and he'd tell me, 'You never reach a goal,' because you only live once and do everything, so therefore you can never reach your goal and you never have too much and never want enough."

At twenty-three, Anthony spends most of his time with the pimping crowd, but they are not his only associates. The boys with whom he used to play basketball in the courtyard have grown up some, and Anthony still likes to fool around with them—playing a little ball, acting as a friend and counselor. "I can talk to young dudes. They be sitting out here smoking reefer. I tell them, 'Hey, why don't you all come inside and smoke if you're going to—you're going to smoke it anyway.' And we sit down and rap and I tell 'em about different things. Talking about they're going to do this and they want to be that and I try to give 'em advice and—'You can still do that, but do this here first. Then you can do greater in this.' "

The Family Scene

At twenty-three, Anthony has been married for five years—"It seems like forever," he says. He and Barbara have difficulties. "I want to do one thing and she wants me to do another. That's the way with any married woman." They work out their problems partly by spending little time together. "We have an understanding together," Anthony says. "But we're still together—she just have her little problems like trying to hold out and say things to try to make me change, but see, she got to realize and I realize what I really want to do and she have to accept it or just leave. There's nothing I can do about that. That's just the way it's going to be. Has to be."

The main thing Barbara wants Anthony to do is get a respectable job. Herself a medical secretary at a prestigious Boston hospital, she (backed by her family in force) does not like the fact that her husband supports them on the profits from his hustles. "She wouldn't care if I push a broom, just as long as I wouldn't—she wouldn't care if it was $80, just so long as she can say to her mother or someone, 'He's got a job.' Fuck that, a job is just a job. The whole thing is getting money. You know what I mean? Don't tell me how to get the motherfucking money, because you're in this white man's world . . . he doesn't give a fuck how he gets his money, so why should you give a fuck how you get yours? Long as you get the money, that's the whole thing."

Several times their marriage has come close to breaking up. But Anthony is proud of his daughters and fond of the image of himself as head of a solid, prosperous household, and he does not want to give it up. "It's not the White House," he says of his apartment, "but I have food, color TV, phone, bank account, clothes, everything else a normal family should have. But don't have, you know. It's cool." But it stays cool on his own terms. "I come in when I want to, go when I want to. That's what any man should do, especially if he's married. Like, most people say, 'Well, do you think your wife's going to go ahead and do this and that?' Well, then, if she do that, she's not my wife. Because if that's the way it happens, she can stay in the house with the kids."

This attitude toward Barbara is little different from his attitude toward women in general, including the prostitutes who work for him. "I always told young ladies when I meet them, especially my—even if I bring them to my house—the door is over there. 'If you don't like what I'm saying, leave.' " Indeed, at times he says it is true of his feelings about people in general. "I have friends, they say I talk a lot, I talk too much, you know, and like I say, 'You—if you don't want to listen, leave. I'm not going to stop talking 'cause you don't like it. That's too bad, what you don't like.' It's just also the way I am."

Anthony's experiences with family life have given him more insight and compassion for the trials of his own parents. He is less bitter than he used to be, and feels now that it would be difficult to blame either parent for the problems of his early years. Of his father, he says, "I plan to go and see him. I see that it wasn't his fault. Maybe like this is the way I was destined; it *must* be, 'cause this is the way, this is what I'm doing. It wasn't a thing where he sent us away. My mother, maybe she felt better reasons that we should be away from him and he felt reasons that we should stay with him, so I can't put fault on no one, all I can say is that's destined. The way I ended up now, or even if I die, I was destined for that, but while I'm destined, I'm still going to enjoy and do things as I go. That's why, like I said before, I'm never going too fast. Like when I go too fast, like slow it down and check myself."

Of the family which saw him through his adolescence and raised him, he says little. He and his stepfather remain distant. "I respect him; we have our hi's and goodbyes." He sees little of his brothers and sisters and their families. But he remains close to his mother. "We cool—you know, anyone that say them and their mother's not cool, they don't know their mother. Your mother is always in your corner. You father get out of your corner, but not your mother. I don't care what you do, you know what I mean? She might not like it, but she's in your corner. So you have to be cool when someone's in your corner. Going back to my friends [the pimps], like times I might have hated my mother, but they talked to me, and said, 'Hey, man, that's not cool what you're thinking now, that's your mother.' I had to be a man to find out why she did the things that she did, you know, and then the same with me, she know I'm gonna do what I want to do, that's why I'm me and that's why I'm a man, 'cause I do what I want to."

"I Do What I Want To"

Now that Anthony has pulled out of his second, severe slump, his days follow a fairly regular routine, centering on the restaurant where his mother works. The restaurant has been a kind of replacement for the family home which Anthony left six years before. "I get up when I want to," Anthony describes his typical day, "and around about 2:30, I go to the restaurant and sit around. It's like, almost like a job. Because I'm not a part of that, 'cause like we're all, like down. And I go over there and sit with my mother, to help so things will be cool. And this goes back to that respect. Niggers have the respect for us, so they'll see one of us there, they won't do nothing while we're there. They'll think twice, you know what I mean? Let's say, Monday—I go to the restaurant and after I leave there, I'll go the barbershop. After the barbershop, back to the restaurant and eat. And then from there I'll wait 'til 8, watch the football game, and then, if I don't go out, I'll come back, watch TV, go to bed. Tuesday's pretty much the same. Only difference'd be Sunday. My Sunday's different. I watch football all day. I might take the phone off the hook."

Anthony feels that he is working things out at last, sorting out what he wants from what he doesn't want, formulating a philosophy that will allow him to live comfortably with himself, that will allow him to "greater myself."

He is pleased with himself for having been able to get off hard narcotics twice, even when depressed. He feels that he had to do the work himself, since his one experience with methadone clinics had been terrible. "They was bullshitting me. Sure enough bullshitting me. And I seen the people that was going there and they was going there for three or four years and no change. Then I seen the people in the street, they been dope fiends for years, they been in the clinics, no change. So the answer couldn't be in the clinic. So I got to get away from that."

So Anthony tackled the problem himself, with the help of some readings from the Health Program. "I said I didn't need this, what I'd been doing, smoking reefer and drink me some wine. Like I was messing with health. I was doing, not a lot of reading, but I'd read what I need to know, and I would see that like the stomach decreases while you're messing with dope—like the reason people don't eat is because their stomach is too small and it cramps and when you start eating then it spreads and that's what cramps. So I pace myself into how I eat, what would make the stomach stretch without giving me cramps—which is liquids. So then I found out what liquids give me protein and help me build my stomach to where I'd be cool. I'd know that reefer would make me eat a lot, so I would get some reefer, maybe just drink some juice in the morning, smoke some reefer and eat at night, and that's how I got myself back to a normal thing."

Along with his pride at having been able to control his drug use comes a sense that he is mature—old and wise for his age. Anthony says that he tries to help his younger friends to profit from his painful experiences. "When I see dudes messing around with dope, I say, 'Hey, man, you did what I'm doing, see' and I'll be wearing my rings and jewelry and 'I lost all this at one time,' and I tell them, 'If you really want to be a slick nigger, go back to school.' I think I really understand black people's problems,

206

young dudes like me, my problems. Or people who's not like me, more educated or whatever, jammed up between this level and this level and want to come down here and can't, I can help them too, see, to go up and down the level. This here I can deal with. I can talk to people on all levels, I can get on the same mind they're on and that's hip, that way we won't have a gap. Like say, you're Professor so-and-so, but I'm the nigger that be on the corner, popping my finger, and we can't communicate."

Anthony now thinks better of himself than he did three years ago. "Like I have very good talents," he says, "I have a good ear for music. I can take mostly any instrument and you give me fifteen minutes and I'll play something out of it. I can take a pencil; I can draw. Have a photostatic copy mind. I really don't forget nothing. I can remember, and have all these kinds of talents, there must be *something* . . . that I could do, you know? 'Cause I know they got jobs for people that just do one thing that I might do. I don't write no numbers down. I keep 'em all in my head. All phone numbers. I have—oh, gobs and gobs of phone numbers. I could sit here and just write you nothing but phone numbers you could call."

He still wants to be someone important. "Even with my schooling, I can't just go jumping into school 'cause they won't accept me, but I want to get in something or get around somebody where I can *do* something or help someone and get myself some recognition, 'cause like, say, around here, there's never no doctors that live around the neighborhood, there's never no one—it's always the pimp or—that's all we have to relate to."

Anthony has tried a variety of ways to realize himself, to be someone. But he will not take just any route. He will not take a menial job to earn the respect of Barbara, her mother, and the square world. "She wants me to get a job, but I don't want a job where—like why should I have that good job where I get wear and tear out of my hands and body. When I know that there's things that I could do that don't consist of wear and tear, because I'm not the wear and tear kind. I'm not big and muscular. I don't have rough, strong hands, which is not saying I'm not strong, but I'm not cut out for that, y'know, and everybody's not cut out to be a hard-working man. I'm one of those that's not cut out for it."

Anthony says he takes a broader approach to the definition of work—"Everything you do is work—if you're hustling, that's a job." But Anthony keeps trying to get back into the straight life, often with the help of his hustler friends. When the restaurant first opened, "I helped them cook and stuff. So they said they'd give me ten percent of the restaurant and help me start my own store and give me the money and everything." His friend "The Gentleman" helped him buy the "refrigerator and everything. It was all mine."

About a year ago, with his friend's support, Anthony set up a fruit and vegetable store in Roxbury. "He worked with me all the way ... like we painted the place; he painted, I painted and we laid it out, we put nets and things up, built our own shelves. It was nice and clean." His hustling friends were full of encouragement, pushing Anthony out of the fast life. "Like doing the things I ... like steal, picking pockets, shit like that, I got away from that. Like they said I got more talents and there's something else I can do if I wanted money. And like this here was something else to do if I wanted to like, go back, being a Player, get established, you can get more broads by saying you're Mr. so-and-so, and you have a store ... "

But the store did not make it, although Anthony feels his prices were fair and his products of good quality. He felt betrayed by his own community. "Probably mainly I quit because I thought maybe even myself that it might flop, the way prices and things were. And people weren't buying as much, and that had a lot to do with it, all the time going and getting this shit and people not buying it. And it was really bad on me because I went around to like my competitors, and I had the same thing they have, better stuff, cheaper prices. I'm in a black neighborhood, there was more niggers over there at whitey's place than at mine."

His failure hurt because he had seen the store as a route to recognition and a sense of service. "We used kids in the neighborhood, let 'em do shit, give 'em anything. 'Cause that's like the way we are. If a kid, if somebody wants something to eat, as a matter of fact, there's quite a few people around there who don't have, you know, give 'em food or whatever. That's the way I am."

His experience with other kinds of work has been a series of frustrations. He doesn't want a "field job," which he describes as the kind of work a "working man" holds down. He says that whites don't want blacks to have computer jobs where they can keep themselves clean, and push them into "field jobs—you work, you don't have time, you can't go out 'cause you're too tired when you come in, you get up too damn early anyway when you leave, so when you come back you know you're going to be tired even if you don't do no work, you're going to be so tired when you come in, understand? And then you're going to have to work all week, and then you'll be too tired to go out Friday or Saturday and then you can't go out Sunday because you've got to go back again early Monday. So he got you on a clock. All the way. But they say they're free. How in the fuck can they be free?"

The road to better jobs is blocked by Anthony's lack of education. "Some of the jobs I've had, the whitey'd say, 'You know, we've had cats we hadda train for this,' and I say, 'Hey, man, there ain't nothing to it,' which is true—you push a few buttons—like I had a job at Drake's Bakery, feeding a conveyor machine with cakes. They took me off the machine because I didn't have a high school diploma, and bullshit, and 'cause I didn't have the so-called degree to run this motherfucking machine. But I could run the machine better than anybody, and this whitey, he got on the machine, fucked it up. He had two years at Tech, but he didn't have common sense, and that's what you need, common sense."

The White Conspiracy

Anthony feels strongly that the white world allows whites to get inside help in competition for jobs and education—he calls this

"standard procedure." If he wanted to get a job, he says, he would have to take a test because he lacks a high school diploma. But his white counterpart would have "somebody just sit down, show them and boom! bam! 'Now, remember that there and remember this here, and don't do that'—standard procedure."
procedure."

Further, Anthony says, blacks have access to "world knowledge," and common sense, but their products and expertise are stolen and packaged by the white world for forced resale to blacks. "Man, we've got the knowledge to know how to do anything, everything. We dance, and no one teached us to be a dancer. But for me to dance on TV, we'd have to go to Arthur Murray or somebody. I mean, how can this motherfucker teach us how to dance? You know what I mean? He copied from me. That's why I tell my women and everybody, even my little brother: 'Don't sell me back my slum!' "

Anthony sees "selling back the slum" as the crux of the white man's strategy to profit from the black man while forcing him to take the blame for crime. "They was into the dope, but now Nixon cut off the dope and they're giving out fifty years for dope, and niggers—whities ain't going to jail—it's niggers going to jail. They robbing the dope—we don't go to Turkey. How can we bring the dope back? But we're the villains." He has nothing but contempt for militant blacks who revile him for dealing dope. " 'You're a dope fiend. If you don't buy it from me, it'll be from the whites, so I'd rather give it to you, 'cause he'll give you something that's going to kill you.' Or say reefer. You know, same thing. I'd rather—if I'm going to see you get killed, if you're my brother, I'd rather kill you myself."

Anthony feels that he is more militant than many members of black community organizations. He says that his attitude is—"I got my hair straight because that's want I wanted to do. And I don't have to be your brother if you don't want me to be. They had a Mau Mau meeting. I went with my hair straight and niggers looked strange, but they're so fucked up, instead of accepting me because now, if the whitey seen me around them, they'll say, 'Oh, no, let him go, he ain't one of them.' " He sees no percentage in maintaining an appearance likely to get him into trouble, but feels that his actions prove his basic intent. "We burnt down, not only the Robie Ford, we burnt down, like they had cars over in the warehouse behind—over on the railroad tracks, and no one ever knew. We burned up 600 cars and that hurt them. Burning the stores didn't hurt them; them cars hurt them. See, 'cause they wasn't sold. See now—that's a militant act, but see, with these motherfuckers, they think they're supposed to go and burn down the local store and the bullshit and wear the green, the red—see, but you don't go out there letting this motherfucker know, 'I'm your enemy.' You know who the enemy is. I know. But he thinks he got a friend. And he bullshit you with that liberal shit— 'liberals are your friends.' This motherfucker's infiltrating you all the fucking time."

The Pimp as the "Free Black Man"

Anthony sees the pimp as the only "free black man," because he is the only black man who can do what he wants. He says, of his player friends, "They're happy. They're free of the mind and like I keep going back to this: when you're free in the mind, you're all right. The only freedom you know you ain't going to get no way, see, 'cause of being black. They've got a stop sign made for you. And this here, not no college professor told me, *They* told me, said, 'Hey, the whitey got a stop sign for you already, no matter what you do.' You know, any black man, they got it already made up for him. So, like they let me know when I get to the road and I see the stop sign . . . you've got to deal with it properly, stop and not stay. And that's what they do—they had a stop sign, they just stopped. But they didn't stay. And most people stop, when they see a stop sign, and stay."

Anthony feels that the pimps have been his only true friends, reflecting a tradition of camaraderie in the profession. Further, he sees his fast life friends as the true community organization. "A pimp is the most hated," he says, "but he is the first ever to establish anything." The pimps, Anthony feels, are the only black organization the whites do not control. "Honkies don't deal with the pimps. Pimps they can't deal with. He can't give him money, they're not gonna take no money from the whitey. But whitey can give all the money to his agencies. That's cool, but then they ain't going to tell you, 'Yeah, kill the honkie." Whitey going to let a man turn you against your own people. The Muslims, they're pretty cool, like they say stop this, but they never really say, 'Black man ain't that bad—talk about the devil.' That's what he, whitey, really is, he's a devil."

Anthony reflects often on pimping as a philosophy—the combination of skills a black man can muster in face of the "whitey's master plan" to control black people. And he sees himself and his friends, sometimes, in a tradition of militant, philosopher-pimps. "You know, like they be talking about Malcolm X—hey, he was a pimp, you know. But he had to do this to dig where the other things were coming from."

Anthony feels strongly that he has been personally victimized by "whitey's plan," deprived of the skills (largely academic) and the opportunities which would have allowed him to make it in the white world. He thanks his pimp friends for schooling him in the ways of the world, the means by which he can get what he wants out of life.

"Like I said, there's a stop sign for every black man, but even with like stop signs—they're like laws, you have to interpret them, you know what I mean? If you don't know what this sign means, you'll just stay there. They'll see to that—see that's one thing the whitey infiltrated in our minds, like 'Halt!' You know what I mean? That just means there's a pause . . . that don't mean forever, you know what I mean? Even if, say, there's a stop sign where a man is saying 'Hold, Stay there!' you know if you just stay there and then don't question, 'When can I leave?' they don't let you leave. You have to leave on your own, the best way that you know how. Yeah, that's freedom."

FOCUS: ANTHONY DOBSON—CONTROLLING DRUGS

In the weeks and months of his post-school "slumps," Anthony Dobson was a junky. He followed a classic pattern—depression, cocaine sniffing, heroin shooting, "resting" in a stuporous daze in his apartment. His appearance disintegrated, his pimp friends began to avoid him. He appeared to have begun the long, slow, downward spiral into hopeless addiction.

None of this is remarkable. Anthony had been through rough times. Drugs were readily available, and, as Anthony puts it, "glamorous." We would expect him to get hooked. What we would not expect, what common drug lore has not led us to anticipate, is that he would get himself unhooked, without benefit of methadone, or Synanon, or therapy, or anything else except his own focused will. But he did—twice—and with far less difficulty than is generally supposed possible.

Anthony used hard narcotics as a mental painkiller, to ease him through life crises with which his unblunted mind could not cope. Drugs appear to have functioned as an escape hatch, which he could use while raw wounds healed and his life sorted itself out. Then, as he became more capable of dealing with the events in his life, he would begin to feel that the cost of drugs was too great— not worth the loss of his sharp appearance, his self-respect, his closest friends. And then, each time, he made a conscious decision to "get straight," and to reclaim the aspects of his life which had always been of first importance to him.

Anthony is not unique in his ability to control the duration of his addicted periods. Many of the young men in the Pathways study seemed able to move in and out of heavy drug use. Josh Miller, Norman Mullen, and Andy Garrison each were heavy drug users during crises in their development. And each pulled away from drugs as he moved into a new phase of his life.

There is a traditional view of drug use, presented by most standard high school drug curricula, accepted by most teachers, parents, and by most young people. According to that view, drugs are a kind of cliff from which the user leaps. Rescue is difficult, painful, sometimes impossible. But for the Pathways young men, drugs seemed to be a train through perilous country. Once drugs had served their narcotic purpose, they were dropped, and replaced by more productive behavior.

Erik Erikson, in his discussions of adolescent identity formation, talks about a period of "moratorium" during which a young person splits off from normal life for an extended period. In college students, this often takes the form of a year bumming around Europe, or picking apples in Oregon. It seems possible that for some black inner-city adolescents, to whom such options are unavailable, a year of drug addiction serves a similar function.

This is not to suggest a casual approach to the use of hard narcotics, nor to imply that drug addiction is a "normal" phase of black adolescence. But it might indicate that drugs have a range of uses and a variety of influences, and that the common reaction of blind panic and despair does not allow parents, teachers, and many youth workers to structure differentiated approaches to young people who use drugs in differentiated ways.

Chapter

7

Josh Miller—Getting Over

JOSH AT FIFTEEN: 1967

Inattentive at the back of the classroom, practicing how far he can tilt back his desk chair without falling into the window, Josh Miller at fifteen is not an impressive youth. He is attractive but not striking—the deep-set dark eyes are watchful, continuously "checking out" people and situations, testing his effect on others, figuring out how to respond. His clothes are clean and within the limits of the Ryan's dress code—the required tie is not always knotted about his rather long, thin neck, but it is always there. Josh is not one of the high-style ninth graders who compete to see who can appear in the most startling and impressive garb. But he is a bright and an unusually efficient student, one of the few at the Ryan who completes his homework regularly and on time. However, he has also gotten into his share of scrapes—fights with other boys, tangles with the law, and one battle with a teacher which he remembers with glee. He is, in other words, an "okay kid," neither scholar nor loser. Josh's ambitions are unusually well-defined for a ninth grader. He is determined to "get over," to pull himself into the prosperity and the status of the black middle class. And he sees education as the best route to his goal.

But, at fifteen, Josh does not seem clearly marked for outstanding achievement. In fact, he has problems at home and at school which seem likely to sap his energies, limit his options and interfere with his firmly stated ambitions. His parents had

215

separated when Josh was in the seventh grade, after years of bitter fighting. "When my parents were living together, I'd say that was kind of the bad years for my family . . . because they didn't get along together. They be fighting every night, throwing pots and pans or shoving [each other] around the house, man, and they'd be suddenly fighting out in the street. That was no good . . . I remember her [asking him] 'What do you do with all your money? It's for bringing home. You don't bring no food home.' I remember once I seen my father down picking up some young whore. That's where the cat's money going. I couldn't tell my mother. Than I saw my mother being picked up at the corner by some man, her boy friend."

The actual separation came about when his father, who must have been watching his wife, saw her getting into another man's car. There was a fight. Mrs. Miller came back to the house with a black eye. "Her eye was, oh god! It was so big and black and blue. I was crying, man. I wanted to kill my father." The fight continued into the night, and the next thing Josh knew, his mother was gone. When he came back from school, she had packed up all her things and gone. He didn't see her for almost two months, when she got back in touch with the family. Only one daughter, Marie, went with her mother. The rest of the unmarried children stayed with Mr. Miller. Jean, Josh's older and favorite sister, took over the running of the Miller household.

Now that things have settled down for Josh, he says, "I'll never get into trouble no more. My father doesn't look at my report card . . . he takes my word because he knows I'm doing pretty good, playing on the basketball team, doing my homework, and he never has to go to school with me. My sister Jean cooks and she leaves my supper on the stove. When I come home at night, I warm it up and eat it. And she sews my pants up, and she wash my clothes sometimes. Me and her get along real good."

Josh fights occasionally with James, mainly when James borrows Josh's "knits" without permission and then gets them dirty or torn; and he hasn't much use for his sister Dolly, who's "kind of evil, kind of mixed up." But he finds his other brothers

216

and sisters generally supportive. He gets along best with his brother William (known in the family as Junior). Although Junior is married and lives elsewhere, Josh feels close to him. "He lets me have parties at his house, wear his clothes," Josh says. But beyond that, Junior is the brother who talks to Josh most, who takes him out driving and helps him work through his problems.

Josh still sees a good deal of his mother and thinks he is a lot like her. "I go over there every Saturday and Sunday," he says. "I tell her, you know, about how my job's going along and all that. I tell her things that make her laugh. We always have a good time, every time I'm around her. And we never get mad at each other. You know, every time I see my mother, I kiss her."

Josh also sees something of his father in himself. "I look like my father. And my father's quiet, and I'm kind of quiet. And my father, he likes to work a lot and I like to work. And he's smart, kind of smart, and I'm kind of smart too." The main difference he sees between them is that his father is very serious, doesn't smile much, while Josh likes to fool around. "My father, he's a construction worker. And, well, he's sort of religious. He like to go to church every Sunday. And he's quiet and he sees that everything in the house is okay. He's kind of old, you know, so he doesn't take us out too much or anything . . . I don't argue with him much, because he's not the arguing type and there's no sense in arguing if he ain't gonna argue back. I don't usually get mad. Only time I get mad at him is when he's drunk or something. I tell him, 'Why do you drink like that?' And he's saying it's none of my business and then I get mad sometimes."

But there is a bond between them. Mr. Miller will ask Josh what he is doing with his homework, and "he likes to watch me do it. And he likes to learn new things, like I teach him algebra sometimes, little by little. And I go to church sometimes, and he likes that."

For his part, Mr. Miller finds Josh "right smarter and different" from his other children. He admires Josh because "he always want to be clean and nice. He don't want nothing nasty around him at all." He remembers the day he taught Josh to drive.

"I took him out in the field and let him drive and, man, he was so happy, he was a happy kid. I'm telling you, that was the happiest day of his life. Oh, man, he rubbed my head and all day he was good."

Although Jean complains that Josh doesn't volunteer to help with housework, she also says she likes him best of all her brothers and sisters because he's been "so bright all his life. When he was just a little bit of a boy, he always was interested in a lot of different activities. Sports, you know, different things." And James says, "He gets along well in school—got a nice personality and all his friends like him," and adds, "if he would ever ask me, I'd be more than glad to help him go (to college) because I feel that's what I wanted myself and I know he'd really appreciate it if I did help him."

The whole family is anxious to see Josh "make it," to have him achieve goals which they have given up. James says, "He's my younger brother. I'm kind of hoping that he does make it . . . The rest of us have grown up now, and none of us have really settled too much in anything. Josh is the last chance, the last one coming up. He's on his way now, so we are just waiting to see if he's going to surpass the rest."

Josh shares his family's hopes that he will "get over." He says his parents want him to be "well-dressed, nice, quiet, a lot different from, you know, the people that hang around on the street . . . like with a suit and tie on going to work, instead of having big boots on, and all that, you know." He says that he is "trying to be somebody," like his Uncle Carl, a successful Detroit minister who "carry a briefcase around, new Cadillac, you know. He has a nice house way out in the woods, got a nice wife. They have a boy and a girl. Plenty of money in the bank. He got everything he wants." Josh feels very close to his Uncle Carl, and says at one point that his uncle is the only person in the family who really understands him.

But Josh would also like to be like John F. Kennedy, "rich and respected." Asked if he would be a pimp, Josh says, "I'm not aiming to be a pimp. I'm going to try to go to school, be my regular self." And being his "regular self" includes choosing a career which would benefit the black community. He sees his three goals—money, respectability, and community contribution—coming together in a social work career. "I saw a lot of people (social workers), how they'd be working and socializing with other people in the community. They'd get things to happen and start the community going and all that stuff."

Josh has decided that the way to get his share of the American Dream is to get the best possible schooling, and he has set himself to make that happen. Josh learned of METCO from a friend, Tom Calkins, and enrolled himself in it.

His decision to go to high school in Newton via METCO was more than his parents could fathom. Both parents grew up in the rural South; Mr. Miller never went beyond the first grade, and Mrs. Miller did not go much farther. Mr. Miller finds Josh's classes at the Ryan totally foreign to what he knew as a boy—"as different as sugar and salt," he says. When Josh moves on to Newton high school and then to the Lebanon high school in New Hampshire, his father virtually loses track of his activities, although he remains proud of his achievements. "He got a good chance to . . . he got a good learning and he's learning good . . . I told him I'll go far as I can with him. That's all I can do. Far as he want to go, I don't mind helping him."

Looking Back at the Ryan

Despite his clear ambitions, Josh's career at the Ryan has been uneven. He liked junior high school, and is less critical of the Ryan than are many of his schoolmates. He liked some of the staff—especially Mr. Hyland, his history teacher, who "liked to fool around and take us places, and he was very intelligent, you know. He taught us a lot of things. And he was fair and he was nice." Josh's grades were good and he always "tried to get interested" in his classwork.

But Josh also got into trouble at the Ryan. He had a number of arguments with teachers, generally over treatment he felt was unfair. He recalls one of these. "Me and my friend Alan, we were in the back of the room doing our homework. When my homeroom teacher wants you to do his homework, you got to do it. So, this particular day, we had to make it home early, to go look for a job. And it took us two hours to do it. You know, we did it through all the classes. It was last period, and we usually didn't do nothing in Science. And everybody was arguing with the teacher, yelling and all that. But me and Alan went in the back, and we were writing our homework, minding our own business. We were almost finished, on the last page. We had about ten examples. So Mr. Herschfeld, all of a sudden, for no reason—everybody was laughing and throwing things and talking out loud—he came up in the back and grabbed our papers, and he ripped them up. That's right. He ripped them up. And he threw them down. Alan said, 'What'd you rip my paper for?' and Mr. Herschfeld said, 'You're not supposed to do it.' I said, 'Listen to all them kids talking. We're going to have to stay after for three hours and we wanted to get a job.' So he said, 'That's not my fault,' and Alan said, 'Ohhhh!' Alan hit him in the face, and his glasses flew off, went on the desk, fell off. They almost broke. And I started to run over and step on them, but I didn't."

Looking Ahead to High School

Josh never regretted his years at the Ryan, and clearly relished retelling stories of friends and fights. But, by the time he had to choose his high school, he decided that this kind of experience was not going to get him out of the ghetto. Josh has a relatively clear and simple view of the link between school and his future, a view strongly supported by school propaganda. He believes that undistracted application to schoolwork will provide him with the credentials and the skills he needs to pave the way to middle class security and comfort. And Josh knows from his Ryan experience that achieving his goals requires getting out of Boston and away from his friends.

The guidance counselor at the Ryan has tried to steer Josh towards English High School, an urban, predominantly black school much like the Ryan. But Josh is confident about his priorities and willing to assert his independence. He told the counselor he wants to go to high school in Newton, because "I think I might have a better chance, you know, if I get away from all of my friends and I go out to Newton. And I could study and get a chance to meet new people."

Josh is powerfully motivated. He is willing to leave his closest friends when he thinks they are a bad academic influence, and he is willing to go to Newton, even though he feels uncomfortable in white settings. Josh says he prefers "Negro schools with Negro teachers, because I understand them best." And his two favorite teachers at the Ryan were black. But he feels he must succeed academically, and adds, "I want a chance to go to a school like that."

Josh says that his school decisions do not mean that he wants to abandon his friends, but only that he wants to separate himself from most of them for a while so they will not tempt him away from study and into trouble. Josh knows about trouble, and is determined to keep clear of it. Three years ago, when he was twelve, Josh and his friends (some of whom later became his junior high crowd and some of whom formed other alliances) got into considerable difficulty with the law. Josh tells the story. "I went with these boys to Egleston Station, near a bike factory. They wanted to break in, but I said, 'No, I'm not going to do it.' They called me 'chicken' and all that, so I went along and we went in through the window, and I cut my leg real bad. I wanted to back out, but we had to break our way outside, because we couldn't get back out. When I was breaking the door, the other two were fixing up three bikes so we could ride out and at least get something. They got the bikes and were bringing them up the stairs. All of a sudden, we looked through the skylight and we saw the cops coming on the roof. And we could hear them saying, 'I wonder how those bastards got in there.' We all ran for the boxes—it was like a comedy show. The cops came down and said, 'Come out or we going to start shooting.' We didn't say nothing.

221

Then they said, 'Okay, go get the dogs.' We started running out.
They came and picked us up and put us in the wagon."

Josh was sentenced to two weeks in the Youth Service Board.
"I . . . you know, my eyes began to get a little watery. I didn't cry.
They just got watery, you know—" and he vowed to his father
that "If I gets out, I ain't never getting in." And, in fact, Josh spent
his junior high school years moving away from the friends most
likely to get into trouble. His brother James describes this
movement as "Josh's two split personalities of friends." Josh,
James says, "used to be with a bad crowd. And he worked out of
that, which is good. He used to hang around with this bunch of
little kids, that used to hook school, go around and steal
everything they could. I don't know what caused him to stop, but
he just kind of tapered off and got back to going to school, and
working, and doing right like he should be doing. And getting
with better friends which his old friends called faggots. He's got
with them. He's being with them and he's doing all right with
them."

Josh's Ryan crowd is a lively bunch, who spend their time
going swimming, playing basketball, riding in cars, going to
parties. The parties are sometimes wild—kids drink, smoke dope,
take pills, fight. But Josh's own friends tend to stay on the fringes
of trouble. They do not go in for serious fighting. If they need
money, they will get odd jobs rather than steal. Josh says, "like
some of us work in a cleaning company. Somehow we seem to
pick up odd jobs, like giving out posters. We make a few dollars."
Then they all chip in so the group can go to parties or for rides.

Josh and his junior high school crowd spend a good deal of
time with girls—usually in groups of girls and boys who flirt in the
school corridors, meet at parties, and get together in the park
where they watch the boys play basketball. The girls come over
and bring record players, dance a little, smoke some pot, and have
a little casual sex. Nothing is taken very seriously. But Josh makes
a sharp distinction between "good girls" and ones who would "do
me rotten." He avoids the latter, even though he feels free to say,
"I just mess around, but I don't take any serious."

Josh enjoys his girl friends and his freedom, but he envisions a future with a wife and children, a prospect many of his fifteen-year-old peers reject out of hand. He plans to wait, "I'd say when I'm about twenty-four, when I begin to get useless," but he has clear ideas about what he wants. "I want one of the nice-looking girls. I mean light-skinned, you know, have long, pretty hair. Seriously, I want a quiet girl, a girl that likes to go out and have a lot of fun. I expect her to stay in the house when she's supposed to, and I expect her to keep the house clean and neat. I don't expect her to work—go out and make money. But I expect her to be a good housewife." This girl—quiet, serious, pretty, middle class, becomes Josh's consistent ideal.

Josh on Race and Self

Josh's description of his ideal wife sounds as though he has bought the "white" ideal of American Society. But he is, simultaneously, deeply concerned with his black identity. In Roxbury, in 1967, few ninth graders are as well-informed about black issues, as firm in their statements of black pride as Josh Miller. He is working through the issues of race and class in an effort to establish his own personal and racial identity.

Like many young people born and raised in the ghetto, Josh had limited experience with overt discrimination. He knows that he is black in a culture dominated by whites. He knows that he is dark-skinned within the broad range of colors characterized as "black." But he says that teachers at the Ryan don't treat black students differently from white because there are no white kids. If you stay in your neighborhood, you don't get burned.

Josh recalls the time he was picked up by the police for stealing newspapers from a white newsboy. "The police took me to the station," Josh remembers. "They called me all kinds of niggers and all that stuff, man. Only ten years old. They were smacking me, grabbing my clothes, and everything. They told my mother that I assaulted this white boy."

223

His other major experience in the white world was with the Boy Scouts. Josh joined the Scouts in Roxbury and accumulated enough merit badges in swimming, first aid, and soil and water conservation, to almost qualify as an Eagle Scout. But then he needed to spend a summer in Scout camp, and, he says, "I blew it. I got messed up with all them white boys. I didn't like them, and I told them. So I had a fight with them. Next day, I called up my father and he came and got me out of the camp, Yes. I had all my merit badges, but I just blew it." After this bad experience, Josh says he began to find out "what was happening," and decided that he was a fool to spend his money on "tents and packs when here's all these nice alligator shoes and all that." So he dropped the Scouts with their forced association with white boys, and moved the focus of his interest back to his neighborhood crowd, their parties, good times, knits, and alligator shoes.

Josh also thinks of how his mother was treated as a suburban cleaning lady. "We couldn't get nothing we wanted. My mother used to get the clothes I wore to school from these rich white people she worked for. Man, I used to *hate* that. My mother used to come home and tell me about the white people and how they embarrassed her. They didn't even know her name. You know, the lady she worked for maybe introduced her to somebody, 'This is . . .' then she'd ask her what's her name. She'd come home and her back be hurting and, hell!—she didn't make that much. She had to do for white people, bring us home some old damn leftovers, man. Bring me her son's clothes home."

Josh is sure that he wants to center his life in a black community. He clearly prefers a black school with a black principal, "because he'd know what we like. He'd probably plan for Negro people to come in and talk to us in front of assembly, or have a dance or something like that." He is looking ahead to Newton, though, because he feels that white teachers might be more naturally inclined to teach subjects like math, accounting, business, history, and the like, not because they are smarter than black teachers, but because they get better preparation in both public and professional school.

Josh has a strong sense of race pride. He believes "Negroes are better than whites, because they [whites] started off in higher positions before we did, but we're catching up. I think that Negro athletes are better than white athletes, Negroes are physically better than whites. I don't know why, but I just think so . . ." He also feels that blacks are more enterprising than whites. "White kids . . . don't like to get out and work a lot, because most of their parents got a lot of money. Most of them aren't too bright that I know of. But the Negro kids I know, they like to get out and work and earn what they get, most of them anyway. They also like to get out and have a lot of fun."

At the same time, some doubt creeps in when he is asked about the differences between whites and blacks. "Maybe whites have a little more in mental, because they have better schools. Most white people got money, and they can afford to put their daughter or son in college and they learn better. I guess they're a little more, mentally, but us, physically."

Despite his doubts, despite some bad interracial experiences, Josh at fifteen is willing to move in the white world, to give Newton whites a chance. "My friend told me that the white people out in Newton are pretty good, they'd like me. I do hear about other places where white people, they hate Negroes, they don't want them in their school, and if they do there's going to be a riot and all that stuff. But, you know, I got a couple of friends that go to Newton and they say it's nice out there."

Josh's comments on race reveal how much he has absorbed the Protestant Ethic. He says that it is better to make your own way in the world, building up a reservoir of experience and capacity to reflect, figure out things on your own, and succeed because of your own determination. But he doesn't identify with whites, and says that if he had to change races, he would be "maybe Puerto Rican or Mexican, because that's almost like being Negro because the white people look down on them, too. They deny them a couple of rights, too." "I would hate to be in the white race," Josh says, "because I hate to be having my way all the time.

I wouldn't want to be going around threatening people a lot, telling them to get out of the country, and always saying don't do that thing."

Josh feels that he is better than most fifteen-year olds at a number of things—sports, rapping with girls, dancing, making friends. He lists as failings only "maybe getting to school on time. Most of the average boys my age don't mind wearing a tie, but I don't like to wear ties. That's all, I think." There is no one in his world that he would care to change places with, because "I don't know any boy that's really better off than me." He says that if he were being brainwashed, the thing he would cling hardest to would be "my personality . . . because if I always had a nice personality no matter what happened, I'd probably be the same."

Josh, as a ninth grader, is basically satisfied with himself and uncritical of his surroundings. His neighborhood, he says, "is noisy, a lot of people walking around, busy and cooperative, pretty industrious. Part of it is pretty clean. There's still a lot of trash around. People's houses need painting, they're old. But other than that, it looks pretty good." Looking at his school, he adds, "I think lots of problems come up in the Ryan because of what people say about it. A lot of people search for evidence, and they can't find it, and they argue over it and all that. What publicity does for it isn't too much. We do a lot of good things, like we might have a good exhibition of science, or something like that, or a pretty good basketball team. Some of our kids are pretty smart, you know. I don't think the publicity does too much."

But, beneath the optimism and general good feeling about himself and his world, Josh worries. He worries a lot about his friendships, saying that he would like to be a "better known person and a better liked person than I am now." He worries about being too dependent on his running buddies who might slow down his progress. But he also worries about what will happen to him if he moves out of their circle. He sees risk of painful loss in both directions, and sets off for Newton High with hope substantially mixed with fear.

JOSH AT NEWTON HIGH

Josh expected that the switch to Newton would change him, but he had no idea how significant that change would be. Newton took Josh away from the familiar people and values of the ghetto, and brought him into direct contact with the world of the rich and near-rich to which he had always aspired. The experience left him more precisely aware of what "getting over" implied, and what it would cost.

First, Josh learned at Newton that his fantasy of a school where he would be away from temptation and magically imbued with skills would not be fulfilled. He did draw closer to his more academic friends; Tom Calkins, who also went to Newton and who wanted to be an architect, replaced hip Sam Johnson (who always knew where the parties were) as Josh's closest friend. And according to Tom, Josh made an effort to be a model student. "He doesn't skip classes and all that stuff, and he doesn't get into trouble. You know, acts real quiet in class and does his work." But Josh's grades at Newton were indifferent, and he had "run-ins every now and then" with openly prejudiced white students. And he suffered a bitter blow when the basketball coach kept him off the varsity team for ambiguous reasons which Josh and Tom interpreted as discriminatory.

Further, Josh's discomfort in dealing with whites has grown more acute in his first extended contact with the upper-middle class white world. Back in Roxbury, he could cope with overt prejudice. He had no trouble threatening Dorchester bar-flies that he'd kick their asses if they called him "nigger." But the half-acceptance of the liberal white is harder to deal with. Josh has become expert at dealing with Newton whites, but his skill has made him uncomfortable. He still covets the life style, but he writhes under its effects. "Like for instance," he says, "I was invited to a party. This white girl, her father is a famous musician. I went over to her crib. Some black stud came to the door and took my coat. I said, 'Aw, man,' and when I got to the house I thought it was some kind of mansion or something. She got maids and all that, and I met a lot of white girls and stuff like that. All their houses are big, man."

This kind of experience has increased Josh's mixed feelings. "Made me feel like that's how I like to live. But in a way I don't really want that. I don't know, it's kind of mixed up, all mixed up. I really don't want that, man, but the things I've seen is making me think that way."

Josh handles his mixed feelings about his Newton classmates and their way of life by exploiting them through a variety of hustles. He says, "I don't want to steal, man. What I do is, I know a lot of real rich girls up in Newton, and I just go out there and talk to them. They don't mind, shit, between five and fifty dollars, like that. I run a little simple love game or something down to them, and they go for that. I tell them something like, 'the reason I came over here is because I'm in a jam. Like, this guy is going to shoot me 'cause my brother had to sell him some dope and it was bad dope, now I got to pay all these guys back.' After I get in good with her, you know. She get high and talk, we laugh and everything, keep on rapping to her."

Josh has developed this hustle to a fine art. "Say if her mother and father is in the room, and they're in there acting up, dancing, putting on square music, drunk and all of that, I act sort of Uncle Tomish. 'Oh, yeah, I heard that music before,' something like that, planning on getting us in a groove. Mother and father, all three of them be digging it. Then I could talk to her when I get ready to leave. Just as she walks to the door, I could break it on down to her like that. Or I might just come right on out and say, 'A friend of mine died and I needed some money to send some flowers. Give me $50.' "

More Trouble With the Law

Going to Newton has not kept Josh out of trouble, as he had hoped. He still lives in his old neighborhood, and spends much of his free time with his old crowd, his hustling friends who have more money and more clothes than he has time to acquire. So Josh tries burglary again and is again arrested. "I was home doing some homework, and a friend of mine came over to my house and said, 'You know, there's this cleaners right across the street from our house, and the man left the window open through summertime.' My friend had a wire cutter. He said, 'Man, all we got to do is snap that screen and get them clothes out of there, probably a little cash in the cash register, man, we could off them clothes like that.' And so, it sounds hip, man. We went up there, go up there and took the screen, be-bopped on in, and I standing there. He passed the clothes and all, and I heard somebody. There was a house behind us. It was dark outside, so you couldn't tell whether people were looking out or not. We had a lot of clothes and he had money in his pocket and next thing I know I hear a door slamming, somebody running. I said, 'Come on, man,' so he came. He was jumping out the window and I seen that they were coming through the alley and flashing their flashlights. They said, 'Stop or we'll shoot!' Man, I must have flew over that fence. I don't know how I got over there, because it was high. So they didn't shoot, but they had to go all the way around the other fence to come through the yard. There was a whole row of houses and a lot of trees and stuff you could hide under. So I jumped under the porch.

"Then I heard them talking. A lady said, 'He ran through here somewhere.' So they were flashing lights and finally they looked in the corner. They said, 'Come on out.' They caught my friend a long time ago. And he gave them the whole run-down on me, man. So then the police say, 'What's with it,' and all this stuff. And I told them my name. So they called up the Newton High School and they called up Mrs. Robinson at METCO. They called up my father—he didn't have no money, he wasn't working—but he borrowed $2,000 and got a good lawyer, went to court. Some crabby old lady, she was a judge, said, 'Two weeks, and then come back and we'll see how long we're going to give them.' "

That arrest was one of the most significant events of Josh's youth. It focused attention and resources on him and his problems. He was already a favorite of the black director of METCO, and his difficulties with the law had also attracted the notice of his class housemaster, a white woman who apparently took a sincere interest in Josh. He appreciates their willingness to bail him out in times of trouble, and says of the housemaster, "She knows that I've had past problems. When I get in trouble, the police call her, because I'd always give her as a reference name. They'd talk to her, and she would help me. When I'd get a B that was unbelievable to her. She'd be real excited and all that. She was pretty happy with the work I'd done."

Both of these women agreed with Josh that temptation was his major problem, and that the best solution was to get him out of his neighborhood, away from his friends. So they arranged to get him a scholarship to the ABC program, a residential academic program in Lebanon, New Hampshire, where he could finish high school at a substantial remove from his "running buddies," under the close supervision provided by a structured, integrated program. As Josh put it, "My friend got two months. I went to school in New Hampshire."

BETWEEN HIGH SCHOOL AND COLLEGE— SUMMER, 1970

Josh in New Hampshire

Josh found the prospect of going to school in New Hampshire exciting. "I thought it would be a beautiful experience," he says, "since I'd never been away from home. So I made that move and stuck it out." But the ABC program was not easy for Josh. Lebanon High School was as demanding as Newton, and the progam required its pupils to study every evening, under strict supervision. There were few black girls in the Lebanon area, and the social life Josh loved was sharply curtailed.

Nevertheless, by the end of the program, he feels that he has learned more than he has paid. "I've learned quite a bit," he says, "especially from the standpoint of getting away, analyzing my whole life, what I've been through, looking at my mother and father, their past. I've thought about my future, being away at school. And, what's more important, I think, is I've been able to see what it's like outside the city, see how people live, where their ideas come from. Like, if they're out in the country, they don't really know what's going on; when they come to the city, say, they go to a caucus with some black students and they make errors—I can understand why they make these errors."

For Josh, one of the best things he got from the ABC program was his relationship with the resident director of his house, a man who was responsible for the well-being of the ABC boys at Lebanon High. The director was a black man who "grew up in a somewhat similar environment that I grew up in, and he got a track scholarship and a contract to be assistant coach. And he got the contract to be resident director. He seems never excited, and his future seems so bright. He's going to stay here about five years. He's saving a lot of money up and he wants to move and have a nice house for his family. He wants to be a veterinarian. He's so much of an inspiration to the guys in the house."

Toward the end of his senior year at Lebanon High, Josh won a scholarship to the University of Pittsburgh. He chose his college carefully. "I wanted to go to a school that had a good reputation, in a city so that when I'm tired of the social thing up on the campus, I can always go down to the city and dig on something down there. I figured in a large institution my chances of getting in between things would be much better than a small school because I know that I am not prepared to go right there and jump right into medical school or law school, but need to meddle around until I finally get half-way settled down. I figure if I went to a school where everybody would be continually watching you, then the pressure might get to me."

He is determined to make college give him what he wants. "I'll go to school until I can really analyze what I want to do in the future and until I get a grasp on the whole situation, so I'll be able to handle whatever I confront. If I can do it in four years, fine. It just depends. Maybe I'll go to two years of law school."

231

By the end of high school, Josh has given up thoughts of a social work career—not enough money in it—and he has abandoned his alternative career as a basketball coach, because it confirms the white stereotype of the "professional" black as either a gym teacher or a musician. "I want to show them whites that I can be something better than that, much better—a lawyer or something," Josh says. "Lots of black people can't afford lawyers. Like me—when I used to get in trouble, I got these rotten state defenders."

Josh is willing to sacrifice a great deal for his personal and professional goals. But he does want to hold on to one aspect of his old life—his closest friends, the old Roxbury bunch whose support and approval have remained critical to his happiness. He is still friendly with Tom, his old Newton buddy, and worries because Tom "ain't been accepted by no college yet, and he's starting to get into drugs. If he keeps on he's going to mess up like most of my other friends did." Two other close friends also worry Josh. "Robert, because he gets caught hustling money downtown, and Willie, because he wants to be a pimp and everything. He's got two girls on the corner and, like, he's my friend. The cat's real hip, man, and it's hard to explain to him what he's doing to his sisters. If I go rapping about the stuff they'll think I'm some sort of square faggot."

In an effort to bridge his worlds, Josh once invited Tom, Robert, and Will up to Lebanon for a Sly and the Family Stone concert at a nearby college. But the bridge wouldn't hold. "They all came up there and we got high. We went over to the field house and we had a good time. It was something new for them. They ain't never been nowhere. Then after we went to an Afro-American Society party. They were kind of looking at Will a little snobbishly because he had on some alligator shoes and dressed real good. They all had combat boots and army jackets. They don't comb their hair and wear all that stuff—black, red and green armbands. They looked at us with that look—'Where do you come from?' I said, 'Oh, shit!' You know that's no good, because all the cats and brothers be doing that. And I see them on

232

a vacation, home from college, and they be out there in white clothes. I don't say nothing.

"You know, when I went away to school—I didn't realize it until not too long ago—but I made a pretty big sacrifice by going up there, because my friends look at me a little differently now. I told them I got a college scholarship and I'm digging about being a lawyer and all of this stuff and, like, they say, 'You've got it made, Josh.' If I come out and hang down on the Hill, they say— well, they won't say it, but they kind of act in a way that what they're saying is—'Why do you need to hang out here with us, man? You've got it made, and I'm just a low-life nigger.' And I've got to put up with stuff like this.

"At times I feel kind of lonely like. When I was home all the cats used to come over to mess around. None of my friends will hardly come over. When I see them it's, you know, 'Hi! How you doing?' Even the broads are different in a certain way. They just kind of turn off when you're talking to them. You don't talk to them like you used to. I don't know, I lost my sense of rap. And when I left I picked up a new vocabulary, so to speak—all this junk, kind of a little ring of white."

Josh does not want to leave his old friends behind. But he says, "You know, to tell the truth, I kind of feel a little above them in a way, because of the things I've been through. I think I know a little bit more than them. I got a high school education, hardly none of them got that. Those cats can't even get decent jobs. All of my friends are all strung out. I ain't really got no real good friends now, except a few. You know, they had the same opportunities I had . . ." Then, almost in the next breath, he takes back his criticism: "I was just lucky. You know, if there was more of those programs that I was in, people could go out and look back at what's happened and see themselves, man. One thing about white people, they make you realize yourself. . ."

Josh has had a lot of opportunity to "realize himself" in white settings. In the summer of 1970, Josh has a job as a truckman's helper, loading and unloading appliances from trucks into stores.

He finds the job "pretty nice" and the pay good at $120 a week, not counting overtime. But he resents the white truckers, especially "taking orders from some of them youngsters. This cat from Dallas—I don't know about him. I think he's an old Klansman somehow. We were in a restaurant eating, and just because he's the driver, he think he's supposed to tell me what to do. He told me to go get his cigarettes out of the car, and I looked at him, I just looked at him and the cat got mad. If he would have said something, we would probably have had it out right then and there. I told him, 'Man, you think I'm going to get your cigarettes?' He said, 'You're supposed to. You're working under me.' I said, 'I ain't working under you. I'm working with Mr. Johnson and the rest of the company. I'm helping you with the refrigerators in the back of the truck, and all that, man. I ain't getting your cigarettes.' And he said, 'Okay.' And I said, 'You'd better do like the shepherd did—get the flock out of here. You know, man, don't come to me with that jive.'"

Josh won that round—the trucker didn't bother him again, but he is constantly on his guard. There were only two other blacks working on deliveries, with 25 whites. Josh says, "We used to quit the job at 3:30, we got to hang around 'til 4:30, and all the white boys is up in the room playing cards and stuff, maybe talking dirty. I didn't want no jive to start. We talk, but we don't talk on a level. So I just go over to the lounge and read the newspaper, fall asleep or something."

He was less guarded at school, although his mixed feelings about whites remained constant through his school years. "When I went to Newton some of the white people treated me real nice. Up until that time, I didn't know any white people, and I got the idea that all white people weren't bad. Then I'd have run-ins every now and then, and I'd change my concept—I'd hate white people. Then in Lebanon, it started all over again. White people were real nice to me. I like them. Then again I had run-ins. They'd talk to me in school, go outside and they're with their friends, they don't really know me. I've been embarrassed by them. It's hard to say. I don't really hate them and neither do I love them, I try to hate them on an individual basis. But you never know what a white

234

person's thinking. So I tend to stay away from white people as much as I can, because you don't really know who's dedicated and who's not. I really can't say I trust them."

At this point, Josh is not sure how he wants to relate to the black community. But he knows some ways he wants to avoid. He rejects the NAACP as weaklings and Uncle Toms who all "seem, like, begging." And he is equally suspicious of establishment black office-holders who, Josh feels, are too likely to be co-opted by their offices, forgetting the people they were supposed to represent. He recalls the time that a black state representative— the first to be elected to high office in his city—came to talk to Josh's black studies class at Lebanon. "He'd go through, talk about fifteen minutes, and end up with nobody really knowing what he said. From the way he seemed he was a black politician in office, not really doing his job in the black community. He's supposed to be representing black people. I don't know if he is or not."

If he is suspicious of black politicians, Josh is equally suspicious of militants. Armbands and combat boots do not constitute what he calls a genuine "black identity." "An Afro's an Afro, man," he says. "It don't really matter what you got on your head. It's what's inside it."

After three years in the white world, Josh has begun to reinterpret the fate of his family. He sees his father now less as a personal failure and more as a victim of the dominant white culture. His family, Josh says, "Could have had it down South, man. My father was down South. He had a farm and all that. He sold it for $1,000—real cheap. Now they got a big skyscraper on the land. Shit, white man used my father. He came up here North, thought he'd get something. He ain't got nothing. I guess all these years, I've been lonesome for my mother and father together. Because all that stuff could have been avoided. When I went to school, I realized it was the white man pressed them so much! They couldn't get a decent job, didn't have a good education."

It's not going to happen to Josh. But things do not seem as simple at the end of high school as they did in the ninth grade, when he planned a neatly compartmentalized life—productively working by day in the ghetto, retiring cleanly to home in the suburbs at night. Josh now understands the distance from Roxbury to Newton and back, and worries about his ability to manage the trip. He has been an activist—more so than many of his Ryan classmates. While at Newton, he arranged a meeting between Stokeley Carmichael and the Afro-American Society to discuss strategies of forming a coalition among Boston area black high school students. The coalition never got off the ground, but Josh's meeting with one of his heroes made him aware for the first time of the need to organize for political effectiveness. He has gone to protest rallies, worked with black community organizations, put his body on the line in a march in Alabama.

Josh is idealistic, but his idealism is tempered by skepticism and doubt that anything significant will be accomplished. "It's confusing," he says. A lot of times I find myself changing my mind about things, then I'll change it back again. It's real confusing, man. It's hard to make an exact decision, you know. I've been through so many things. I've been through SNCC, I thought about joining the Black Panthers, I've been on the verge of joining the separatists. Anybody can be black. Anybody can just run down words. What's actually being done can be seen. And so, I don't just acknowledge every brother that goes like that." And he raises his fist in the black power salute.

Disintegration at Home—Josh Moves Out

The years Josh spent at Lebanon, finishing high school and working out his own identity, were not easy ones at home. Josh feels he left for New Hampshire just in time, because "I wasn't too happy with the way things were going at home anyway." The reasonably balanced life he had with his father and Jean ended when Jean moved out, to be replaced by Josh's stepsister and two other sisters who returned home after bad marriages. To Josh, they didn't match up to Jean's standards, or his own. "Like, man, I never had dinner there hardly," he complains. "My sisters won't cook. I had two sisters there, and they both on welfare. They wouldn't clean up the house . . . do none of that. They got rats up there, roaches. Garbage all in the house, all around the sink and, shit, dishes they never washed, roaches crawling . . ." Then one night, he came home to find another sister sleeping in his bed. "She had all her clothes up there. Josh decided to live with his mother. His father asked him to stay, saying, "Don't move out, you can sleep on the couch," but Josh says, "I was tired of living like that, any old way." So he moved into his mother's clean, modern apartment, with a shower—"I like to take a shower. I don't like taking no baths"—where he was convenient to his friends and to the bus to New Hampshire.

The move didn't alienate him from his father, any more than his original refusal to go with his mother premanently separated him from her. Josh says that he visits his father every week or two, and, he says, "We laugh, talk, slap each other on the back, like we're boys on the street, get along fine."

Josh admires his father in many ways, and feels a great sense of indebtedness to him for keeping the household together after his mother left. "He worked, took care of all of us, man," Josh says, " 'til most of my brothers married and went off. We had to find a smaller place and he stuck with us. When I'm in school, my mother won't send me money. My father sends me money, even though I don't need it. Sometimes I send it back to him. I know he can't afford it. My father—he really cares, he's concerned. He hasn't any education. He doesn't really know what's going on, but, you know, my father cares, more than my mother, I believe."

But at the same time, Josh constantly worries about his father. He worries about his heavy drinking, about his lack of education, about Josh's sense that his father "never seems to be enjoying himself—like something's always bothering him." Josh thinks that perhaps his father cares too much, tries too hard. "You know," he says, "I wish he wasn't so tired all the time. He's always tired from working. And he's real skimpy, skinny, from not eating. You can tell, no one's been taking care of him. He drinks a lot of liquor to kill off some of his problems. I wish I'd get him off that. He smokes a real lot. I don't even know if the cat's got cancer. He don't know. He might." Josh feels that "My father's the kind of person that could easily get conned. You know, anybody walks up to him and says something to him—he'll listen and smile. If someone came out of nowhere and said, 'Lend me $10,' he might just do that." Josh is distressed that his father has continued to support the disintegrated household on Hollis Avenue and says, "My sisters, they really don't care about him, don't cook for him, wash his clothes, and the cat is paying all the rent and everything. They just living off him."

Life With Father and Mother

Josh now recalls his life with his father as burdened with premature independence. "Like I could cut out for a weekend and they wouldn't even know I'm going. I used to stay at my friends' houses. He'd think I was at my mother's house." And he recalls weekends when his father "stayed on the streets, got drunk. So I used to hang out in the street, and I'd come home late at night and he'd probably be in bed, drunk. I'd just go to sleep and get up in the morning and go and I usually didn't see him. Then come Friday night and Saturday night, he'd cut out and would come home Sunday night. Who knows where he is?"

Josh now feels that under the easy camaraderie, the "boys on the street" relationship, there is no deeper communication. He doesn't believe he could confide in his parents about his street life or his "messing around with girls" because they wouldn't understand. He says of his father, "It's because we never got down to real talking ever since we've been together. We never went nowhere and I can't talk to him. If I could, I don't think he could understand."

Josh's relationship with his mother is equally complex. Certainly he prefers his mother's orderly house and appreciates her concern for him. "My mother, she cares about me, too. Like she can't send me money at the school, but at least when I come home, she's always got food on the table for me and all that, bed's always made up. She cleans my clothes up and all, she buys me things. I notice she thinks about me a lot."

Josh admires his mother's formidable willingness to scramble. At 55, she has accumulated a small but impressive store of the world's goods—a color television, a hi-fi, a "nice rug she got at a discount place," a decent five-room apartment with a shower, a French Provincial living room suite. And these comforts have not come easily. Josh says, "My mother's slick, getting those welfare checks. She was working, man, working her ass off. Plus she was working for white people, slaving over their stoves and all that. But all this stuff, she do down payment on it. My mother just wanted to live, have something she could enjoy."

Nevertheless, Josh has come to some unpleasant realizations about his mother. He has always known she was moody—"she changes like the weather; sometimes she's kissing on me and all that. Next minute I come home and she start yelling at me for nothing at all"—but he has just come to realize that she is "very sneaky." "I used to work (at age ten or eleven) selling newspapers, make about $25 a week, have money in my pocket, and I'd wake up the next morning and I'd have $15. I used to yell, scream, be hysterical, try to find out who did it. One day I saw my mother take my money out of my pocket. We had a big argument, and she was telling me, 'Be quiet! Don't tell nobody.' You know, she'd pay me back, she just needed it now, and all that stuff. And then I found out she was doing it to my sister. She went collecting welfare money from her, from her sisters. And she was keeping it. I was mad about that. I said to myself, 'My mother must be no good to do something like that.' My sister wasn't gettin no money. She was supposed to get $60 every two weeks. She was only getting $30 from my mother to take care of her and the baby. My mother told the city people that my sister is incapable of keeping her baby, so that way she'd collect more money. She was keeping it, man. I think she's kind of been deceiving."

Josh has nearly total freedom and independence at his mother's house, just as he had living with his father. He likes the fact that his mother lets him go to New York by himself, and that she trusts him to look after the apartment and himself when she is away. But with his mother as with his father, Josh tends to perceive their

239

apparent trust as a lack of caring. He says, "I'd say to my mother, 'I'm going to stay with Dad for the weekend.' She wouldn't know—I could be dead and she wouldn't even know. She would still think I'm over there."

Looking back at earlier times from the vantage point of his New Hampshire experience, Josh has begun to feel that things had been much worse for him than they had seemed at the time. At fifteen, he felt reasonably good about himself and his home situation. He said his family loved and looked after him, and stated firmly that he wouldn't change places with any boy his age. Now, at nineteen, he remembers himself as acutely poor. In a community where clothes were very important, Josh says he never had a suit until he was fifteen, and then he paid for it himself. Other boys in his Scout troop, many from low-income families, had parents who paid for their uniforms and equipment. Josh had to buy his own. "It's a wonder I ain't no crook or nothing now," Josh says. "I used to hang out on the street stealing everything. I had a little messed-up jacket, no shoes."'

In fact, from his new perspective, Josh wonders if he had really been loved as a child, "because if anybody loved me, then I wouldn't of went to the Youth Service Board three times." He clearly associates his troubled record with lack of parental love and trust—a shift from his ninth grade sense that he was led into trouble by his friends. Now, he says to his mother, "Ma, I think when I started stealing and all that, it really began because I became so furious at you and Daddy for what you all did to me that time when I got caught stealing. I was ten years old. I got caught stealing something and you all beat me but you all never listened to my story, just listened to what the police said."

Now, he feels that he can no longer trust his parents, that they would interpret anything he did on the street in the worst possible light—"take me for some kind of junkie or something, just jiving around wasting time, messing around, stealing." The only person in the family that he feels he can confide in is Junior. Junior would give him advice and keep secrets when his mother would just "go gab-a-gab-a-gab—you should have done this, you shouldn't of done that . . . I told you a thousand times," and his father, "even if I told him it'd just go out the other ear."

At the end of high school, Junior is the only one of his brothers and sisters that Josh feels close to. "He was the only one that would help me in school when I was small. Now that I'm older and bigger he knows about what an education can do for you. He's the only one in the family who can help me with my future, because he knows what I'm into. My older brothers either don't care or they don't really know what I'm doing. They think I am just going to school to mess around, to kill some time."

This assessment of his family's feelings was not quite fair, Josh would admit later. His brothers and sisters sometimes gave him money and talked to him more seriously now that they knew he wanted to make something of himself. But in that lonely summer between high school and college, Junior was the only person in the family for whom Josh felt uncritical warmth. The two brothers spent a lot of time together, leaving the rest of the family to their own quarrels. "I have brothers and sisters in my family that wouldn't even speak to each other in the street."

Josh, at nineteen, harbors much bitterness about his past, about his parents' failings. But he remains loyal to them. "My mother knows that as soon as I do make a lot of money I want to help her out and take care of her. I'll probably move out, but I'll see that my mother is doing well."

Josh's greatest regret as he looks back over his family life, remains the breaking up of the household. By the time Josh graduated from Lebanon High, his parents had been separated for about seven years. But he still says, with the freshness of recent loss, "It's been kind of bad since they broke up, my mother and father. It seemed awful strange, you know." He wouldn't want to go back to the times when he remembers locking himself in his room to stay clear of the "total pandemonium" that was his family. But he cannot give up the vision of a different kind of life. "I used to go to other friends' houses and, like, their family would sit down to dinner and everybody was just talking about what went on in the day and everybody was interested in what each other was doing. Whereas, when I went back home, like, if dinner was on the table, well, it was there, and if it wasn't, well. It was never like a family sitting down together and just talking and laughing and having a good time."

Occasionally, he has a glimpse of what it might have been like for his family. "I remember once we went to the airport," Josh recalls, "when I went to Lebanon. And my mother and father went to take me there. They were in the back seat sitting next to me, on either side, you know, and they were talking and laughing. I was so happy tears went in my eyes and all that. It was the first time in a long time that they were laughing and everything."

Josh's Ideal Neighborhood and Family

Josh is determined that his children will not be subjected to this kind of upheaval and sorrow. "I want to have a family that I can come home to, sit at the table with, have dinner, talk about things. I want to be able to look after my mother and father and keep contact with my family. I just want to be able to have peace of mind."

Josh can define "peace of mind" in very specific terms. He wants to live in a pleasant, urban, black, residential neighborhood—the kind that impressed him when he went visiting in Atlanta. "It's like out in Newton," he says, "only black people out there, man. I didn't believe black people live like that." On the other hand, he is reluctant to cut himself off completely from his roots. "I don't want it to be in the upper middle class," he says. "Nothing like that. There's something about them people. They can't relate to the people on the bottom. Since that's what I grew up with, I always like to be that way. I don't want to put on. I like to live with people that grew up in the same background I did."

He has an equally clear vision of the kind of wife he wants, made clearer as he begins to find girls who fit his vision. By his senior year in high school, he has begun tentatively to think of marrying his current girl "in about two or three years, maybe." He describes her warmly. "She likes what I like. She likes nice clothes and all of that. She's interested in helping people in the ghetto. She's very smart. She's a music major, and I kind of dig that. I don't know, she's just hip to what is going on today. And she's real sweet, she don't lie or nothing. Her father's a preacher, you know, so she's the daughter of a preacher."

Unfortunately, the girl got pregnant, and Josh was faced with a major conflict between affection for her and his compelling desire to go to college. She had the baby and moved to New York. Josh acknowledged the child and visited them for a while, but then "things developed to the point where we just stopped seeing each other. It was best on both of our behalfs. I was not ready to make a move and go down there and stay with her and she definitely did not dig coming back and forth. I'd come there and my attitude wasn't the way it should have been. I was just digging on her and the baby, but I was not seriously thinking about my role of helping her out. And I think she made the right move because I was not ready to deal with it. I made the decision that I should've stayed in school and I tried to explain it to her that things would be okay, and I would be back. I meant that, but she couldn't dig it. She has a nice job and is living out in the suburbs of New York with some nigger. The baby's doing okay, he's growing up and she's having a nice time."

In the ninth grade, Josh said that the only thing that might prevent him from going to college would be "if I got married and had a couple of kids." He isn't about to let it happen.

JOSH AT THE UNIVERSITY OF PITTSBURGH—
SENIOR YEAR, 1973

By the end of his college career, Josh has made his break with his past life. Now he is more involved with issues of his own future than with the old concerns for family and friends which dominated his earlier years. He still thinks about the old days in

Roxbury, but he is more reflective and less bitter than he was when he left high school.

At twenty-two, Josh still spends his vacations with his mother. But by this time, it matters less where he lives. His mother's apartment was more a base for his social life than a home. His occasional quarrels with his mother now center on her "old fashioned ways of thinking about things"—such as Josh bringing a girl up to his room and closing the door. On one occasion, Josh recalls with amusement, "she came in and kicked the door in, like John Wayne or something like that. It seems like she just don't want to see me get out and do it myself."

He has moments of resenting his continuing bonds with his mother, which are linked with his fears that the years of school have made him less capable of making it in the real world. "I know I'm independent enough, but running back and forth to school and staying to help my mother makes me feel like she's pulling me on a puppet string, back and forth. Just having to not accept some responsibilities makes me question if you can really make it on your own tomorrow. And I think I could see things a lot clearer once I get on my own and understand how things exist, and how I have to deal with them."

Josh is sad about how far he has drifted from his brothers. "I mean, like, me and my other three brothers, we're all starting to see each other much more clearly. Like how we should have stayed together and how we could have started a business or something like that. But I don't know, they all got hung up into a lady too early in life, I guess, and the consequences are coming out." Although some feeling of solidarity remains in the family, it is understood that they have all gone separate ways, and Josh feels "it's best that I work whatever problems I have out myself at this point."

He wants to work out his own problems, and usually feels ready to handle them, but he is sometimes haunted by confusion, by fears that he might make the wrong choices, by a sense that he carries a burden of expectations which might be too much to bear. He feels, on the one hand, that he has never had a solid family base to depend on, and on the other, that he has been given so many golden opportunities that failure is impossible and unacceptable. "If I got strung out," he says, "I guess at this point nobody would probably understand. Like they'd say, 'Damn! This nigger and all those breaks, you know—all those things going for him, like why?' "

Josh feels obligated to continue the struggle to "get over," but his vision of the future, of the goals he is struggling toward, is no longer clear. In the ninth grade—even in the twelfth grade—Josh thought he knew his long-term goals. He had picked out a career, a kind of neighborhood, even the kind of girl he wanted to marry. Now, with fuller knowledge of his options and limitations, he realizes that "getting over" will not end with college, and that his most crucial decisions are yet to be made. He now says that he does not know what he will do next year, "but I do know that I want to help other people. I can't say that my goal is clearly defined at this point, because I have so many obstacles to go over, so many things to check out for myself."

But he rarely considers the possibility of failure. Instead, he keeps his focus on short-range goals, which he knows he can attain. "I imagine that as soon as I get some things complete and as soon as I see what's available, I'll be able to be more for real than when I say, 'Well, I'm going to do this and that immediately.' My immediate goal right now is to be out of school this time next year, and to really find out what's going on in the world, and how all the things I learned in college and Roxbury, and all of that mix together and how I'm going to use them to get over and help somebody."

The College Experience

The University of Pittsburgh has not been easy for Josh. Suddenly confronted with a new system, with new rules to learn, new demands to meet, Josh felt lost in his freshman year. "You're on your own," he says, "and it seemed like the pressure mounts,

245

especially on black students, because things go at such a quick pace. I don't know about a lot of the other dudes I hung around with, but I'm sure that they weren't used to the system of writing papers in a college fashion and rapping to a professor, or just having to deal with a lot of exams and things like that."

Josh tried to adjust. There were black upper-classmen "hipping us to how to get over," which were the gut courses, how to arrange class schedules so one could sleep late, which professors to watch out for. Grasping for survival, Josh set no specific goals except to "stick with this for four years. It would be slick to get around the system, and then I'd have a piece of paper to show somebody. That right there entitles me to a job at such-and-such a salary."

Josh felt pressured by the demands of college work, and equally pressured by the demands of his new friends, a set of upper-middle-class, black, "swinging dudes" with "the best reputation among the ladies. The niggers down in the city looked upon us with respect." This group was deeply involved in the college drug scene, and Josh drifted along with them, pushed by his desire not to be left out of anything, and by his need to escape the anxieties which beset him. In the early seventies, drugs were hard to avoid.

"It's really fucked up, man," Josh says, "because you find yourself into it so quickly, almost like you're riding out on a surf, where everything is calm as you're going out. When you're coming back, you're on a wave fifty feet high and the chances are you might drown. Most of my friends were on to the same thing. It's kinda hard to keep your head straight. It seems like everybody is having a real good time, but they're all under the influence of something that's making them have a good time. When you try to be down to earth, man, with somebody, it's kind of hard when you find that you're left out in a way. There was some people that it was almost like [drugs were] a must to associate with them. It's a lotta pressure. There's so many cliques, a lotta dudes just can't dig where you're coming from, man, and accept what you got, and what you have to offer."

Josh has always had a hard time balancing his ambitions and his need for approval from his friends—and he tends to select his friends from the hippest, most swinging crowd around. Yet his push to "get over" has made him cut himself off from the swinging world. This break was made easier by a terrifying drug experience. "We were all sitting in the dormitory room, rapping and talking about this bitch and that bitch, and let's get clean and go to the party and hang with her. I guess I must have took more different kinda drugs—I was so high I was almost like a pig, man, just zooming. I didn't know I was really fucked up till I went outside and saw the world. Then I realized I was by myself because there wasn't anybody else as high as I was. But I couldn't dig it. It got so heavy into me I thought that I was on the brink. I think I learned a lesson that night, just by indulging in too many drugs and just trying to be like the rest of the fellas. You know how much a person can extend himself till they finally find out what it's all worth."

So he broke away from the good-time crowd. "I realized I had ten brothers and sisters, and only two of them finished high school, and how much it probably meant for them that I keep on going. I tried to set a goal for myself at that point, to prove to myself that I could finish it, and not only just finish it, but really get something out of it. The most immediate thing was that if I left school and went back home and went back out on the street, I'd probably end up doing something I had no business doing."

Josh's friends in his junior and senior years came from less affluent backgrounds. He began to pick his "tightest buddies" among those who had come up the hard way, going through his experience with ghetto elementary schools and parents with little education. These were the black students who had "to fight in order to get over, coming up, and we seen a lot of things go down around our way that taught us a lot in life. You can tell, a lotta dudes had their mother and father lead them by the hand. We tried to reach out and be friendly and shit like that, but some things just clash."

At the same time that Josh was pulling away from his middle-class friends and their games, he was falling in love with a girl he

247

met through that crowd. Jeanette was the embodiment of his ninth grade dream. "She's just sweet." Josh says, "You know, understanding. She wasn't really strong . . . I guess you would say her parents were black middle class, maybe upper-middle-class. Just by knowing her, you could tell she had a very tight growing up. Everything she done was carefully planned by her parents. Seemed like the whole thing was programmed, all the way to the person she is, to her personality. You could tell that she had much enjoyment in her life. She was enjoying every minute that she was living . . ."

Jeanette had what Josh considered the best possible education—in the South at an Episcopal parochial school with "like about nine black students in a class of five hundred," and a family which was "close-knit," warm, and secure. "She was a very open person, even though she was closed to some things. I think she was closed to a lot of things intentionally. I mean she knew a lot of the things she went through were sweet water compared to what I had to go through in life or somebody else. I don't think she really wanted to get hung up on what somebody else was into, [she wanted] to dig on how things are right now. Just enjoy yourself and forget the past, make everything brighter. There was so much happening in her. From what I could see her whole background was based on people being honest with themselves."

Josh met Jeanette at a time when he was heavily involved with the swinging scene, with drugs, often behind in school, often disgusted with himself. When he met her, "I didn't give a fuck about much and I was looking for a good time. I wasn't looking for any lady with airs about her, or any type of fancy clothes or hip talk that would like impress them. The thing that she had going for her was just that it was natural, you know."

"Main thing I noticed was how uncomfortable she was at the party. I think I dug that right off. It was a thing where she was looking around, expecting somebody to pull up her skirt. She was like jump into if somebody did it. Whenever I saw her, I would just stare at her—not just stare like I was hypnotized, but stare in a way like saying 'I'm checking you out. I hope you're digging it.'

248

After we got to know each other, she told me she dug me just staring at her. It wasn't a thing of just getting over on her. I felt very satisfied for once, because the other young ladies I was hitting on wasn't nothing like a satisfactory type relationship at all. I felt like I had her under my powers, and that helps every nigger's ego. I said, 'I'm really slick—here I am, got a nice lady. Ain't none of the other hip niggers got a square lady that looks good. I was thinking I was unique. She had money and I was convincing myself I wasn't taking advantage of her money or whatever. Her being there was very necessary to make my thing work."

Jeanette became more and more "necessary" to Josh, and during his last year at Pittsburgh, their relationship became less public and more intense. "As soon as me and her began to see each other, it wasn't her and her girl friends and it wasn't me and my fellas. It was just me and her. That was what made it so beautiful. Everything was so nice. She seemed to sort of settle me down and relax me. Things started to come together. Things seemed just a little bit clearer."

Clarity is precious to Josh, whose life has been a maze of confusing and pressing decisions. But in 1973, Jeanette is in Georgia, at home, and Josh is about to go to Paris. As he is about to leave, Jeanette calls him to say "she felt that like we being away from each other so long that there is a good possibility that I might forget her and things will change. She thought it was best that things ought to take its course as it develops. We had an understanding that if we ran across someone that we thought was the one to make the move with, then our relationship would have to be a thing of the past."

Josh is bitter about Jeanette's decision. He wanted her to wait for him to work things out for himself. "I wish there was a contract I could tear up. Or something like that. Or renege on smoking the peace pipe. But it's an understanding as far as me and her talking on the phone, so far away from each other. I have no choice but to understand."

Even in the face of losing Jeanette—beautiful, gentle, secure, with the capacity to "balance things out for me," Josh's resolve remains clear. His commitment is to his future. "I just have to put things like that aside. Of course I feel alone, in a way, because I'm not doing the things I should be doing. I'm not 45 years old and realizing that next year, ten more years, I'll be 55, pushing on 60. But y'know I think that I went through that much shit, I guess you could say that I have to do it for my own good. I just can't go out and deal with everything without it. So I just made up my mind that it was best if I concentrate on my inner energies, I guess you might say. To find myself out. In a way, it was a sacrifice."

But it is a sacrifice Josh feels compelled to make. He saw his brothers get "hung up on a lady" too soon and destroy their futures for relationships that did not last. It isn't going to happen to Josh.

Looking back over his growing up, Josh is more concerned with what he has learned, what he has accomplished, than with how hard it has been, or what he has lost. He says that he has always been lucky. "My parents didn't have no education in the first place. They could offer me only so much as far as the future. Naturally we didn't have everything we wanted. Rather poor, as a matter of fact. The schools I went to wasn't too tough, either. The things that interested me when I was young, I'd probably have ended up being a criminal or something like that. Then drugs. And seeing my sisters and brothers all fucked up. Just a whole lot of things around me that made me want to turn my head and put everything away, for good, including me. But I always sort of want to play things by ear. If I saw a break, I would lay on that until I see something a little hip or whatever. I'm lucky because there were so many things that diverted my attention from each step. I just tried to gain my self-control at the right time, when it was necessary to try to put things behind. I'm lucky that I also realized that in order to get what I want, I have to set some sort of goals, whether real or unreal, and work for something . . . have something to go on, man."

FOCUS: JOSH MILLER—
FORMING A BLACK IDENTITY IN A WHITE WORLD

Josh Miller spent his adolescence picking his way through a minefield. He wanted to adopt the values of the middle class, but also retain the respect of his ghetto friends. He wanted to live in a comfortable suburb, but also remain part of the inner-city world. He wanted to move easily in a white dominated society without losing a trace of his black identity. He wanted, in other words, to be both a traditionally successful person and a firmly black man in a society which considers the two mutually exclusive.

For Josh, defining his own identity was a tormented process. He could take his Uncle Carl as a role model, but Uncle Carl was far away, almost as distant from Josh's life as the black entertainers and civil rights leaders whose lives, however admirable, are too extraordinary to be useful to a ghetto youth making everyday decisions for himself. There were black teachers at the Ryan, but Josh knew nothing of their lives away from school. Television did not provide the models Josh needed. In the late sixties and early seventies, there were no black situation comedies, no documentaries about the black middle class, few opportunities to see blacks in realistic non-subservient roles. So Josh had to invent his own models, piecing them together from aspects of people, places, and situations he encountered while growing up.

It was not easy for Josh to synthesize a positive racial identity from his diverse experiences in Roxbury, Newton, Lebanon, and the University of Pittsburgh. In Roxbury, he learned the skills which allow a young man to survive and prosper with his friends, but he also learned that those skills would never allow him to "get over with the Man." In Newton, he learned to hustle the white world, to perceive himself as slicker, tougher, more agile of mind than his white classmates. But he also learned about the loneliness of living near suburban affluence, with people who neither love you nor hate you because you barely brush against their comfortable lives.

251

Josh learned a lot about whites in Newton, and he learned a lot about being black. Like many of the young men in the Pathways study, his increased contact with the white world did not breed sympathy and understanding, although it did break down stereotypes. For Josh, this meant moving from vaguely positive expectations, through a state in which he perceived whites primarily as objects for his various hustles, to the point where, as he puts it, "I try to hate them on an individual basis." With the changes in his perceptions of whites came alterations in his feelings about himself as an individual and as a black. He was always determined to believe that blacks are as good as anyone else—and that he, himself, was a little bit better. That confidence is critical to the particular way he wants to operate in white society. But his determination to move in white settings brought him in constant confrontation with the apparent superiority of whies. The whites in Newton, and later in Lebanon, are comfortably rich, while he (and most of the blacks he knows) is painfully poor. His suburban classmates have acquired facility at studying, while study for Josh requires learning a set of skills not taught in the Ryan classrooms. Intellectually, Josh knows the economic and social bases for the advantages he sees around him, but emotionally, they are difficult to manage, day after difficult day.

The move to Lebanon made things no easier. It was positive, because it gave Josh his first close and continuous association with a man with whom he could identify—the resident director of the ABC house, whose origins and ambitions were close to Josh's own. But moving also took him permanently out of the ghetto, dissipating the skills which had made him a survivor there.

Josh's sense of isolation at the end of the ABC program and in his first two years at Pitt is difficult to communicate. "Getting over," requires a gigantic risk, a blindfolded leap into space with only a prayer that there will really be something on the other side. Once Josh left his friends "hanging down on the Hill," there was no going back. The skills which insure survival in the ghetto—fighting, jiving, stealing, constantly renewing the rap—are counter-productive in the white world. They must be systematically rejected—unlearned—and replaced with a new set of abilities. But there is no guarantee that any particular person will be able to develop enough skills to succeed in the white world. And if he cannot, then what? Ghetto style changes so fast that the old skills rust quickly—the rap gets "a little ring of white." And habits unlearned do not return easily. The ghetto youth who makes the leap towards white success has no guarantee that there will be a good life, or even a recognizable self on the other side.

The level of this risk is hard to overestimate. When Douglas Jones snatches a purse, he chances arrest, a beating, perhaps jail. These are painful risks, but they are familiar ones. He can calculate their costs, weighing them against the excitement of the robbery and the value of the receipts. Douglas's personal identity is never in jeopardy. But Josh cannot weigh the risks, because he does not *know* with any certainty what lies ahead, what the white world will permit him to make of himself.

Josh took the chance, and apparently won. At the end of college, he is still piecing together the person he will become, but he has survived his major crises. It seems that he will achieve the combination of black identity and white comfort that he has always sought. But others are not so lucky or so willing to take risks. When students like Anthony Dobson drop out of the Health Careers Program, when others, like Norman Mullen, refuse to take the exam which would get them into prep school, their teachers are bewildered and sometimes irritated. "These young people are being given every opportunity," they argue. "How could they be so ungrateful as to refuse?" But "every opportunity" has massive costs. It is less bewildering that so many refuse options than it is remarkable that so many are willing to risk taking them.

Chapter
8

Brian Henry—Hiding Out

BRIAN AT SEVENTEEN—NINTH GRADE AT THE RYAN

Brian Henry, walking the halls of the Ryan looks like the dark ghost of an earlier era. In the hip, jive ninth grade of 1967, silent Brian with his glasses, his briefcase, his shambling walk, is noticeable and apart. He is "The Professor," the oddball, the scholar.

One non-admiring classmate said of Brian, "He carries this big briefcase everyday, wears this funny looking cap. Everybody laughs at him. Girls come into the room and say, 'Where's Brian?' They don't know who he is, and they heard somebody talking about him. Then all of a sudden Brian is coming through the door. I said, 'Boom, boom'—that's the way he walks. The girls said, 'Oh, that's Brian.' Brian was real embarrassed. He'd go straight through the door, let down his briefcase, clip off his hat, he'd say 'Huh!' Take off his coat. Then he'd go straight to his seat, open up his briefcase, slip out a comic book or something, and start reading it."

Brian never bothers anyone. He rarely speaks outside of class, and then only to a few teachers who show an interest in him because of his studiousness and talent in art. He never steals anybody's girl, beats anybody up, tells lies behind anyone's back. But despite his efforts at neutrality, no one seems indifferent to Brian.

255

His teachers are generally positive about him, praising him for being "quiet, industrious," and "the only one in school with a briefcase." It doesn't seem to matter to anyone that the briefcase is full of comic books as well as homework. Everyone sees it as the sign of maturity, seriousness, good grades. Yet the teachers have little sense of Brian as a person. They speak of him in the abstract. Only the art teacher realizes that something might be going on inside. "He is so terribly talented," she says, "even though he is a very quiet, reserved person. Nobody is going to try anything on him or tell him anything, because he has a great inner fire that could explode at any time."

Brian's classmates have no clearer sense of who he is than do most teachers. But their attitudes toward him are generally less positive. Some look upon him with remote approval as a virtuous but alien being. "He never bothers nobody," one boy says. "Always does his work, pays attention in class. I think his mother is real strict and made him do things like that." Others have only contempt for Brian. Anthony Dobson describes him as a "real bull-thrower. He's, hell, he's no good. His tie is all choked up in his collar. He looks smart carrying all his books and shit and he reads his ass off." Only two boys, both neighbors of the Henrys, see Brian as anything but a self-satisfied scholar. "Brian ain't that smart," says Manuel Garcia. "He just do all the work. He's real quiet and just sits there and draws or reads a book. He never comes out of his house." And Norman Mullen, who was Brian's chief tormentor, is even more scornful. "I wouldn't say he's smart, but . . . all you got to do in the Ryan is sit down, don't talk too much, do your homework and your school lessons, and you get an A in every class. His life must really be a bore."

Brian does nothing to make himself more accessible. After school, he loads his briefcase with schoolbooks and comic books and goes home by one of two unvarying routes. One is the direct route home, which he walks alone with his thoughts, though often physically accompanied by three other boys. Ever since entering the Ryan three years ago, Brian has shared the sidewalk with these boys, but he knows scarcely anything of their lives. One is the son of a friend of his mother's; another stays in school because "if he doesn't, he'll be in Viet Nam." The third companion is so remote from Brian that he can't even remember the boy's name, although he knows he "likes to have fun, which who doesn't.

The alternate route Brian travels all by himself. It takes him along a narrow path through a large area, from store to store where his favorite comic books are sold. He knows the issue dates for all his best "books," and the stores most likely to carry them first. He will go miles to get a new edition of "Batman" or "The Avengers." Occasionally, Brian will vary from his routes to pay a solitary visit to the park, but usually he either goes straight home or detours to the comic book stores.

Brian At Home

Unlike Doug Jones, who is happiest on the street, or Josh Miller, who wants to stay out with his friends, Brian is only comfortable at home where life is highly routinized and for the most part under Brian's control. Most of the boys, when asked what they would tell a double who secretly took their places for a day, could give only general guidelines. Brian provides his stand-in with circumstantial blow by blow directions. Coming home from school, "he stands outside the door and tries to get the lock open, because it takes around fifteen minutes to do that. Then he gets in the house and drops his briefcase which weighs around a hundred pounds. Then he takes off his coat and hangs it up. That's the main thing, takes off his clothes and hangs them up. Then he takes the card table, sets it up in his room, takes all the books out of his briefcase and lays them on his bed so he can get to them easy. Then he picks up the subject which is most hardest, and he starts to work on it. Oh yes, he gets interrupted in the middle of his homework because he has to eat. He watches television. He goes to bed. And that's it."

The single constant companion in Brian's circumscribed life is his mother, Vesta Henry. Since her husband died seven years ago, her whole life has revolved around Brian, Jr. "I think when a mother is not working," Mrs. Henry says, "she should be home. I

257

have always tried to make it a rule that if I'm going out in the morning some place, I usually tell him before he goes to school where I be. I have always made this a habit to be home when he comes home from school because I think it makes a child feel good (of course, he's a young man now) when the mother is home to greet them when they come in from school."

According to Brian, his mother is "kind, considerate, and, like a mother should be . . . she's the best mother in the world." And to Mrs. Henry, Brian is "wonderful," because he studies hard and "if he's going out any place, he always lets me know." She feels that they have an almost mystical ability to communicate. "Sometime I can be in the kitchen or any place in the house and I can be thinking of something and he'll walk in, 'Mommy, you know such and such a thing,' and I say, 'You know something, Brian, I was just thinking the same thing.' "

In the years since his father's death, Brian and his mother have come to share more and more of the household responsibilities. On the first of the month, Mrs. Henry goes out to collect the pension check on which the two of them subsist. When she returns, they figure out the month's finances. Although money is always short, Mrs. Henry says that "I usually allow him to make a menu of certain things that he wants to eat. Some people, they just snaps anything on the children, but I always figure they have a desire for something as well as you do."

The two of them shop together. "Brian and I will sit down and discuss, like what we going to buy." But Brian has a $10 a month allowance which he may spend as he likes. "He never spends all his money," his mothers says. "It's very seldom that he spends it all. Unless he's going to buy a gift or something for me, say for Mother's Day. I don't really know how he saves his money anyhow, but Brian, he's very close with his money. I like that about him, too."

Aside from financial planning and occasional shopping expeditions, Mrs. Henry doesn't ask Brian to help much around the house. "Brian doesn't do a whole lot in the house," his mother says. "Like take out garbage and mop the floors, clean the stairs and all that—he doesn't do that. There are some boys that do those things, but I try to arrange it so that he can have his time for his studies, since he have so much work and since it take him so long." Nor does Brian have a part-time job. One reason is that the terms of his father's pension (which is supposed to support mother and son) preclude regular work by either of them. But both agree that Brian must save his energies for his school work.

Brian and his mother share a commitment to his education. Mrs. Henry's happiest memories are of her own schooldays in the tiny Alabama town where she grew up. Her mother had died when she was a baby, and she was raised with three siblings by an unpleasant stepmother, all that remained of a sizeable family. School was her sanctuary. She speaks lovingly of "Mrs. Williams, my teacher. I will always love her. She taught me through the seventh just on her own. She wasn't supposed to, but she did. We used to have so much fun, and we used to enjoy helping the teachers decorate for the plays and things."

Mrs. Williams offered to get Vesta into the state normal school, which would have allowed her to earn a teaching certificate. But, "my daddy, he felt that my sister and I, we should stay together." He refused to let her go. Mrs. Henry now looks back wistfully on the lost opportunity. "I had my choice that I was going to be a nurse or a teacher." She tries to make Brian's chances better.

Brian has made up his mind to do well in school, although what he calls his "short memory" makes studying a tough, slogging business. "Most of the time it takes me all night to do my homework, because I have so much," he says. "Every night I have to memorize something that's hard for me like geometry. I have to memorize something in biology like this Saturday for this Monday, then I have to do English, memorize the definitions . . . I have to do health, health . . ." His voice trails off at the prospect of his work load. But he gets it done. Ever since he was kept back in the third grade "because I wasn't smart enough I guess," Brian has been devising ways to make up for what he thinks is his lack of intelligence, ways which demand more and more effort and will.

259

"I don't get sick," he says. "I have to go to school. I can't get sick."

Brian and his mother bicker at times about how to preserve the long hours needed for his homework. A major source of contention between them is the amount of time Brian spends on comic books and television. Brian loves television and avidly follows the "good stories like Star Trek. I like to get away from my home and the only way I can do that is by watching television." But his mother, concerned that he might not do enough homework, limits his viewing time. She says that she lets him watch if "it's a special program that I know Brian really like during the week, I will tell him . . . 'Well, when such and such a program is on, you can watch it; when it's over, that's it,' and he know I mean it, you see." Brian says, "When I'm looking at television and she hollers for me to do something, I have to concentrate real hard to keep from getting mad."

On the whole, though, Brian agrees with his mother about the temptations of television and says that he is glad when the set is broken. "If it comes a good story on television, I want to see it. That's one of the main reasons why I'm glad that television is off, because if it's off, I can't see it, and in that way I can do my homework. But if it's on, I want to watch it."

Comic books are not as much of an issue. Mrs. Henry restricts her seventeen-year-old's money for comic books when she thinks he isn't doing well enough in his classes. Both Brian and his mother link comic books with reading, and reading with educational progress. Brian sees his "books" as a legitimate alternative—perhaps the only one—to unremitting attention to assigned school work. "I read comic books because that way if I read them I don't have to do my homework, you see. Now you can read comic books just for enjoyment. That's the whole reason why I read them. When I'm reading a comic book (and I read them at least for half an hour) that's half an hour a night that I don't have to sit and do my homework."

The few other things Brian does in the afternoons and evenings, must be wedged into homework time. He makes models with precision and care. He keeps a diary. "I know it's strange to keep a diary," he says, "but it's the only thing I ever do because I don't really have that many friends. And there are some things I don't like to talk to my mother about." He will not reveal the contents of his diary to anyone, not even with assurances of secrecy. "It's classified information here," he says. Finally—and remarkably for a boy who says "English is one of my bad subjects"—he writes stories modelled after the science fiction shows and the "Fantastic Force" comics that fascinate him. He is as secretive about his stories as about his diary. He describes them cryptically and shows them to no one, not even his mother.

All this intensive activity goes on within the walls of the Henry apartment, particularly in Brian's small cluttered room. Scattered about are boxes and boxes of comic books, models in various stages of development, odd bits and pieces of things he collects to see "if I can make something out of it." His mother considers the room a mess. "I tell him, 'I have to keep behind you just like a two-year-old,' " but Brian knows where everything is and does not want his mother to move anything.

Once when the bedroom ceiling began to leak, Mrs. Henry moved Brian's bed into the living room. Brian had one of his rare outbursts of anger. According to Mrs. Henry, "I said, 'Now you want your bed back and have your bedroom looking like . . . I thought you could go in there [the living room] and have that little corner for your workshop, you know.' " But Brian said, " 'No, I want my bed back in there.' Well, I said, 'I tell you what you do—you want that bed back in there,' I said, 'Help yourself and put it back there. I'm not moving it.' " And back it went.

Brian's room is his workplace, but it is also his sanctuary, his retreat from his mother. Although they show the outside world only love and mutual dependence, inside their own small world they often grate on one another. Small irritants assume large proportions. Mrs. Henry says that Brian has a habit of making "sweet water," from tap water and sugar, and "one thing he do get on my nerves with stirring in the glass." Brian says "There's always a big discussion in the morning, my mother wants me to eat my breakfast, and I don't want to eat breakfast. We have a fight about that every morning . . . Yesterday I gave in and I ate corn flakes."

A major source of argument is Brian's occasional afternoon venture to the bookstores or the park. "The bus stop, it's across from the store, and I go downtown, and I look at the books there. I come up Blue Hill Avenue, and I stop at Alaska Drug Store and look at the books there. Then I have to go all the way up Blue Hill Avenue to Grove Hall—I have to stop and look at the books there, and from there I go home. One time I got home at five o'clock. She screamed and yelled at me. It's very irritating."

"She says I shouldn't go out, that I shouldn't be out late. I can't agree with her all the time. Sometimes I like to go out and be alone in the park. I watch the pigeons. And there's usually two dogs in the park that are running around. I like to watch twin engine jets go overhead. I don't think of nothing. I mean I go to the park so I won't be thinking of anything. I just like to watch people pass by, the birds . . .

"Well, when I get home, she's going to start screaming at me— 'Why did you stay out so late, you know I worry about you!' "

Brian hates the "screaming and yelling" but he never questions his mother's right to be angry. He is far more concerned with controlling his own rage. "I hold my breath, and I count to ten . . . the main thing is to keep myself from thinking things. I usually go in the room and close the door and jump underneath the bed, put the pillow over my head. Anything to keep from hearing her screaming."

He says that there is no way to get her to stop. "You just have to wait for a long time. If I say anything to her, she'll just scream louder." He says he must exercise great restraint to keep from getting mad and "kicking things around." Sometimes he uses a concentration trick he learned from Star Trek, in which "Mr. Spock recited the multiplication tables until you get to the more complicated ones. The idea is to concentrate all your thoughts on that one problem. That way you can't think about anything else. That's what I do most of the time when my mother is screaming at me."

Although she wants Brian to come straight home from school, so that she knows where he is, Mrs. Henry worries about his reluctance to go out anywhere once he is home, especially his unwillingness to go visiting with her. They have a running argument about such ventures. "Sometime, I'd like to get out and go see friends," she says. "Like on a Sunday, and when there's no school. And he says, 'I want to stay in my room.' So I say, 'Oh, well, never mind, we'll stay home.' We are home mostly all the time."

Brian recognizes his mother's needs and says, "I wish she'd go out more," but he will go to great lengths to keep from having to accompany her. "My mother tries to get me out of the house, but I don't want to go out. When she wants to go out, she always wants to take me with her. Once in a while I go in my room and I put on my clothes and everything and when my mother wants me to go out, I say 'No.' If I don't go with her, she won't go either, so she says she won't go."

Mrs. Henry's drinking poses another problem for them. She says, "I don't drink like I used to, because I used to every time I'd get worried. I'd get out and find me something somewhere to drink. I was drinking quite heavy before my husband died." Even after Brian was in junior high school, she says, "Maybe on the first of the month I used to, after I paid all my bills, and I got to thinking about all that money gone, I'd get me a bottle and drink something. But I would be home. I'd drink beer and whiskey and everything, when I'd be fixing supper. I'd be as happy as a lark and playing music. There's no use of lying."

Mrs. Henry says that her drinking is no longer a problem, but Brian disagrees. He says that his mother handles the money for the household when she "is not intoxicated. But when she is, she lets me hold the money until she gets to where she's going and when she wants to buy stuff, and also when she's intoxicated, I take the money and I hold it. That's when we have the real battles, because she wants to go out and get something else to drink, and I don't let her have the money. She screams at me. She gets real violent about it.

"The next day, she's still got a hangover. Usually the day after that she forgives me. She knows that I was holding it for a good reason so she wouldn't go out and blow it all, as the expression goes. It's very depressing because she hollers at me a lot. And I just stand around and take it. She screams really loud, and what really bothers her is that I just talk like I'm talking now, I don't be mad or anything. That really bothers her." Brian has many uses for his self-control.

But even during their worst or most petty quarrels, neither Brian nor his mother ever thinks of living with anyone else. Mrs. Henry currently has a boyfriend, but she says she does not trust him and plans to "give him the street." She says, "As long as Brian was single I wouldn't marry nobody. Brian would have to be married also. I would always have a hard time meeting the right fellow, because these mens today want to come in your home and they wants to beat and boss your child around. If a man ever put a hand on him, I'd go to the electric chair."

Marriage, in any case, has little appeal for Mrs. Henry. She has been married twice, once for six years to a man in the South whom she left "because he was unfaithful and I found the deep truth, and I gave him another chance and he didn't accept it." She had a little girl by that marriage, who was hit by a truck and killed at the age of three. Her second marriage, to Mr. Henry, was not much happier. A railroad worker, substantially older than she and ferociously jealous, he monitored her every movement. "I think some of the reason why Brian is quiet now and doesn't like to go out is because he knew that his daddy never like for me to leave him anyplace, not even with his sister," Mrs. Henry says. "I think that has a lot to do with a child."

Mrs. Henry says that her husband was even jealous of Brian, and once "it came up in argument that it wasn't his and all that, and I told him, I said, 'Well, the only way you can prove that, I tell you what you do. There's your son and there are you and here is me. Let's go down and we'll have a blood test, that will tell you everything.' And after he kept on rousing, I said to him, 'I am not worried about who his daddy is, I know who his mamma is'— because I just got tired."

Even now, seven years after his death, the jealousies and concerns of Brian, Sr. seem to affect the lives of his wife and son. Brian claims that he doesn't "know too much about my father, because I was small then. He died when I was ten years old, so I don't remember too much." But he recalls his father's death as the beginning of their endless moves from apartment to apartment. "My mother said we got to move from there because I don't want to see ghosts walking around the house, and I said, 'No, I don't want to wake up one night and go into the kitchen and see a sandwich float out of the refrigerator . . .'"

But the moves do not seem to have gotten them far from their ghost. Mrs. Henry has little desire to bring a new man into their lives. "If my husband had passed on when Brian was about two or three years old," she says, "I probably would have accepted a marriage. But Brian was ten years old when his daddy died, and knew his daddy well, and everything. No I wouldn't dare unless Brian was married." Besides, she adds, "I'm used to my own way, and I would have to start all over getting used to their way and change my way of living and everything. I'd rather stay on by myself."

Marriage is not for Brian either. At seventeen, he says, "I thought of it, but I rejected it. It doesn't appeal to me because of the children. I don't have anything against children, except that when they're small, they're dangerous. I don't like the idea of having to dry babies, and then clean them up and wash them, and then they start crying. You have to figure out how to stop them, and then if it's late at night and the baby starts complaining, you're in trouble. Then they can walk around the house, and they often break everything, not intentionally, but by accident. Then as they get older . . . well, they're just dangerous, period." And, responding to the suggestion that he could delegate all that responsibility to his wife, he replies, "Ah, but suppose she wants to delegate it all to me?"

Brian's visions of the future are all extensions of the present: he and his mother sharing a small apartment, arguing about whether or not to go out, determining what to spend their money on. The card on their apartment door, which reads Mr. and Mrs. Brian Henry, seems emblematic of their determination to stay together in a kind of mother/son, husband/wife relationship.

It's a relationship that keeps them aloof from the people around them. Brian says his only reason for regretting that he has no friends is that "I can't cheat like other kids. I have to do my homework, because I haven't got any friends who are in the same class, so I can go over their house and copy from their work, or they can copy from mine." Mrs. Henry says that she used to have some good friends (Mrs. Mullen was one who speaks warmly of the nice things Vesta Henry used to do for her), but everyone has moved, leaving her with "some people around that I know, but I wouldn't call them real, real friends. They're just people that I've met since I'm up this way." And now, she says, she prefers to keep her relationships casual, to avoid intimacy. "I like to have friends come in. But let it be different, not the same person, because I think you can get along in life better. I think in order to make a good friendship, try to stay away a while and then visit." She despairs of finding a "woman that you can confide in."

She feels that she is a constant target of gossip and disdain from people who thought she would not be able to manage when Brian, Sr. died. "When his daddy died, a lot of people said things that they shouldn't have said—'I wonder what will become of his son, now?' And that's why you see me struggle. I work harder now. If I had to work my fingers to the blood, I would go down for him . . . if the blood come over my head."

But despite her struggle, she can barely manage on the combined pensions granted by the railroad and the Veteran's

Administration. One of the poorest families in Dorchester, they cannot keep staples in the house until the end of the month; Mrs. Henry cannot afford to heat her home adequately or to have her teeth fixed, or even to repair her reading glasses.

She says, no one (especially no one involved with her church) appreciates her struggle. "People say, 'She ought to do this, and that boy ought to do that,' but they not going to give you one penny to help, you see. When it come down to it, you don't have a friend in the world.

"Now a lot of these people, they go in town, they get a whole lot of new clothes, they go to the show and they see what you have. And you wear a hat to church two Sundays, they say, 'Gee, don't she never got tired of wearing that old hat?' That's no Christianity. If a person looks like they need and you start making fun of them—you ought to try and help them. That's what you call a Christian. That's no good making fun of other peoples. I don't go for that."

It is because of her fear of gossip that Mrs. Henry agonizes over Brian's refusal to change his necktie and his insistence on walking to school rather than spending a dime on the bus. She is sure that people assume that she doesn't clothe her boy properly or give him busfare, but instead spends the money on liquor.

Pointing to stacks of packed boxes which line the apartment wall, she speaks of "moving away from all these gossipers." She and Brian have moved four times in the six years since Mr. Henry died, and it doesn't seem to have helped. "If people don't get you one way nowadays, they try to get you another way," Mrs. Henry says. "Some way or other, to hurt you. I ain't finding none to try to help me. It's always the other way around."

Brian is similarly unhappy with the neighborhood boys, who congregate to tease and harass him. "I was having trouble with the kids, because I sit in the house all the time. They think I'm some kind of nut or something because I don't like to go out.

267

Well, anyway, they sit around all the time outside and they start making jokes about me and about the way I walk. Of course, I don't mind them doing that because I know they can't help that part.

"I didn't do anything about it last year, but this year I'm gonna see what happens when I go outside and say something back to them. I want to see what their reaction would be. That way I'll know which way to be—whether just to stay in the house when they say something about me or whether I should do something about it."

The threats go beyond words. A year ago, some neighborhood youths threw stones at the porch of the Henry's triple-decker building and broke some windows. Brian plans some vengeance, but will not say what it is. His mother, he says, told him she didn't want him to fight with the boys, and Brian agrees. "I don't want to go out and fight them either, because there's more of them than there are of me. They get a gang together . . ."

In the meantime, he says, he has "to keep a close watch on them. I don't trust those teenagers out there, they might try and do something to my mother. I don't mind them talking about me that much, I mean it doesn't hurt me that much, but then they started to talk about my mother. That's when they started to bother me. But I let that go. They didn't do that too much either. I'm gonna see what happens, like I said—when I say something back to them."

Mrs. Henry says she worries about Brian's lack of friends, complaining, "It's not my fault, because I have pleaded and begged him to try to have some friends to come around until I have really just got bored of trying, really." Brian says, "When I was small, I didn't go out then, and then as I grew up, I stayed in the house more and more." His mother confirms this, saying that he would never go out to play with other children, although occasionally he would play with the sons of her friends if they came to the house. "Oh, he played with them around the house, but he was never for going out." Despite her concern for her son,

Mrs. Henry cannot really disagree with his position. She says, "I'm kind of 100 percent with Brian on that. You really have to be kind of careful, because a lot of peoples now are doing things that they have never did before in their lives to make a dollar. So in visiting in the homes of people, you really have to be careful. Sometime it's better to be by yourself." She sums up the feelings of the two of them. "That's a true saying with anybody, 'Stay by yourself, you stay out of trouble.' "

Brian and the Outside World

Much of their mutual sense of the dangers of the outside world comes from first-hand experience. They have both been gossiped about, treated as eccentric. They have had rocks thrown at their windows. Mrs. Henry lost one child and came close, she feels, to losing Brian in an automobile accident which left him with his shambling limp.

According to Brian, the accident occurred when a driver, swerving to avoid some boys on the street, hit him on the leg. The driver then drove him to the hospital, where they found an injured kneecap. Mrs. Henry sees that accident as "a kind of planned thing," partly because, when she reported it to the police, she saw two men talking to the authorities after overhearing her, and partly because there was no subsequent investigation into the accident, although there were eye-witnesses. "People can have so many ways of trying to get even with you, you know. And especially when you have a child, because a child have to walk the street, when you be in the house sometimes."

Brian says the accident "depressed" him, but he does not share his mother's dark thoughts about the circumstances. Brian seems less frightened of the external world than his mother. He doesn't "trust those teenagers," nor does he want their friendship. But he doesn't want to "waste" them either; he simply wants them off his back so he can get on with his life.

At times he'd like to exclude his mother as well. "Sometimes," she says, "when he comes in and he's real tired and I says something to him, and he'll act like he didn't want to be bothered. He be tired and he just don't feel like talking, and I'll be sitting here all day and I'll be lonesome." On those days, Brian goes directly and silently to his room, understanding her situation, but needing his privacy more. "I just don't like to be bothered with Mama when I'm too tired. Mama wants to talk; she be lonesome." Both recognize that their reclusiveness has its costs, but these seem less than the costs of taking on the outside world.

Brian, of course, confronts the outside world every day in the halls and classrooms of the Ryan. And in school he also has to cope with his own pervasive sense of his limitations. He wanted from childhood to be a scientist, but decided in the fifth grade that such a career was beyond him. "You have to be smart to be a scientist," he says, "play around with test tubes, remember chemical formulas. Well, I'm not that smart, so that knocked out being a scientist, see."

He sees his success at the Ryan as a kind of sham, based on a "smartness" of another kind. "As far as teachers go, I go over okay," he says. "With my teachers it's the fact that I'm smart and when they ask a question I always raise my hand and answer it." But he does not believe the combination of classroom docility and relentless toil will take him very far. Perhaps this is why Brian turned down a remarkable opportunity to take a scholarship course at the Boston Museum of Fine Arts. Brian never mentions the scholarship offer himself, but several teachers do, although none of them knows why Brian did not accept the offer.

But Brian knows: instead of taking the art scholarship, Brian has decided, by the ninth grade, that he will be a draftsman. "It's an easy subject," he says. "All you have to do is memorize the stuff and then do it. Along with my being able to draw good, it made things simpler. I'm going to have to go out in the world and get a job, and it's not going to be as an artist. So I thought I would switch to something that would prepare me for going out in the world and getting a job."

Brian's art teacher, perhaps the only staff member at the Ryan who has developed a genuine, personal relationship with him, thinks "it's a pity. He should be in a course in fine arts where it would be an expressive type of deal, not any sort of commercial art. He's not a designer, he's an expressionist. Even though he designs everything beautifully, layouts and things like that are not for him. It's more of an inner expression he's after."

Although Brian shows uncharacteristic self-assurance in acknowledging his excellence as an artist, he prefers to follow a safer route to a livelihood. He hates memorization, but knows he can memorize the mechanical rules for drafting. So he has decided to become a draftsman rather than to rely on his artistic skills.

Brian gets on well in almost all his classes, although he likes some teachers more than others. Like many of his classmates, he most respects the teachers who combine sympathy with serious-ness—often defined as "strictness" in the positive sense. Of Mr. Hyland, a general Ryan favorite, Brian says, "As a teacher, he was hard—that's the kind of teacher all of them should have been like. Mostly everyone liked Mr. Hyland at the school." In addition, he admires Mr. James, the black vice-principal, because he shared with Mr. Hyland the "ability to handle themselves. You wouldn't find the kids talking back to either Mr. James or Mr. Hyland. When either of them gave an order, they'd carry it out." The teachers Brian does not like were less competent because "they didn't get the respect that they wanted," and without it were unable to handle their classes.

In his three years at the Ryan, Brian has been in trouble only once—with the gym teacher. They had a running argument about Brian's gym participation, "and I always lost the argument," Brian says. "That figures, yes it does. It wasn't much of an argument, of course. First of all, he'd ask me why I wouldn't want to take gym, and I'd tell him, because I didn't like it. Then he'd ask me why I didn't like gym, and I'd tell him because I didn't feel like getting up there and putting the ball in the tiny teeny-weeny basket that they have to throw it into. He said, 'Well, you have to take gym.' And I said, 'I don't see why I have to take gym, there's no need for it.' Then he'd tell me, 'Yes, it's in the curriculum wherever you go.' And I said, 'Well, they shouldn't have it in the

271

curriculum. What's gym got to do with education? It doesn't make sense to me.' He said, 'It's in there so you have to take it.' "

Brian refused to take it because "it's in there," even under the threat of an E marring his straight A record. With a combination of active and passive resistance, he managed to avoid gym almost completely. Sometimes, he reports, he went to sleep on the stairs. "I used to have to stuff my ears, so I got some special ear stoppers so I could go to sleep and have a nice nap." Or he would begin to do homework and wait for the period to end. Occasionally, he'd dress for gym and run around the gymnasium while the others were playing basketball. He didn't enjoy it, but it was better than having to participate. His classmates seemed to respect his rebellion. Although he was often taunted and teased, no one seemed to torment him about his refusal to participate in the gym class.

Brian sees himself as more able to get along with his teachers than with his schoolmates. "As for my own age group," he says, "I don't get along with them too good, because I don't talk to peole, because I don't have anything to say to them." In fact, Brian perceives himself as more disliked than he actually is. With the exception of a few boys—chiefly Anthony Dobson and Norman Mullen—Brian is regarded as inscrutable but inoffensive, "smart, good drawer, won an award. Don't say nothing to nobody."

Dobson and Mullen, the two leaders of the class, are his main tormentors. Norman Mullen, who is also Brian's neighbor on Claremont Avenue, is especially inventive and cruel. "I like coming to school to look at Brian," he says. "I used to walk up behind him and just watch him, just watch him, you know." This behavior was well calculated to drive Brian crazy. "When Norman talks to somebody," Brian says, "he tries to make fun of them in a sly way. He says to me, 'How are you feeling?' And he asks me, 'Do you feel fine?' I know there's some kind of catch in that, that he's going to hit me with if I say I feel fine, so I say, 'No comment' and he says, 'You mean you don't feel fine?' or something." Brian suspects that Norman was involved in the assault on their Claremont Avenue apartment, and worries about what he might do next.

Brian's alienation from his peers may be the source of his detached description of the trouble at the Ryan during his ninth grade year. He says there was disruption at the Ryan, with "teachers getting beat up, having their tires punctured, and maybe having the windows broken out of their cars." But he sees the city-wide publicity stemming from these incidents as disproportionate. He blames students for the disruptions, but says, "You know, it's only a few of them that cause trouble—like four or five, disturbing classrooms. You just have to have one person and that will disrupt the whole class."

He describes the disruptive few as being, like Doug Jones, kids who "don't like to go to class; they like to hang around in the corridor. Or they run around the corridor, disrupting classes. They liked to talk back to the teachers just to be smart. Or, in the cafeteria, they'd take some ice cream and throw it on the floor or they'd leave their tray on the table and turn over the milk or something like that."

Brian does feel that some students who "act up" could be helped, possibly by special programs, "like the Boy Scouts, the YMCA." But, he adds, "I don't think those kids go for the Boy Scouts or the Y too much unless they have something really spectacular to offer, like maybe free karate lessons." Basically, he feels that those kids are "rotten," but "it doesn't mean the school has to be rotten also."

Although Brian talks freely about conditions at the Ryan, it is clear that they are not his first interest. He prefers to focus on his own progress, to keep tabs on his own achievement. And his mother is close behind him. Little as she likes venturing out into a world of strangers, Mrs. Henry is a frequent visitor at the Ryan. The teachers like her and respect her concern for her son. One recalls her as "pleasant, not too sure of herself, probably a woman not too well-educated. Certainly interested in Brian doing the best work." He adds that Brian is "the only child, and she wants the best for him."

Brian and Race

Brian does not see the problems of the Ryan in racial terms. In fact, racial issues are not central to his relationship with the world. He does not particularly identify with black people, nor is he as interested in black history, culture, or current events as he is in science fiction or comic book characters. Asked to name a famous or well-known black figure he volunteers "Joshua, you know—at the battle of Jericho," and "Noah, he saved the people from the flood that God created and he brought the world back to the beginning again." But he has to think for a while before coming up with anyone from the last few centuries. Ultimately he produces "Bill Crosby [sic], he was going to become a football player, but he changed his mind. He's in television . . . *I Spy*."

He can't remember being hit with racial epithets. He says the names he is called reflect his odd walk and academic habits. At a time when academically able students like Josh Miller and Norman Mullen are expressing a desire for more black teachers and administrators in the all-black Ryan School, Brian consistently maintains that there is no difference between black and white teachers in their ability to teach or to relate to black students.

Brian declares firmly that there is no difference between blacks and whites, that both are people "with just a difference in the pigment of their skin." But a note of doubt surfaces. "Sometimes I get the feeling, they [whites] have a little better brain power. Their brain may be better for understanding things. First of all, everything that is invented is mostly invented by white people." He adds, however, that times are changing, "I figure that there will be a change in that [the comparative inventiveness of blacks and whites] by the year 2000, because black people are coming up in the world."

Brian prefers to withdraw from any consideration of racial issues. There are no racial problems in his room. Asked what he would like to be if he weren't black, he says he'd like to be an ancient Phoenician, and abandons even that, saying he'd like a "plain, ordinary desert island, out in the Pacific, where nobody was except me. No colored, you know—just neutral, all colors mixed together."

Although Brian says that whites have economic advantages, he feels no discomfort about being black. He would not want to be white, nor would he want the human race to be entirely black. His ideal world would be one in which everyone was "half and half," so that racial strife would be impossible. Until that utopia arrives, he chooses to know as little as possible. He says that neither he nor his mother ever watch the news, and he denies much knowledge even of the uprising in his neighborhood which followed the death of Martin Luther King, Jr.

Nevertheless, he can understand the anger of some of his fellow ghetto-dwellers. "Let's say some people have good reason to do their riots . . . because living gets on your nerves, and they get lousy-paying jobs, and they have to feed their family because the dumb idiots got married. And then they get down in the dumps, and get paid lousy and they have a white employer, and then they bunch together and start a riot. Some of them, not all of them, have good reason for rioting. Like some people just do it so they can get the stuff free. It's a real easy way to get the merchandise."

Mrs. Henry, by contrast, is less temperate in her analysis of the racial situation. Contrasting her Southern youth with her adulthood in Boston, she says that in the South, "if they [whites] like you, they like you and vice versa. Here they pretend like they like you, but at the same time they hate your guts. It's worse, because they are sneaky here. At least [white Southerners] are plain. All they want you to do is stay on your side and they stay on theirs."

She feels strongly that "whites have been keeping us back," and agreed with Martin Luther King when he said that "Negroes have to keep pushing for themselves." At the same time, she sees divisiveness within the black community. "A colored person, if they see one down, they try to put you further down instead of trying to help others, but when they become successful, they usually don't." Like Brian, Mrs. Henry is unfamiliar with most contemporary black figures and organizations, but, also like her son, she deplores the assassination of Martin Luther King, Jr., the aftermath of which still haunts Roxbury.

Brian and His Privacy

Brian seems reasonably content with his limited life, shuttling between school and home, between fantasy and homework. Certainly, he declares himself happier than his mother, who says that she spends her days "around here in this shack . . . Wishing . . . Wishing that I was working." But he feels unique in his relative comfort with his way of life. Brian cannot conceive of any other boy his age taking his place in his household, not even for a day. "He couldn't do it," Brian says. "It wouldn't work. It would drive him mad if he knew how to. He couldn't take it, after being normal, after doing what other kids do. He couldn't take it.

"Most people are used to having contact with others; they go to other people's houses and stuff like that. Me, I stay in the house all the time, except for when I go out and get my books, and then I come back home, and that's about it. See, so, if he had to sit up in the house as much as I do, he'd go nuts, especially in the summer when there's no school. I hardly go out then. No contact with anybody except my mother." He shakes his head. "He'd go nuts."

How does he manage? "Simple. I was raised up that way. See, it's a matter of adjusting to the environment, and because I did it all the way from childhood, it works out for me."

At seventeen Brian says that "patience" and self-control are the keys to his personality. But his matter-of-fact, pared-down approach to his own life appears to come not from coldness, apathy, or indifference, but rather from a desire to control his mind and concentrate his energies on what he can take care of and manage. His art work, his dreams of being a scientist are relinquished as career aspirations, although he maintains his interest in both in his leisure time. Much of Brian's expressivess, his fantasies and his ingenious, even humorous, qualities are locked away in the privacy of his bedroom, because he does not care to transport them into the classroom or the future world of work.

BRIAN AT DORCHESTER HIGH

The shift from the Ryan to Dorchester High was agony for Brian. Always an A student at the Ryan, always "The Professor," the substantially higher academic standards of even this weak high school have shaken his academic self-image. "I wish I had a better memory," he says. "I'd like to have a quick mind. I've never been sure of myself, and I'd like to have reassurance."

He studied hard, even at the Ryan, but now, he says, he studies "mostly all the time. That's from the beginning of the morning to the end of the night, mostly from when I get home till ten or eleven o'clock." He says he now has little time for television and comics, because he has to spend so much time painfully memorizing his homework. "I don't like to study anything now," he says. "I don't mind reading about it, but reading and studying is different. When you study, you have to remember, but when you read all you have to do is read. You don't have to really remember unless you want to." His mother worries that he is exhausting himself with study, while he fears that "when she sees the E I'm going to get from Spanish, oh, that means it's hollering time."

Brian chose Dorchester High, with the help of a vice-principal at the Ryan, because "it has one of the best art programs in the city, and also it was close to where we live." Brian never says why the Dorchester program seemed preferable to the Museum School curriculum. But his mother says that "the counselor told me, he said, 'Brian doesn't need to go to art up there, because what they taught in the Ryan, that's what they're teaching there, so he already knows that.' He was going to take the real oil painting, but he had so many subjects that it was just too much for him dragging all those books—those books are too heavy—and then coming back about six o'clock, got to stay up till 11, 12, 1 o'clock, you know, to get his work. So I just had it cancelled."

Once Brian got to Dorchester, however, the counselors there placed him in the college course rather than the art program. Brian found the college course homework murderous, and "wanted to switch courses so I wouldn't have the college course. At Dorchester I thought they had a course in drafting. I wanted to take a drafting course, but then, after we talked about it for a while, I decided to stay with the college course." He was reluctant to do so, but the combined pressure of his mother and the Dorchester guidance counselor was more than he could resist. "He said I might not want to take up drafting after I got out of high school, and if I stay with college, I would have more of a variety of jobs I could get."

But, by the end of his sophomore year, Brian had tired of the relentless homework load, and switched to the business course. This will not prepare him for the drafting job he still wants, but it does make life easier. "If you were in the college course," he says, "you had enough homework to kill you. Then again, if you were in the business course, which I was in, you had enough homework to keep you busy, but it wasn't enough to kill you."

The business course also seemed the more rational choice to Brian. To go to college, he says, "You're going to have to have the money for it. Then you're going to have to have the incentive to go. And that's as far as I can see it." Lacking the incentive himself, and doubting his own intellectual capacities, continuing the struggle didn't seem to make sense to Brian.

In Dorchester High Brian remains the model student who always comes to class prepared. He says he has learned to read all assignments ahead of time, because "if you read through the chapter it gives you a better understanding, and sometimes on a test they have a question from the homework, and by doing the homework you know what the answer is."

But, if he has the formula for academic success, he still feels that social abilities elude him. He says that he gets from school "the only thing that's available from going to school, which is knowledge. Friendship . . . oh, well, I haven't got it but it's available." He doesn't feel that he will ever change. "I'd have to be brainwashed. I'd have to have a complete new set of values put in my head. I like to be by myself because that's the way I've been all my life. So I'd have to have ideas about being around people . . . I seldom venture too far away from the house because I don't have any place to go."

He expresses more desire to have friends than he did in his junior high school years. The reasons he gives are essentially pragmatic. "I've noticed that if a person has friends they are more likely to be on top of what's happening . . . like around each school. Take, for instance, the fact that there's going to be a holiday one day. A week ahead of schedule, everybody else in school knows there's going to be a holiday but me, I don't know. If you have friends who are also trying to get a job, they may not be trying to get the same job that you're trying to get, but they may have heard of some place where they can get a job that is the kind that you're looking for." Beneath the practical reasons, lies a more general desire for more social life. He says that if his mother could change him in any way, she would want him to be more sociable, and he adds that if he could change himself he would want to "be able to socialize, have friends."

He has formed a friendship at school with a white boy, David White, which seems more significant than Brian will admit. He initially refers to David only as "the guy I play chess with," and denies knowing much about him. "He's got a dog and he's got a brother. A dog bit him," Brian volunteers, but that is all. Nevertheless, Brian refers to David as his best friend, and says later that "we're in the same homeroom and we usually roam around the school together whenever there's no class. And we play chess together. We always play chess. 'Cause I'm trying to beat him, you see. We don't wander around the school too much, because the corridors are patrolled by teachers. And you have to make like secret agents to get through one part to the other. So we play chess most of the time."

In addition, Brian says, he still sees the two boys who used to walk to the Ryan with him, and says that they have changed since junior high "for the better." He describes both of them now as "nice guys," and reports their future plans in some detail. Even if Brian feels that it would take brainwashing to make him gregarious, he seems much more socially aware at twenty than he was at seventeen.

Brian came to Dorchester High at a time of increasing black awareness and protest, but his militancy remains low. He is dimly aware of the Black Student Union, but never participates in their activities and does not feel competent to comment on them "since I don't know enough about it." He knew that there had been a demonstration in the school, during which black students had staged a walkout, but he says, "I'm the silent majority. I don't like the news, so I don't know what happened."

Discussion of racial issues seems to irritate more than stimulate Brian. He says he refers to himself as Afro-American, but doesn't have "any feelings about it, one way or the other. Sometimes the colored kids get carried away with being colored. They put on an act. They start saying 'I'm colored and I'm proud of it.' When they're talking to white kids most of 'em talk like that, but they be kidding around."

Brian believes in school integration, because "that way we can learn to live together in peace. I've heard that when they're children [blacks and whites] play together and everything. But as they grow older they begin to break away from each other and go to their separate race. And they stick together as far as parties and stuff goes. And the only place they ever get together is at school and it's the only place they can find out about one another's life and that they're both the same."

Although Brian separates himself from both racial interaction and racial conflict, he says that he has come to understand the meaning of the Roxbury riots. Once, he says, he thought the destruction of property was "rotten," but "now I have to change my tune. Because the riots brought about a lot of good things.

They brought recognition to the colored people. Even though they had to get arrested to do it, they did it." And now, he says, things are "changing for the better," for blacks, "at least it seems that way."

Brian does not think that an increase in the number of black teachers would improve the education of black students. Except for black history, where a black teacher would "naturally take more pride in it than whites would, I can't think of anything they might teach best." He says he doesn't care about the race of his teachers. "I doesn't make any difference to me. I'm not prejudiced." His favorite teachers in junior high and high school have been both black and white.

He views discipline as far more important than race for quality teaching. He liked his high school history teacher because "he kept the class in line. We had one boy in particular who was always the clown. Sometimes Mr. Jameson would joke back at him and make him shut up." The good teacher, according to Brian, is nice, not "one of those Gestapo teachers," but one who will "try to get their attention and make them work."

Brian blames school disturbances (which he still sees as the work of a few students) on poor parental discipline. Some parents "feel that when they were being brought up by their parents that they didn't allow much freedom. So they decided that they were going to give their children some freedom. The trouble is they gave them too much freedom.

"And it got out of hand and they did whatever they wanted to. And they got no respect for authority. And so they decided, what the heck, if I don't obey my parents there's no reason why I should obey my teachers. That's the way it comes out."

Brian clearly differentiates his mother from such parents. He is less critical of her now than he was in junior high school. Her "personality is nice," he says. "Easy to get along with. Most everybody on the street likes her. She likes to do things for people. I tell her not to do this. She's got to help everybody. She gets carried away with being nice."

281

Brian says that they get along well, without as much fuss as formerly. "She's very nice. She doesn't give me a lot of trouble. She doesn't tell me to do this, do that, and make me do a lot of things that I don't want to do. There's no generation gap as far as my mother's concerned. We agree on everything."

Brian appears to have won the privacy battle, and Mrs. Henry seems to have learned that if she wants to go out, she will have to make her excursions alone. "I don't have anything to talk to my mother about," Brian declares. "Bills, that's about it. I talk to her about everything, whenever we start talking, that is, You see, we don't get too much talking done, even though we live in the same house, because I like to stay in my room and she never comes in my room. She usually cooks or goes out. So I don't have to talk to her."

Mrs. Henry is working now, as a nurse's aide in a home for the elderly. She doesn't like the job, Brian says, "because they're so messy," but it takes her out of the house during the day, and gives her a little spare money to spend when she goes out—without Brian—in the evening.

Brian describes them as content with their parallel lives. "She likes it when I get up and wash the dishes," he reports. "Take out the garbage and stuff like that. She gets sloppy and she kisses me. She'll bring me a present like some jelly roll." He pauses. "I like the jelly roll," he adds, "but the kissing has got to go."

Only two of their old areas of conflict remain—Mrs. Henry's drinking and Brian's occasional poor grades. Brian says that the only time his mother upsets him anymore is when "every once in a while she likes to go on a spree, and she gets carried away. It doesn't really bother me except when she decides she's gonna go out in the street and sing and talk and everything. You know, it's stupid." But he does not feel that he should take any action. "I suffer, that's what I do."

Brian's rare poor marks bring the old maternal response. "She screams at me and yells at me." But he has perfected his controls.

"Luckily," he says, "I have a defense against that. It doesn't bother me. You see, I make believe she's talking to somebody else, and I laugh at the fact that they're getting bawled out."

Brian has so minimized his own needs and desires that there is virtually no way his mother could punish him now. "She thinks she can punish me by taking away the television and not letting me watch television, that's one of my favorite things, but I can do without it. Or she thinks she can take away my comic books and punish me, but it wouldn't really bother me. The only thing that she can really do to bother me is to make me go outside. That's punishment, wow!" But he isn't about to reveal that Achilles' heel to his mother. "What she doesn't know about, I'm not going to tell her."

Brian and his mother have moved twice since he left Ryan. He says his present neighborhood is a "very good one now that the lady who used to live across the street from us has moved out. She used to be out on the streets fighting with everyone and swearing and such in the summertime. During the wintertime she was kept inside because of the cold and it was nice and quiet." As for the houses, "On the outside, they all look in good shape. Of course on the inside, it would be a different story." Their present building is a brownstone, which Mrs. Henry prefers because it doesn't get as cold in the winter as the triple-deckers in which they have generally lived.

Brian is content. "I like the room I'm in because it's dark in the morning and I like to sleep late and I hate sunlight coming in on my eyes and waking me up. I like it nice and dark. That takes care of it right there." But even if this is the nicest of all the apartments in which the Henrys have lived over the last few years, the same boxes, packed and ready, line the walls. Mrs. Henry is looking for a better place, even if Brian says, "I wouldn't mind living in an apartment like this one for the indefinite future."

Brian spends most of his spare time in his room, studying and reading comic books and movie magazines. Recently, a new interest has taken over his comic-reading time—popular books and magazines about science. "I always found science interesting, especially biology. I started reading medical books and science books and novels—anything I could get my hands on." Now, he says, "the only thing that interferes with my reading is television."

His principal outside entertainment, other than the chess games which are confined to school, is walking alone at night, "because I like the dark—can't stand the sunlight," and going to movies. He likes the James Bond movies and has "seen all the Clint Eastwood things. They're beautiful. Especially the first—*A Fistful of Dollars*. I thought it was going to be lousy, because most of the time when they give them a big build-up, and I go to see it, they usually are lousy, but this one really deserved the build-up they gave it." His voice quickens as he talks about the movies he likes, but he adds, a little defensively, "You wouldn't consider this exciting, but to me it is."

BRIAN AT TWENTY—A GRADUATE OF DORCHESTER HIGH SCHOOL

Poised between high school and work, Brian is anxious about his future. School was under his control. But getting and holding a job requires skills he doesn't think he has. "I graduated from high school. I now have to go out and get a job. I don't like the idea of having to go to work because then I'll be stuck—I'll have to be around people—I'll have to deal with them. I just haven't had the experience to deal with people."

Brian has had only two jobs in his life, neither of which taxed his social skills. Early in high school, he augmented his allowance with an occasional Saturday stint helping his mother's boyfriend, Frank, move barrels in a meat-packing plant. In that job, he spoke to no one but Frank, who even collected his pay for him. Then, in the summer after his junior year, he got a job in a medical laboratory through one of his cousins, as a "caretaker for the equipment and for the general surrounding area." He worked only five hours a week—alone—and felt himself a responsible member of the medical community. He says of the equipment in his care, "I had to keep it clean. Because they were sort of in the medical profession and they had to have it clean. Otherwise it would mess up the blood test analysis that they ran."

But now he sees himself faced with the need to find a "real" job, and the prospect is unnerving. He has always wanted to be a draftsman, and it is still true that his "first choice is mechanical drawing. I thought it might be good as a profession. I like to draw, and drafting requires a certain amount of drawing. And it's interesting."

But he has no training in drafting, other than an introductory course in the ninth grade. The only job for which he has applied is as a file clerk at Boston City Hospital. He says he doesn't mind filing. "It's nice and easy going." He had two courses in office practice at Dorchester, so that he has some confidence that he knows what he is doing. He thinks he will get a filing job, when one opens up, "as long as they don't have the questionnaire filled out with the color, and as long as I'm not going to have to run up against anybody who might be prejudiced." He plans to keep trying, going down the list of city hospitals, "and if they don't have it for me, I'm going to another place which might get me a job."

If he can't get a filing job, Brian says, he will look into other kinds of clerical work. He has no real second choice career; he will go where the work is. But he has very clear ideas about what he doesn't want to be. He says his least favorite job would be as school custodian, "because it sounds like a terrifying and boring job. An accountant is another boring job. I don't think I'd make a good lawyer. Do you ever watch television and those lawyer shows? All that research they have to go into. And they have to walk in front of the people in the courtroom and present a case. No good."

Even though his high school program did not prepare him for the drafting career that was his first choice since junior high school, Brian still feels that his education was crucial to his future. He got through high school with a B average, despite his homework difficulties and his poor preparation at the Ryan, and he cannot understand why some of those around him, including his cousin, dropped out. "They dropped out," he says, "these kids I know, who were nearly finished with school, and I can't understand why. My cousin, he dropped out of school and he only had one year to go. Some other kids I know dropped out and they only had two years to go, I don't understand why they go and take a chance and throw away their future by not finishing high school when it's only going to take two years. It's not really that hard to pass. It seems like a stupid thing to do."

At seventeen Brian felt that no one could take his place, even for a day, without going mad from the isolation of his life. Now, at twenty, he declares that a human replacement would not even be necessary. "I wouldn't have to have anybody replace me," he declares—not without a trace of humor—"because I could go away without being missed. The place where I am mostly at all the time is in my room, so I close the door and lock it up so that she can't get in. Then I set up the tape recorder and I tune it, and I set up this special attachment which, if anybody knocks, it goes off, it goes off and the tape says, 'I don't want to be disturbed, go away. I'm not going to talk to you. I'm not going to do anything, so don't bother me.' And then she'd leave, hopefully."

BRIAN AT TWENTY-THREE—
FROM BOSTON BUSINESS SCHOOL TO WORK

At the end of high school, Brian was prepared, whatever his fears, to launch himself into the world of work. But now, at twenty-three, he is still in school, facing once again the prospect of job-hunting and job choices. His application for a filing job at Boston City Hospital never came through. Brian says, "I went up there to apply for a filing clerk. Because I had taken it up at school. They didn't have any jobs like that open so they asked me if I wanted to push patients around the floors. I didn't want that. Before I went to look for a different job, my mother found out about this school for accounting. I decided, since I didn't really

286

have any trade it would be better to have something that you could get a hold on and so I went to that school to take it up."

Boston Business School seemed to be a good choice to Brian because tuition is waived for Boston residents and they have an active job placement service for their graduates. But the school is demanding, and Brian says that he "did terrible that first year. It's a hard course up there, and aside from that there's a lot of memory involved. And I didn't really have to do that much memorizing when I was in high school." His worst subject was English, which seems unlikely in such a persistent reader and writer, until he explains that "you have to memorize at least three hundred words or something like that so you can pass the test."

He didn't complete either the English or the math course that first year, and had to make up several units during the following term. Nevertheless, he says that the second year was easier. "I didn't pass all the courses the second year, but I didn't have any real difficulty." That year he took courses in accounting, math, psychology, law, office practice, filing, data processing and English. Although he failed some units in law and in English, he says, "I was good at accounting, except for when we got to mathematics. I was good at some of the English, like punctuation. I like punctuation. I didn't understand punctuation when I took it in elementary school, but I liked it when I took it up there, because I always wondered how they figured out the different types of punctuation.

"I liked office practice. That was working with calculating machines and mimeograph machines. Math was all right. Law, yeah, I liked law. And economics was nice, too, because I liked my teacher. She was a nice teacher."

Brian has more to say about the human side of his teachers than he has ever said before. He liked many of them, and remarks that some of the young women instructors were pretty and one was "super-cool." He says, "She didn't go along with the usual standards of teachers. At least when I was there the first year. We had a lot of fun in her class. She used to joke around with the kids.

She wasn't solidly strict with them. See, there was no real reason for her to be real strict with the class because one of the students "could do mathematical problems quicker than she could." Brian laughs. "She would sit up there sometime and say, 'How did you do that, Renato, so quick?' "

Brian has found Boston Business School congenial and speaks of his classes and the people in them with relaxed enjoyment. "We had a fun class the first year," he recalls. "We just mostly kidded around. During a typing class that we used to have a ten-minute break in, we'd come in the room and start shooting rubber bands. Would you believe this? Graduated from high school and shooting rubber bands?" He shakes his head in amused derision. "We talked about anything," he adds, "football, baseball, what was happening in the news and stuff like that."

He still denies having any friends outside of school, but says that he has made several casual acquaintances in his classes. "I just don't have any long conversations with them," he says. "An on-and-off conversation is the best I can do." His first year he became fairly friendly with Renato, the math whiz. They talked about mathematics and "sort of collaborated when we had a problem. Or when I had a problem. He was *very* good in mathematics."

Although Brian still frets about his poor memory, and comments on the difficulty of some of his courses, he does not seem as tense about his academic achievements or failures as he used to. "I don't take things as seriously as others do," he says. "I know my teacher was telling me one day that there was a girl who had studied for the test all night and she came into the school and was so nervous that she started to take the test and her mind was a complete blank." That would never happen to him, Brian repeats, "because I don't take things as seriously as others."

Brian attributes his comparative lack of seriousness to the fact that he does not pay tuition. "It's kids who come from other cities or towns," he says. "They have to pay, what is it? Tuition is $500, I think. That's why some of them go into cardiac arrest the day of the test." Further, he feels that his lack of interpersonal entanglements saves him from such emotional excesses. "Other people," he explains, "they're around other people and they get themselves in trouble, well, I don't mean trouble with the police or nothing, just trouble with their own friends. They'll say something to one friend and another tells another friend and the next thing you know that friend is coming after him because they told them something. Like my mother, she gets upset over little things. I marvel at the way she gets upset over such minor things. Like her boyfriend's coming in the house and not saying anything to her. She goes into cardiac arrest."

At seventeen, and again at twenty, Brian seemed uncertain about how sociable he wanted to be. He said, then, that he hated to go out, to be with people. But, on the other hand, he said that if he had children (which he had no intention of doing), he would want them to "definitely socialize, so they'd not be like me," and he envied his mother's easy way with company. Now, at twenty-three, his position seems to have hardened into what he calls "anti-social," which "really means that you do not make the effort to socialize with people. Because you never have." In fact, he has come to feel friends would only create conflicts and complexities in his otherwise well-ordered and well-controlled life.

Brian says that he never gets angry at anyone, because he has no friends to get angry at. "You see, you pick up things from a friend, see. Feelings, the way you react to situations. Since I don't have any, I can't pick up those feelings and ways to react. I think that's one of the major reasons that I don't have any conflicts as far as friends go—like if I tell somebody I'm going to do this and then I don't and they get mad about that."

He says that he was invited to a party at the business school once, but he didn't go, because "I just didn't want to. I'm not used to being around people I don't know, basically, except for in school." And in school they don't bother him, because "I don't have to socialize with them, they're just there."

Brian thinks he might have had an "alteration of personality" if he had not been an only child. "If I had had a brother or sister, it is

289

possible that I would not have been anti-social," he says, but not with any particular regret. He says that he has no desire to go out with girls—if a girl asked him to go to the movies with her, "it would be a choice between her and my comic books; she would have to lose." And he remains firm in his intention never to marry, never to leave his mother's house. "I'm what's known as a confirmed bachelor," he says. "I'm not into that thing about carrying on a name onto another person. That doesn't interest me."

As Brian has consolidated his position on external relationships, he has become more relaxed about his privacy at home. He and his mother still live at the apartment that they moved to three years ago (although the boxes are still stacked against the wall, and they plan to move to a new apartment in the summer). But Brian is no longer so protective of his room, nor so eager to retreat to it at the end of the day. "The kitchen is the base of my operations," he says. "I use the table . . . for my homework, drawing, reading. See, I've got a table in my room, except that I got books on it, novels that I haven't read, and I got my radio and I got my watches and my pencils and pens and I got my tape and I got my notepads and a can and I got my hat and all kinds of things piled on top of it, so if I was gonna use it, I'd have to move everything off, and it would take me half a day to do that. So it's easier to go to the kitchen."

Brian says that he and his mother get along "fine" these days. She has stopped drinking entirely, because of an illness which makes her vomit whenever she "tries to drink a pint or a half a pint." He has taken on more household chores. "I wash the dishes sometimes, the floor sometimes, that's about it. Sometimes I warm supper."

He says that his mother is sometimes irritable, perhaps because "she has stopped drinking," and periodically "she just gets mad and starts screaming." The issues are familiar ones. "If I leave something out on the table or put something on the stove and you get a couple drops of oil on the stove, she says, 'You wipe off the stove. Wipe off the stove. It's dirty. I wiped off that stove and now it's dirty!' " But Brian no longer gets angry. "She cracks me up," he says of her fits of rage, "Because it's so minor and she's getting so upset over it. I tell her she is too sensitive. She shouldn't take things so hard. They're minor things."

The only time his mother really annoys Brian is when "she'll get up early in the morning to go shopping and she'll want me to get up in the morning to go shopping and I like to sleep late." But, he says, he generally gets up and goes with her, "unless I can do it on my own. Like sometimes we have to go pick up government food, you see. So if I go by myself, I don't have to get up early in the morning and go with her. She wants to go out when it's cool. I don't care if it's hot or not, just as long as I can stay in bed and sleep."

Part of Brian's desire to sleep in the morning stems from his peculiar schedule. In the summer, he says, he stays up until three in the morning, and then sleeps until one in the afternoon. "I just like to sit up late," he says, "because sometimes I'm reading a good story and when I'm reading a good story I hate to leave it so I have to sit up and keep going until I finish it."

Brian feels that maturity has changed his taste in reading and in television viewing. He still reads comic books, "but I don't read funnies, like Archie, stuff like that. I never liked those. I like the adventure type, like Batman and the Avengers. This is a group of superhumans who band together to fight crime. That's my kind of comic books—superheroes." He appreciates the superhero comics as an artist as well as a reader. "They hire some really good artists, like Neal Adams," he says.

In addition to comics, Brian reads more fiction now—"science fiction novels, space or secret agents, or stuff like that. I like adventure stories." He estimates that he reads thirty books a month, and most of his allowance (which is still $10.00 per month) is spent on reading material. "Luckily," Brian says, "books is practically the only thing I have to spend money on, except when I go to the movies occasionally."

291

His books are not as easy to find these days as they were when he was in junior high. Urban renewal and urban uprising have shifted Brian's book-buying route. "There's been so many changes to the city," Brian says. "They knocked out my drug store that was on Blue Hill Avenue. Put up something new, because they got burnt out a couple of years ago. Let's see, they closed down my store that was on the Harvard Avenue route for books. I think they caught them making book in there. They just used the books as cover, you see, so when the police came in there they would think everything was legitimate. And then there's the bookstore that used to be down at Dudley; they closed out. So they knocked out most of my bookstores." Now Brian has to go across town, to Harvard Square or Kenmore Square to locate his favorites, which he finds annoying but necessary.

Brian still watches a lot of television, especially movies, but his viewing habits have changed. "I got old," he says. "My sense of humor has gone down some. I mean, I don't find things— cartoons—as funny as I used to. I still have to get up now, on Saturdays, to see *Star Trek;* they have a cartoon version of it out now. It's straight science fiction, whereas the cartoons are supposed to be funny."

Actually, he says, "I like to listen to radio better. I can listen to that twenty-four hours a day," especially when they play soft music. He likes records, too, but can never afford to buy them, except when they go on sale.

At seventeen, Brian spent nearly as much of his leisure time producing drawings and writing as he did consuming television and books. Now, the balance seems to have shifted. He doesn't draw much anymore, he says, because "I'm a perfectionist, and if I can't do something perfectly, then I don't want to do it at all. I spend too much time reading; I don't have time to draw."

He is much more public about the contents of his diaries and about his stories now, but he says that he is writing in his diary less and less. "Last time I wrote in that diary was . . . last year," he says. "I keep entries in it once in a while. I don't read it for a long time. If I read it over again, then it won't be interesting, but if I wait a long time, like maybe a year, then I go over it and it's interesting to find out what happened to me back in the past. Sorta like isolated details which I forget."

He has several stories in various states of completion, but he does not have confidence in himself as a writer. "You see, for a writer to be really good, he's got to have a good vocabulary, and since I don't have a good vocabulary, I don't think it's that hot. I mean, I think the ideas are good, but as far as the writing goes . . . I don't think so."

One story, his most polished, he likes enough to consider submitting to a magazine. "It was about a kid and a cat that he had. His mother was trying to get the cat to eat, right? So she couldn't get him to eat. So she was talking to her husband, and they had a conversation going on." The mother sends the child upstairs to get ready for supper, telling him to take a bowl of food for the cat with him. He took it and he went upstairs.

"The parents remain in the kitchen, talking about the cat's habit of clawing people who are trying to help it. So while they were talking and they were discussing taking the cat to a vet, the son was upstairs playing with the cat, and he was trying to get it to eat. Then all of a sudden, the cat jumped at him, and then we switch back to the parents.

"So they're talking, then the kid starts crying in his room, and he starts to stagger against the wall and he starts walking down the stairs. And anyway, the punch line to the end of it is that when he stumbles into the kitchen and is bleeding from where the cat clawed him and neither his mother or father is really looking at him—they know he's come into the kitchen, but they haven't looked at him yet—so, anyway, his mother is at the refrigerator, no, his mother is at the stove and his father is at the refrigerator, and he says something to him and so he doesn't answer, see, and then he says something to him again, and he says, 'What's the matter, Billy? The cat got your tongue?'

"And, you see, that's the whole punch line. They turn around and they see the kid laying there on the kitchen floor with blood dripping out of his mouth. 'Cause that's what happened, the cat got his tongue." Brian laughs. "That was the punch line. I think I'll send it in to a magazine and see if they'll buy it. In to a horror magazine."

Despite the endless hours that Brian spends "basically safe behind the walls" of his mother's apartment, he says "I like the outside. I like to watch buildings under construction, jets, clouds." But, he adds, "There's not too much you can do by yourself, you know. I really don't get around that much, so there isn't too much I can say about that."

Nevertheless, he has an elaborate fantasy of another life, one which he would live if he were a millionaire, or maybe a billionaire—"I don't like to take any chance of becoming bankrupt"—which would be outdoor-oriented and utterly different from his present existence. He would travel, Brian says, "I'd start off in this country and then I'd work my way up to Canada and then I would go . . . well . . . out to California, then from there, I would angle my way down to Mexico and then from there, I would angle back to America and go back to my base of operations and think of a new plan. I like the idea of going deep skin diving in maybe the Caribbean, or something like that, or mountain climbing—that sounds interesting—sky diving . . ."

Even in this purest fantasy, however, Brian envisions himself alone. He would not even take his mother, he says. "I prefer to go by myself, to tell you the truth."

But, pushing fantasy aside, Brian contemplates the reality of going out to work. He has two units to finish at Boston Business School. Then he will graduate, and that means "trouble. I have to find a job in the first place, and then I'll have to keep it." Brian does not care what kind of business he works in, as long as it is a "nice, quiet office where there isn't any company." His financial goals are equally modest. He wants to bring home $90.00 a week, which, he figures, "means I'd have to make at least a hundred and thirty dollars, taking taxes into account."

Brian seems less disturbed by the prospect of job hunting than he was three years ago. He has some confidence that his training will outweigh his interpersonal difficulties. If accounting seemed incredibly boring in high school, it was, and remains, marketable. "It's a good occupation," Brian says. "Besides, I heard that it pays fairly well."

Further, he has had some independent job experience during the summer between his two business school years. Alone, he went to the Jordan employment agency, and emerged with a job as an inventory clerk in their suburban warehouse. To hold the job he had to get up early every morning and take an endless trolley-ride to work. But he earned $2.15 an hour—which he considered not bad for summer work—and he enjoyed the work, even though it meant working closely with six other men.

Brian saved $10.00 a month from his summer pay, and gave the rest to his mother, "because during the month, we're broke." His mother is no longer working and the railroad pension was cut in half when Brian turned twenty-two, so his pay was a critical supplement to their meager budget. He is looking forward to being able to make a more substantial contribution to their finances.

Brian's concerns about getting a job center in his worries about himself as a personality, not himself as a black man. He thinks there might be a "possibility" of job discrimination, but says, "that is a question I will have to answer in the future, because I haven't really had to go after those many jobs." He says he has simply had no experience with discrimination. He dismisses the notion that teachers might be prejudiced with a snort. "Ridiculous! All my teachers always liked me, because I don't cause them any trouble." He says that he does not encounter racism because of "lack of contact with people. I don't have to go through that."

He knows, however, that his experience is unusual and takes a detached view of racial conflict. "I think that black people have a good reason to, at times, be down on the other side, because the other side, some of them, are bad guys. And then the same thing

295

goes with the other side—they have the right to be down on some blacks because they're rotten. But they shouldn't put them down just because their skin color is different—that goes both ways as far as I'm concerned."

Brian does recall, with some effort, one racial incident. "I was downtown," he says, "and there was this white guy. He says something—he called me a name because I was black. Yeah, I remember that now. Guy was drunk, dirty, looked like a bum. He called me a name, so I called him one right back." But Brian says that he didn't get angry at the man. "First of all, the guy was drunk, and second of all, he looked like a bum, which means he probably didn't amount to anything, so he was probably down on everybody, and he took it out on me just because I happened to be black, you know? I found it a most interesting experience, because I never ran across one of them before."

In fact, Brian says, nobody can really make him angry anymore. Even at twenty-three, his mother will fuss if he leaves the house without his jacket or his watch. Brian says that "cracks me up, sometimes," but it doesn't anger him. His strongest emotion, he claims, is irritation, arising when his mother gets him out of bed too early on the weekend, or when she smokes cheap, smelly cigarettes, or when the television stations change the programming schedule so that there is "football and baseball on TV when my movies are coming on. That irritates me." But, he adds, "That's just a minor irritation."

Brian says that total temper control would be the chief characteristic of anyone who tried to take his place in his household. He says that the person would only have to sit around the apartment, reading and watching television, saying very little, and the switch would never be noticed. "Tell him to grump a little when asked to take the garbage out, that's all." But "when she yells at him, don't get mad. That's very important, don't get mad, 'cause then she would know right off that it wasn't me."

FOCUS: BRIAN HENRY—FAILING THE SUCCESSES

When semi-literate Doug Jones dropped out of school in seventh grade, after years of intermittent suspension and continuous failure, nobody was surprised. Doug was deeply troubled, an unwilling partner in the educational enterprise. He and the Ryan expected—and got—little from each other. In fact, it may well be that schools, as they are presently organized, can do little for young people as problem-laden as Doug.

But how do we explain the Ryan's failure to educate Brian Henry, that compulsive student, diligent, attentive, rarely absent, a model held up to his peers? Brian almost always got A's at the Ryan. Nevertheless, he was neither well-educated nor well-counseled. Brian was, perhaps, the school's greatest failure, because he played by the school's rules and still lost.

Brian lost academically because the Ryan simply did not teach him enough. For all his A papers and correct answers in class, he entered Dorchester High (a quite undemanding high school) with skills so poor that he had to redouble his studying to keep from failure. And later, when he entered the Boston Business School, the gap between the skills he gained at Dorchester High and those demanded by a relatively simple business course was equally great. Brian never blamed the schools for his deficiencies. He believed what schools too often communicate—that everything is taught, and it is only the students who fail to learn, limited either by their laziness or stupidity. Brian knew he was not lazy. It never occurred to him to question the practices of the school. So, he assumed that he was stupid, and limited his aspirations accordingly. This is not the least of the Ryan's failures.

But the Ryan served Brian as badly in the guidance office as in the classroom. When Brian thought about his future (which he did more systematically than many adolescents), he saw two possible routes for himself. One was to develop his considerable artistic ability, a path which seemed to him attractive, but without job possibilities. The other was to learn drafting, an occupation which built on his skills and his personal preferences, and one he could think about concretely. Brian felt that he *knew* what it would be like to be a draftsman, as a result of his introductory course in the ninth grade.

The guidance counselors at the Ryan, and later, at Dorchester High failed to identify either route. The Ryan counselor killed the first option by misinforming Mrs. Henry that the first-rate Boston Museum School of Art could not teach Brian any more than the Dorchester High School art department. When Brian, at his mother's instigation, gave up his full scholarship to the Museum School, he gave up his perception of himself as an artist. Not only did he cease to consider art as a possible career, he stopped drawing and painting even for pleasure. One door was closed, possibly forever.

Even after the Museum School scholarship decision had been made, however, Brian still had an alternative career route. Drafting might not have called upon Brian's richest creativity, but it seemed a reasonable career for an artistically skilled, somewhat reclusive young man. But again, counseling intervened. Instead of being sent to a high school with a solid drafting program and a good job placement record, Brian was channeled into Dorchester High, which had no drafting program at all (something Brian was not informed about until after he was there). At Dorchester High he was placed, against his inclination, in the college program.

Now, if there is one thing Brian did not intend to do, at the end of junior high school, it was to go to college. College is expensive, he reasoned, and he and his mother had no money. Further, he did not perceive himself as smart enough for college, nor did he want to do anything with his life for which college would prepare him. In Brian's eyes, the college program only meant more homework in an already overburdened life. It comes as no surprise that he insisted, finally, on dropping the college prep course. It would not have surprised his Ryan art teacher.

How did this happen? Why was a boy with such clearly defined talents and such careful plans so badly guided? Why were so many Ryan students so poorly served? Apparently, Brian was a victim of his own good behavior. Ryan students who were well-behaved and who got good grades were automatically counseled into the college-prep program of a nearby high school. Students with poorer grades, or with less docile behavior patterns, were tracked onto business programs. Actively difficult youngsters, like Douglas Jones, were not counseled at all about the future—it was hard enough to deal with them in the present. There was little individual differentiation built into the counseling process, little attention to the perceptions and needs of specific boys. If you were smart and artistic, you went to Dorchester; if you were "medium-smart" with no obvious skills, you were steered (as was Josh Miller) towards Boston English High; if you seemed to be good with your hands, like Andy Garrison, you might be pushed towards Boston Trade.

Ironically, the student who most believed that the school knew what was good for him was the one most likely to be deceived. Brian Henry and Anthony Dobson—the most fervent advocates of "education" as a life goal were, in different ways, the most victimized by the Ryan's stereotyping. And students such as Josh Miller and Norman Mullen, who suspected and resisted every effort of the school to steer them in any direction, were the most successful in getting what they wanted and needed.

Schools cannot deal with all of the problems posed by life in the ghetto. But they should be able to distinguish between Brian Henry and Norman Mullen, between Andy Garrison and Douglas Jones. They should be able to help individuals design individual paths towards future goals. When schools fail to do this, they fail their students, whether they have been pushed "up" towards a college prep program they will never complete, or "down" towards vocational skills which do not meet their interests or their needs.

PART III

SO WHAT?

Chapter
9
The Way It Is

INTRODUCTION

There is a legal doctrine that "the thing speaks for itself"—that an event is so clear in its meaning to all reasonable people that it requires no interpretation or explanation. In a way, that is how we feel about the lives of the young men whom we have described—as they grow, change, cope, succeed, or fail in ongoing encounters with their families, friends, teachers, the ghetto and the larger society. The different meanings and pathways of their individual lives seem clear.

Yet, as social scientists and as citizens, we also recognize several important ways in which these young men "speak" not only for themselves but for tens of thousands of others in similar circumstances. We wish to draw implications and to make suggestions to teachers and schools, to policy-makers and politicians, and to other young men. We do so not from the distant perch of the detached observer (a role we never played and one we believe as fictitious as it is pernicious) but as fellow members of a society that simultaneously encourages all to aspire but denies some of the means to achieve their aspirations, that prides itself on valuing individual dignity and freedom but that denies some the chance to realize their human possibilities.

What should be done? What can you and I do? What can the schools do? To answer—proximately, partially, diffidently—

such questions, we begin by teasing out some broad themes from the Pathways materials, drawing not only upon the six cases presented above but upon data from the other young men with whom we talked.

In what follows we discuss the stereotypes and myths about black youths and about family life in the ghetto—and then examine some of the realities. We see how these stereotypes warp the perceptions of teachers and others in the ghetto schools and thereby reduce their ability to relate in the here-and-now to the needs and possibilities of their students. We examine black and white teachers in the ghetto schools, asking why teachers are so puzzled by their students and why the problems of classroom discipline and structure appear so difficult. We discuss the widespread belief in the ghetto that education is a magical key to success, point out how educational pathways are sometimes dead ends, examine the lures of the street, and describe some ghetto characteristics that make it a high risk area. Then, we describe what it means to these young men to be black in a world dominated by white people and white institutions.

Finally, we discuss what can be done, how institutions such as schools can be made more fulfilling and more consistent with the American dream. The questions seem simple: what can I do? what can the schools and teachers do? how can programs be designed to meet individual needs and respect individual differences? The answers, as will become clear from our extended discussions of the possibilities for and limitations on the changes schools, teachers, policy makers, and citizens can undertake, are not so simple.

STEREOTYPES AND MYTHS

The most striking and probably the most significant conclusions about the sixty-one young men studied in the Pathways project and about their friends, families, teachers, and surroundings are the pervasiveness of stereotyped thinking about them and the destructive results of such thinking. Evidence abounds in our data for the heavily stereotyped mythic thinking which underlies what is commonly called "racism." The phrases used convey in themselves the absence of thought, the cessation of perception, the presumed futility of attempts to change: "these children," "the black child," "the black family," "whiteys."

Not to see Anthony Dobson or Norman Mullen or Andy Garrison as a human individual but solely as a "black male adolescent" is to deny him his right to exist and grow as an individual person who can define success and failure in his own terms. Adults in American society share fears about adolescent males. When maleness and adolescence are combined with black skin, these fears fetter thought, inhibit appropriate action, encourage blind reaction, and often perpetuate the presumed conditions they purport to correct.

BLACK GHETTO FAMILIES: MYTHS AND REALITIES

A Pseudo-Villian: The Matriarchal Black Ghetto Family

One of the most pervasive myths about family life in the ghetto identifies a supposed mother-dominated, father-absent black family as the prime origin for the hypothetical "tangle of pathology" that mires black youngsters in the self-destructive ways of their parents and programs them in their turn to perpetuate a way of life supported by welfare and marked by anti-social behavior. Juvenile delinquency, school dropout, alienation, out-of-wedlock births, pimping, homosexuality, excessive dependency, mental illness, crime, poor work attitudes, and a host of other social and personal ills have been "explained" by the shakiness of black family structure.

Not only the writers of scare headlines in the papers, decriers of calamity from the pulpits, and other professional alarmists pound hard on this theme. It has also permeated the social sciences and, to a distressingly large extent, been supported and perpetuated by the "findings" of social scientists. The famous

"Moynihan Report" of 1965, written as an in-house Department of Labor document by Daniel Patrick Moynihan and his staff to draw support for a national family minimum income plan from a reluctant Congress, stated the thesis baldly:

> The white family has achieved a high degree of stability and is maintaining that stability.
>
> *By contrast, the family structure of lower class Negroes is highly unstable, and in many urban centers is approaching complete breakdown.*
>
> . . . [The] Negro community has been forced into a matriarchal structure which, because it is so out of line with the rest of the American society, seriously retards the progress of the group as a whole . . .
>
> . . . [It] is clearly a disadvantage for a minority group to be operating on one principle (matriarchy) while the great majority of the population . . . the one with the most advantages . . . is operating on another. Ours is a society which presumes male leadership in private and public affairs . . . A subculture, such as that of the Negro American, in which this is not the pattern, is placed at a distinct disadvantage. . .
>
> (Moynihan, 1965, pp. 5, 29, emphasis in original)

The Moynihan report argued further that father-absent homes, supposedly so common in the black lower-class, could not teach their sons how to be adequate and effective men able to take advantage of opportunities for employment and self-sufficiency. Children from such homes were more likely to have lower I.Q.s, to be troublesome in schools, to be school dropouts and delinquents, and to evidence psychopathology, alienation, and withdrawal.

Even in the presumably few intact black lower-class families, according to this argument young men were inadequately reared, because the black mother was dominant, relegating her husband to a subservient role and depriving the young black male of the necessary effective masculine role model.

All Negro youth were in trouble, because even middle class youth:

> [often] as not must grow up in, or next to the slums . . . They are therefore constantly exposed to the pathology of the disturbed group and constantly in danger of being caught up in the tangle of pathology that affects their world . . . Many of those who escape do so for one generation only: as things are now, their children may have to run the gauntlet all over again. That is not the least vicious aspect of the world which white America has made for the Negro.

> (Moynihan, 1965, pp. 29-30)

Moynihan believed he was arguing for the blacks, not against them, by promoting a federally supported program of family assistance.* But he and the even more numerous policy makers, public officials, and teachers who espoused these pseudo-explanations and stereotypes, although neither malicious nor stupid, surely provided fuel for others who were both.

The Pathways data suggest that the realities of family life in the black ghettos are more varied and complex. The differing family patterns of the boys we studied show no consistent relationships between the behavior of these young men and father-absence or father-presence.

The Presence of Absent Fathers

Even where fathers were regularly present in the homes, most Pathways mothers we talked to, far from subjecting children to

---

*The details of what Moynihan was doing to whom and why are so complex and controversial that they go far beyond our present concerns. For details, see Rainwater and Yancey (1967). For an alternative view, see Moynihan (1973).

periodic demeaning of their absent fathers, seemed very sensitive to the possible repercussions of such talk, and took special pains to allow their children to maintain positive feelings about their fathers. As one mother said:

> The children haven't been told anything against him. After all, he is their father and they should love and respect him. So, for that reason they love him far as I know. [Frankie will] say to me, 'Daddy is telling some more of those funny things he like to tell me. He says he gonna send this, that, and the other.' He hasn't got to the place where he don't believe he's going to never send him anything.

Or, another mother:

> I never downed their father to them. I never make it a subject in this house. If they ask me a question, I try to be as truthful with them as I can, but I don't go out of the way to say he stinks, or he's no good, or this or that, because one day maybe they may run into their father, and maybe he can explain it to them. I don't bother with that.

In some situations, a mother will allow herself the freedom to criticize her children's father, but will soften the criticism to the point where sympathy for him and even humor is possible:

> If I say something like 'You don't think about nobody but yourself, just like your father.' They say, 'Oh, ma! That's your husband. *You* got married to him! And I say, 'That's your daddy. He's more related to you than he is to me.' And they don't never just get down on him. They always say something in both our behalf.

While some "absent" fathers of the Pathways children (usually those who had left Boston) rarely saw their children and did not help support the family financially, about half of the fathers who were separated or divorced sent money regularly for child support, even though they were not always forced to do so by a legal separation agreement.

The data do not indicate that a father (or mother) is necessarily "absent" from the lives of his or her children simply because the entire family does not physically dwell under the same roof. Statistics based on physical proximity are not just misleading but so gross as to be almost useless. For many of the young men their "absent" fathers were more present in their experiences, thoughts, and fantasies than were many fathers who lived with their children.

For example, Thomas Short's mother was dead set against any contact between the children of her first marriage and their father, from whom she was separated. When we first met Thomas, he was visiting his father secretly because, he said, "My mother would kill me if she knew." But the closeness between Thomas and his father never abated, even when his father went to prison. When we re-interviewed Thomas he was nineteen, living at his mother's house, but spending a great deal of time with his father, who had remarried and moved to a nearby town. Because of his father's recent illness, Thomas had just returned from two weeks of caring for his convalescing parent. "He had to have an operation and had a blood clot on his lung, so he was in pretty bad shape. So I stood on to make sure he was cool, take care of his kids and his house."

There is a wide variety of relationships between absent fathers and their wives, ex-wives, and children. Only a minority of absent fathers behaved according to the stereotype, and only a minority of present mothers behaved in the domineering matriarchal style. The "father-absence/mother-dominated" stereotype ignores the importance of the *true relationships* between parents (present or absent) and their children. Sophisticated interview techniques or intensive clinical interviewing are not necessary to realize that a father who was indifferent or abusive to his children while he lived with them would more likely negatively shape their development than an absent father who was perceived as loving and who continued to support and participate in his family's affairs.

Extended Families in the Ghetto

As our six case studies suggest, in many ghetto families the members and kinfolk give each other extensive support. Some even approximate what anthropologists call the extended family system, with its highly developed patterns of child-rearing and economic interchange going far beyond those in the simple isolated family unit of mother, father, and their offspring. In such "extended" families, the "absence" of a father may be replaced by the presence of a grandfather, an uncle, an older brother, a close family friend, or a grandmother, for that matter.

The anthropologist Carol Stack, in an illuminating study of black ghetto families in a midwestern town, among whom she lived, summarized her conclusions in terms which strongly resemble our finding about the Pathways families and which stand in sharp contrast to the stereotype:

> Black families in The Flats and the non-kin they regard as kin have evolved patterns of co-residence, kinship-based exchange networks linking multiple domestic units, elastic household boundaries, lifelong bounds to three-generation households . . . These highly adaptive structural features of urban black families comprise a resilient response to the social-economic conditions of poverty, the inexorable unemployment of black women and men, and the access to scarce economic resources of a mother and her children as AFDC recipients.

> Distinctively negative features attributed to poor families, that they are fatherless, matrifocal, unstable, and disorganized, are not general characteristics of black families living substantially below economic subsistence in urban America. The black urban family, embedded in cooperative domestic exchange, proves to be an organized, tenacious, active, lifelong network.*

(Stack, 1974, p. 124)

*Stack lived for two years in the black ghetto of a midwestern town, sharing the family life and participating with her small son in the exchanges she so

310

In the ghettos there are complex networks of personal relationships among kin and non-kin that can provide tremendous emotional and financial support for youngsters growing up in deprived circumstances. Along with a tangle of pathology, there is a tangle of health, warmth, and growth—and there is no direct or convincing correlation between the bare bones of the marital relationship or the physical proximity of parents and children and self-sustaining pathology.

But the myth is monolithic and remains powerful. It lingers on, and many intelligent, dedicated teachers in the ghetto are too often misled by it in dealings with their students.

How the Myth Affects the Teacher

For some teachers, the myth about the black family substitutes for detailed concrete specific information about the diverse family backgrounds of the youngsters they teach. "Those kids" come from disrupted homes. Therefore, "they" lack adequate male models and can be expected to be disruptive, to be hard to teach, to be slow learners, to drop out of school. The misperceptions caused by the myths are evident throughout our cases. Douglas Jones's intact family did not keep him from raising hell in several schools before he was pushed out. Nor did Anthony Dobson's stay-at-home preachy mother keep him from becoming the pimp he didn't want to be. Nor did Josh Miller's rearing in an almost classic "disrupted" home prevent his getting through college.

But facts do not alter deep-seated beliefs. Witness Mr. Ferraro, middle-class teacher of Italian-American descent, who came to

graphically describes. Members of the community were her informants, her research assistants, and her friends. At the same time, along with her "participant observation," she carried out systematic surveys, including a statistical study of kinship and residence patterns from 188 records of Aid to Families with Dependent Children in the county where she did her research. This survey includes data about 951 children and 373 adults. (Stack, 1974)

teach at the Ryan under the mistaken belief that it was a middle-
class school in Dorchester. Mr. Ferraro was interviewed in 1967
when the Boston white community was at the height of its alarm
over black demands for a greater voice in their destinies and their
schools. Disowning overt racism, Mr. Ferraro expresses a more
subtle stereotyping:

> . . . it is amazing that you can first go there and be teaching
> a Negro class, and as the year progresses you turn out to be
> teaching *children*. I think that is good, it's what is needed. But
> if you are going out there to teach Negro children all year,
> you're going to have a tough time. That's for sure.

But for Mr. Ferraro, "these children" were a mix of
contradictory attributes.

> They are very finicky children, as you know. They are very
> emotional and artistic, I find. But as far as educating them
> they are very ashamed of their meager educational back-
> ground. They are afraid of questions, as you must know, and
> if your questions aren't phrased correctly, you will only get a
> yes or no answer. I found it very difficult teaching them.

> (Interviewer: When you say they are very emotional, you
> think that Negro kids are more emotional than white kids?)

> Ah, yes. I think that maybe it's the pressures that they are
> under community and society, very emotional. They are
> much more artistic in drawing, music, and rhythm, very
> creative.

> They are very proud, and most of them are very cocky. They
> think they are the smartest things alive, in most cases. They'll
> get all Ds and they will say, "Well, I *could* do much better."
> They are very cocky about their ability; they can do anything.

> (Int: But earlier you spoke about some kids who were
> ashamed of their deficiencies?)

Yes, but in general they still strive to be the first one done. They are very competitive people. They strive to be the first one done and have their papers done correct.

(Int: So then, are you saying that the kids do work hard and well?)

We still have to force knowledge on them. They are not very receptive to knowledge.

The interviewer asks "Why do you think that is?" The myth of the black family takes over.

(Ferraro:) Why? Because of the home pressures. I think they don't have enough pressure at home. I think it's a problem in the Negro family. I think the root of all their problems is the family unit. All the other ethnic groups, they had to fight their way up. You're Jewish, I'm an Italian—we had to fight our ways up. Sure, we got into ethnic situations in our work. But we had family units, and they are honored.

And there is no such thing as the ideal Negro family. Now, everything is geared to their mother. The mother is the center of their family because of the fact that the father is not around.

And, I think you are going to find that even the child that lives with both the mother and the father, even though he will respect both parents, he'll still identify with the mother because of the perspective of friends: 'John's father is a son-of-a-gun,' and therefore the child thinks, 'my father must not be any good.'

The interviewer inquires, "How do you get to know so much about the families?"

(Ferraro:) I think you hear from the other teachers that had them before. You gain a lot of knowledge as far as the family life is concerned. Some of them had their families in school—

brothers and sisters. Like, if you have the Johnson family, which is one of the toughest families to handle in the whole school. If one teacher had Karen Johnson and another Johnson was coming up, you would watch out for the Johnson family. Because, there again, this is evidence of a family problem more than anything. Why does one family act up more than another? You look at their family. It is a broken home, so of course you can imagine what is going on.

(Int: But what kind of direct contact do you have with the parent so you can find out what's going on first hand?)

(Ferraro:) I talk to parents. They want to know, 'What's happening here? What's the problem? Are my kids getting sufficient education?' And always they asked, "Whose fault is it? *But they will never take the blame themselves.* They want to blame the teachers. They want to blame someone.

You might say they do care about their children in this respect, but will they sacrifice their good time to help them. This is what I found was very difficult. If you could catch them at a working hour, fine. They will take time out, but do they want things to be good for their children? Do they want to work for it? If *these people* all cared about their children, I don't think we would have a problem ... if they cared in a *working* sense, if *they* wanted to strive to help their children, we wouldn't have a problem.

(emphases added)

Other white teachers, like Mr. Corcoran, accepted the myth more grudgingly. Corcoran was dismayed to have become convinced that "the kids who are good in school are from good families, and the ones who are having trouble are not, and I haven't been able to help them one bit." Some teachers saw around the edges of the myth. Thus, Mr. Morris, the seventh grade guidance counselor, believed the presence of both parents in the home was less important than the attitudes of older brothers and sisters toward school, and concluded that "Sure, it goes back to the home again. But by the same token, you'll also find another individual child that has one parent at home, circumstances unknown as to where the other parent is. Her mother will be working as a nurse's aide, working nights some place, and the child will still perform every day up to snuff."

The myth of the black mother-dominated family is but one element in the stereotyping that occurs in the thinking of some teachers, but we believe it is an important element in what went to make the Ryan the tortured school it was in 1967, and which continues to make it a place where far less formal education occurs than parents, students, or staff wish for.

EDUCATION AS MAGIC:
SCHOOL AS THE ROYAL ROAD TO SUCCESS

Among all the young people and adults interviewed in the Pathways project no belief was more universally held or strongly shared than the firm faith that education—a high school diploma, further job training, higher degrees—would unquestionably lead to a good and decently paying job, opportunities for promotion, and the "good life" of security, dignity, status, self-realization, and satisfaction to which all Americans aspire. Norman Mullen said it bluntly:

> If you don't have a high school diploma, you might as well forget it . . . you gonna be in a hell of a jam! Everybody is gonna have something. You ain't gonna have nothing.

His words were echoed by all—by the college graduates; by parents regretting educational opportunities they missed and which they wanted for their children; by the dropouts, both those who struggled to stay in school but failed and those who left as soon as they could. Most striking, even those who had experienced the inadequacies of the schools they had attended (and who had many friends and family members with diplomas or job training who were unemployed, under-employed, or in dead-end jobs), wholeheartedly endorsed Norman Mullen's paean about the virtues of education. Josh Miller, the college graduate,

315

saw his four years of college as a way to "get around the system," to have "a piece of paper to show somebody . . . that . . . entitles me to a job at such-and-such a salary." Doug Jones, the junior high dropout, reports, "I've gone to a lot of jobs before, and I couldn't get into them because I didn't have a diploma."

There is little doubt that educational credentials are indeed helpful, if not indispensable, in "getting around the system," for they have in fact become an integral part of it. The myth of the "self-made man" with a third-grade education has given way to the reality that the more pieces of paper an individual accumulates attesting to the length of his endurance in school and college, the greater will be his chances of success in the job market.

Although the odds have always favored whites over blacks by a considerable margin; nevertheless, blacks with college degrees tend to be better off than those with only high school diplomas, and those with high school diplomas better off than those without them. And the propaganda generated by the statistics has been pervasive. It has penetrated the ghetto as well as the suburbs. Brian Henry's widowed mother, for instance, remembers her husband telling Brian when he was a young child that he should "get all the education he could." And to help bind the future, Mr. and Mrs. Henry bought Brian an encyclopedia when he was still only three years old. More than half the boys in the Pathways Project got their high school diplomas, and many of them continued into some form of post-secondary education. The question is: what did they actually learn en route in the search for credentials? There is a kind of "double vision" in their perceptions that enables some to accept their own often negative, bitter, and unrewarding experiences with the formal education system and yet to retain their faith in the overall desirability and goodness of education as a goal. If there is any other generalization that applies to these young men, it is this: much, probably most, of what they "learned" was the product of their experience in the home, in the streets, and in those school-related encounters that had little if anything to do with the school curriculum.

316

The Academic Pathway to Success Sometimes Goes Nowhere

Despite the "double vision" that sometimes enables the dream to remain viable, the grim realities of ghetto life affect everyone. Andy Garrison's educated and highly skilled father remains stuck for a lifetime in a succession of poorly-paying and insecure jobs. Similarly, the young men growing up in the ghetto confront in their daily lives the often visible irrelevance of education to material success.

The grim realities are that some who go to school, work hard, and toe the line remain where they started—at the bottom. Others engage in illicit activities and wind up with highly visible material rewards. The numbers runner, the pimp, the dope dealer can show they have "made it" with their Cadillacs and country houses. Anthony Dobson's pimp counselor even had a helicopter to attest to his success as an entrepreneur. Education as the preferred pathway to achieve a goal that is widely shared in our society—economic success—is not as available to black people as to white people, and even where it is available, it does not always work. The black child who is taught that schooling is the way out of the ghetto and towards the American Dream, often discovers later that it isn't always so—and perhaps blames himself as a "failure," even though he may recognize how discrimination and prejudice handicapped him from the start.

LIFE AT RYAN:
PUZZLEMENT, DISCIPLINE, AND CULTURE SHOCK

The young men we studied showed a complex variety of life styles, ways of coping, and kinds and qualities of relationships with family and friends. Their connections to schooling were often ambiguous, contradictory, and without clearcut pattern. These ambiguities, perplexities, and contributions were reflected in the Ryan's teachers as puzzlement about their students, as problems of discipline and "law and order" in the classroom, and as "culture shock" when confronting students with different attitudes, behaviors, and life styles.

317

Puzzlement

If some of the white teachers and a few of the black teachers at
the Ryan saw "bad kids" coming from "pathological" black
families, many others were more puzzled than fearful or angry.
They often felt impotent, bewildered, unable to cope with or to
understand the seemingly erratic behavior of their charges.

Some of the children are seen as a mystery to all of their
teachers all of the time. Daniel Raymond was described by one
teacher as having an "attitude that was negative . . . sort of sullen
at times . . . when I first had him in class I said to myself, 'This
kid's an odd-ball.' I just had to figure out how I was going to try to
get along with him . . . He was not a typical kid." Another teacher
saw Daniel as "sort of like . . . he was living in a shell . . . I don't
know about Daniel."

Other children look inconsistent. They appear to be different at
different times. For example, one teacher described Reggie
Thomas.

> Reggie at the beginning of the year was beautifully turned
> out; dressed well, starched and pressed and clean. And then
> one time he went through a stage there, he just didn't . . .
> wasn't the same boy; slovenly and looked like he didn't . . .
> just stepped out of a battleground, and we couldn't under-
> stand it. Then he seemed to go back to the other way again,
> but never quite captured the sharpness and that peak that he
> had. And he was very, very sullen. Sullen boy.

Sometimes a teacher would perceive a child as intelligent and
abe to do the required school work easily while another teacher
would see the same child as completely incompetent. John Short,
for example, is described first by his English teacher then by his
history teacher:

> (*English teacher:*) John Short is a sharp kid. He's real dark.
> I had him in 7K. He's a smart kid. He's a real smart kid. I
> really liked him.

318

(Int: What kind of work did he do?)

He did good work. As a matter of fact he always did good work. He'd never come in with any materials. I'd always have a pencil for him. I'll never forget it. I always had him do work because I knew he could do it. He definitely . . . he'll do the work for you. Only if he likes you. I think this is it. And he likes me.

(Int: What kind of school work do you think that John should be capable of?)

(*History teacher:*) Why, heaven knows? I don't think he should have been in the 5th, 7th, or 6th grade. I think he's been pushed on, passed on. I think his age was for that grade but his ability was not. I think that his early education on up I think it wasn't too good. And therefore he wasn't ready for the work. So he would hide behind his behavior.

(Int: What's the highest grade you feel John is capable of completing?)

I shouldn't really say, but to me he should go back as far as the fourth grade and redo it up from there.

(Int: In general how has it been being John's teacher?)

Puzzling. I say puzzling because if I can't reach a child I do worry about him. You worry about trying it some other way. And you wonder every now and then whether it's your fault or what. It is puzzling.

Some teachers escaped their puzzlement by embracing the myth of the black family, others turned to other stereotyped explanations, and some remained like John Short's history teacher—baffled and unhappy about their bafflement.

In the early stages of our teacher interviews, we were amazed at the widespread use by the teachers of inadequate social science theories about the relationships between family background and student performance. Later, our surprise abated, when we realized what few cues were available from the behavior directly observable by the teacher in school. Teachers, feeling over-whelmed and bewildered by school behavior which they cannot predict or understand, use the meager cues available and extrapolate from them to currently fashionable developmental theories.

Most disturbing was how fantasies, or even accurate knowl-edge about the out-of-school experience of black children, were used by some teachers to *exclude,* downgrade, and avoid the necessity of analyzing and understanding the *classroom ex-perience,* the milieu for which they were largely, if not completely, responsible. We do not mean to minimize the problems faced by teachers in confronting the turbulence of many inner city schools. But we cannot afford to underestimate the need for teachers and educators in general to develop greater understanding of classroom dynamics rather than to explain away behavior with inadequate generalizations about the family life of the ghetto child and its inexorable effects on school performance.

Discipline and Culture Shock

Part of the teachers' bafflement, their premature closure in the efforts to perceive the differences among their pupils, and their inability to attend to the here-and-now of the classroom situation may come from culture shock—the upset both physical and mental that we all feel when we encounter the natives on their own turf and discover that not only are they different from us, but they are different in ways which they value as highly as we do our own. The white middle-class teacher stepping into the Ryan was more likely than the black teacher to experience such traumas, but even some black middle-class teachers were not wholly immune.

One black female teacher at the Ryan, discussing her colleagues' difficulties, stated the problem that faced most white and some black teachers.

In some cases I feel that some of the [teachers] were not the type who could get along under those circumstances even with a stronger principal, that they weren't the personality that would go along with the urban child. They had probably come from a very nice background and gone to nice schools, and they weren't used to hearing children swear.

One of the things that really seemed to upset a lot of the people were the threats the children made quite often. I think that if you live in a community, or work with children in a community such as this, that many things that they say like, 'I'm going to kick your ass,' to them don't mean a thing. Someone else might recoil in horror and think that they really mean this sort of thing, but to them it's just a way of talking and of showing how much emotion that he's displaying. I really feel that a lot of people took things that the children said a lot more seriously, and they probably worried about it and wondered if they were going to get cut up, beat up.

A lot of this had to do with their performance in the classroom too. I felt that many of the people, not just people who were fired, but people who were working there were really afraid of the children. And this is really bad.

This teacher, drawing on her personal knowledge of the black community and the lives of the children at the Ryan, could—without denying the physical threats that a minority among the children present—distinguish far more realistically than could the white middle-class teachers the genuine threats from the rhetorical styles.

She went on to comment on the relationship between the home life of the children and school discipline problems.

If a child does something that really is wrong, there's no need saying "boys will be boys." A lot of these children really lack and need discipline. It's surprising sometimes that those that seem to cause the most problems are those who are *not* let run wild at home. Their parents really do care about what they

321

do, and what they say. In some cases the parents are very strict on them, but because they put on this bravado in school, and they say 'My mother won't do anything,' the teacher probably has an image of a mother who doesn't care.

Culture shock is a major teacher problem because cultural differences become too easily tied up with issues of classroom control and discipline. A lower-class student uses an obscene word in front of a middle-class teacher. The teacher, accurately by his own lights, translates this act as a test of classroom control. He responds with a disciplinary act. The student reacts with outrage and with consciously provocative behavior. In terms of his own culture, he has done nothing wrong. The teacher escalates the punishment and classroom control becomes rigid and counterproductive. Misunderstanding leads to threat. This cuts off the possibility of communication which could clear up the initial misunderstanding. Some teachers become obsessed with control issues and have little energy left to understand the unfamiliar culture in which his students live and learn.

Some teachers coped with their culture shock and their discipline problems by imposing rigid standards of behavior and decorum, occasionally enforced by physical sanctions (a feat not always possible, especially for white teachers). Others managed to captivate the interests of some of the students by a genuine concern for and involvement with them. Still others coped not at all, but either fled the Ryan Junior High in disarray and sometimes in tears or struggled in fear to the end of the school year.

Mr. James, a black male teacher, successfully preserved classroom order and was fairly widely respected among the students. He put his case for strict discipline:

> You gotta have heart. You can't let these children run over you. I don't care how much a teacher tells me that he loves these black kids, if he lets them run around the room all day and doesn't teach them a damn thing, he should automatically leave himself. He shouldn't wait to be rated as a

poor teacher or they ask him to leave. He's sabotaging the program. This is what these kids need. You got to get control from them to be able to learn. I know children who come [and ask], 'Mr. James, may I sit in your room this period?' They say 'I do better reading one of those books on your table than to go in some of these other rooms, cause I don't want to get in any more trouble and it's nothing but hell-raising in [those rooms]!

A young, white, middle-class colleague of Mr. James described the "James approach" as "a paddle, with a loud voice" and went on to note that he could not use that technique because he was "not a Negro and I don't have twenty years of teaching experience and ... I don't want to hit the kids anyway." Mr. James was "stern and tall and authoritative." The younger teacher had come reluctantly to the Ryan and looked forward to leaving at the end of the year. He did not find Mr. James' no-nonsense approach either available or desirable, but could discover no alternative that worked for him.

Mr. Feliciano, a teacher from a Hispanic background, managed to achieve a common ground with his students as fellow "persons of color" and developed close personal relationships with some of them. He stated his philosophy thus:

> ... I think that the type of teacher that goes to the Ryan school should be like a missionary. By missionary I don't mean idealistic in the sense of applying their ideals but missionary in the sense of a worker, someone that is really going to try to accomplish and to put a few ideas in.

> Let me give you an example. Many of my children have a warped concept. The epitome of success is a pimp, a hustler, or a prostitute. You can't go in there and say this is awful, this is dirty, bang bang.

> Many of these children come from homes obviously where the father is a pimp or the mother is a prostitute. You can't destroy the one thing they love, and say this is dirty, this is

323

awful. You have to go about it easier in a softer manner. You have to reeducate them.

You ask them what happens if they contract a disease. Some of these diseases are so bad to kill. What about when they get very old, who supports them, what do they do. It seems to me like a secretary would have a better life than she would. Of course it is very glamorous to sit at a bar stool and listen to music all night but beauty only lasts about how many years, would you say? I would ask them. And they would say maybe 8 or 10 years. I would ask, 'Then what?' You have to destroy this image of success that they have of something and try to reeducate them. You try to establish different concepts without a direct frontal attack.

The same thing about the idea of being a pimp. Well, it is nice to be a pimp, you live well, you drive a Cadillac and wear silk suits, but for how many years? What happens when you get too old and ugly and none of these pretty women want to work for you? Who is going to take care of you when you are old?

I get very involved with all my children. I talk to as many as possible. For instance, before school they wait for me outside the school. I bring in about 8 or 9 with me into class before school and talk to them.

At the other extreme was an idealistic young female teacher, a Harvard graduate, who quit after two months at the Ryan. Almost totally unable to communicate with her students, or to prevent them from hurting each other or her, or to teach those students who wanted to learn, she finally noted in despair in her diary:

Today I started hitting kids with a stick. In my homeroom. Not hard or seriously but just to shock them. That is a sign that I should quit. The kids say Mr. James always hits the boys with a stick and hit the desks of the girls real hard. Some of the girls were telling me about the rattans some of their grade school teachers had. Even using a stick is silly because the kids know I would never hit them hard enough to hurt them.

I am becoming more and more convinced that I can't do my thing at the Ryan School.

The royal road to success has many potholes—not only for those who try to travel its twisting and sometimes tortuous routes but also for the caretakers and for those who try to assist and instruct them about the route.

SCHOOL VERSUS STREET

Just as many teachers are torn by conflicts and sometimes bewildered about how to behave in the school, puzzled by the students and confused about the meaning of it all, so many students—who are trying to find the path—exhibit contradictory and sometimes conflicting attitudes and behaviors. On the one hand, parents, teachers, and matchbook covers urge with varying degrees of stridency "stay in school, get additional training and you will get ahead and succeed." On the other hand, there are the potent lures of the peer group, the gang, the swinging life of the streets, the euphoric ups and downs of drugs, the excitement and adventure of petty and not-so-petty crime, the *machismo* and high living of pimping.

Many of the Pathways young men expressed their fears about succumbing to the lures of the streets while at the same time worrying about the satisfactions they would miss by not succumbing. They spoke almost as if street life were a contagious disease rampant among their friends, which had to be avoided if they were to make the most of themselves. Josh Miller spoke for many of the young men when he said, sorrowfully, "Well, I'm just going to have to not be around my friends as much as I want in order to pull to myself some things that I want to do." On the one hand, he asked himself, "What if all the niggers I came up with reject me?" On the other hand, he feared his vulnerability to the

325

self-destructive ways of the past: staying high, dealing drugs, petty thievery, short-run pleasures. "I don't want my understanding of what they are going through mixed in with my ideas and the way I'm headed. I think sometimes I am susceptible to going toward them . . . Sometimes I just feel like giving up."

Stanley Stewart, another young man we interviewed, shared Josh's fears. "The guys I hang with now are a lot better than the ones I used to hang with. These guys don't get busted, don't get hurt. They're just doing the right things. No crying, no sighing—they're doing straight things but they're still hip too." Terry Thomas pointed out to us that between our first interview with him and our third interview, two of his closest friends died from drug overdoses, and went on to say that, "Well, I figure I've seen all these dudes be shooting up. Two of my friends have died. A life goes so quick, man, it's not for me . . . Next thing you know, you've got a Jones [habit] for it. You'll be out there, ripping people off and jiving and getting yourself shot at. It's not worth it." His conclusion: stay away from other people who might get you into trouble.

Yet the swinging life has its allure, as this graphic description by John Robins makes clear:

> Well I had been fucking around with drugs and shit, man, orange sunshine, all kinds of shit. I took [acid] for about two weeks. That high is, I don't know, it's out of this world. The first time I took it was like you be out in the desert. All you see is miles and miles of desert. That's just how it was out in the street. All you see is miles and miles of houses. They be *bright*, man. It seemed like there ain't no shade nowhere. I took it. Shit, the whole class was taking it. You wouldn't even know you'd be doing it. Just walk around the corridors laughing and joking around, chasing each other. Used to have some fun. *Plenty* fun.

> Gambling, you ain't never seen gambling till you dug the trade school. There's a locker room, they be three, four

326

niggers from another class, five, six niggers from a different class, and everybody be up there betting five dollars, ten dollars.

A clear statement of the problem as many saw it was given by Clarence Meredith, who by his final interview had been in and out of jail, on and off drugs, in and out of several jobs and programs, and was trying to get his life together.

The attitude that I have is I want success and I want it legitimately. But the possibilities of having it working out are very slim. I'm trying to get into a position like construction. I'll try to get into that position or some other type of legitimate position.

But like if I get a shot, you know, at some off-the-wall position that's the position I would take. If I could see a lot of daylight in it, I would rather do it on a different level, like a business type level or something. It carries more strength because people have different attitudes toward you. That's the way I like to do it.

The young men we interviewed seemed very much aware of the precariousness of their positions and of the drastic and sometimes permanent consequences of just a single slip. For those who were determined to get ahead, to see Clarence Meredith's "legitimate position"—what Anthony Dobson called "clean work"—the costs were high. Sometimes a seeming "failure" to seize "opportunities" simply represented an assessment that the costs to their personal lives if they chose to move up and out from friends, family, ghetto, were too high. It was better to stay put.

THE GHETTO AS A HIGH RISK AREA

Reviewing our data about the sixty-one young men, we were startled to discover how many of them had suffered from major life catastrophes. Eight had a parent who had died before we began our interviewing, and two more parents died in the interval between our first and last interviews. Eight of the interviewees had lost a total of nine siblings through illness, accident, fire, or fighting. Douglas Jones's father was imprisoned for murder. Douglas himself was hit by a truck and had to spend time in the hopital. Brian Henry was hit by a car, causing a permanent limp or shuffle and his father died when Brian was very young. Norman Mullen was terribly burned by fire as a child and an aunt to whom he was very close died. Andy Garrison was in a car accident. Anthony Dobson had a paralyzed hand for a year.

The impression one gets is of great vulnerability among these ghetto youth, of their lives as being precarious, a sense among them that what you do or how you struggle or try to be good doesn't really make any difference. You can be ripped off or burned out or arbitrarily arrested and jailed or in an accident at any time. This produces surprisingly fatalistic attitudes among what are, after all, very young persons. For example, one young man said:

> From the minute you're born your life is laid out and nothing can stop it. There's no use crying over people when they die. My mother used to say that older people used to cry when a person was born because they're coming into a world of trouble. And they're supposed to rejoice when they die because all their problems are gone. I thought these people got it all backwards. Then I started thinking you're supposed to die at a certain time.

> I used to read Greek mythology about the Fates. Everything was Fate. Your life is like a string and it's at a certain place on the string where you're going to die. Along the string each and every day of your life is prepared.

> My mother would like me to be a good boy, but how can you change if you was raised up in that kind of environment? If you was living in Roxbury and in the South End, and all the friends you met—everybody was out stealing things and things like that? I could change if I could get away from the neighborhood.

328

There is a feeling of the arbitrariness, the chanciness of life, both in good things and bad. Another young man put it well.

> I mean like right now I'm not doing anything. I'm laying around. But in a couple of days, maybe even today or tomorrow, things might change. I might have a bit of scratch in my pocket or I might just run into the right person— unexpectedly, you know. But I'm getting pretty sure that it'll come along any day now.

Perhaps this accounts for what almost seems to be a sense of survivorship among those who do get out, who are making it or trying to make it. Those who get ahead find it hard to believe that it was their talent or hard work that gave them their rewards. Going to a good school or getting a good job was just luck. They often see themselves as survivors helped along by random events other than by any efforts of their own.

BLACK IDENTITY AND THE WHITE WORLD: MEETING THE MAN

In their attitudes toward both blacks and whites and in their sense of racial pride and identity the young men we studied displayed divergences, differences, and seeming contradictions. Their attitudes toward whites ranged from a combination of ignorance, indifference, and hostility in Douglas Jones, through the sophisticated perceptions of Josh Miller making his way through the white educational system, to the color-blindness of Brian Henry as he constructed his self-contained world.

Their attitudes toward their own race reflected the same fragmentation and variation—a tinge of anti-black sentiment in one of the most articulately militant young men; a fellow feeling for other blacks in a youth who was withdrawn and frightened but little conscious of race; a willingness in an avowedly anti-white young man to join the "white system" to exploit it for his own ends. To further compound the complexity, in many families the parents shared a specific orientation toward race, while their children, often close in age, differed among themselves in their attitudes toward their color, the black community, and the white world.

Thomas Johnson, in our final interview with him, gave a view of the relations between the races shared by a number of the boys. When asked, "What do you think would be some things that you'd want to communicate to white people?" he displayed awareness of stereotyping by both blacks and whites and a sort of sad resignation about the limited possibilities for change.

> I would like (whites) to be aware of what some of their own people is doing to blacks. Why black people are the way they are. What makes them against white people. White people do things and they're not aware of it because not *all* of them do it, but just some of them do it. It's like if a black man killed a white lady, then they blame the whole black nation. White man kill a black woman—black man blame all white man.

> I would like the white men to see his stupidity in life, how to treat human beings. That would be my main thing. For him to be aware of what he's doing.

> The black man don't like to be bugged. He know he's qualified to do a lot of things. Lot of times the white man's staying in the way and obstructs the black man. Therefore, he goes to violence. I'd like the white man to see what he's doing. But still it don't mean they're going to change. And what makes me mad is when the black man goes looking for a job for which he's qualified and they deny him.

Other young men forcefully expressed blanket hostility. For example, John Patrick said:

> The only thing whites have got going for them is that they can cheat people. There's plenty of corruptness. They can perpetrate so many crimes on black people and get away with it.

> They are beasts. They eat odd foods. All of them are fat and we are a slim, trim beautiful race of people.

330

Some young men saw white adolescents as weak and soft. One said:

> . . . they are faggots . . . squares. Most every whitey I know, they can't fight or nothing like that. Mostly all the colored people I know, they can fight. They think of defending themselves and whiteys think of getting rich.

> Colored kids are down. White kids act like they came up soft. Colored kids come up hard and they still act better than whites do.

Perceptions of white hostility sometimes convinced the black youths that education was the way to get ahead in a white-dominated world. One said:

> You learn how to live early, how to take care of yourself. The white, it takes him a whole lifetime and a half to live and realize that he's living. You learn how to take things as they come, how to do without, how important education is.

Education and Coping with the White World

When black youths leave the ghetto to rise in the educational system—whether they go to suburban schools, to prep schools, or college—part of their nonacademic learning experience is how to cope with the white world. Some of them learned about whites when younger, often on a job during the summer. Many also gained knowledge through their exposure to white teachers. Anthony Dobson certainly gained much of his expertise as a con artist by working his routines on his white teachers at the Ryan and on the white youths he met in the bars he frequented. Exposure to and sustained interaction with whites simultaneously increases among some of the boys a sense of their own racial identity as blacks and their hostility and militancy against whites. For Douglas Jones whites seem undifferentiated. They are a class of objects to rip off or beat up. Other Pathways youths who were, like Douglas Jones, heavily into crime and delinquency, manifested similar visceral anti-establishment attitudes without clearcut racial consciousness or awareness.

On the other hand, Norman Mullen, skilled at hustling overlapping multiple scholarships, saw his knowledge of the white world as something uniquely valuable, significant, and indispensable to his goal of getting ahead. His conclusion that "You got to get out with these whiteys and get into their shit," was preceded by a dissertation on why this is so important.

> Through education I learned a lot about what the world is about, what these white people are about. When I know what these white people are about I think I can deal with them better. A lot of these blacks around here they don't *know* what these white people are about. They might read about white people in the Muslim paper but you got to deal with them to find out about them. You going to be in your own world anyway, because you're black and you don't *think* like no whitey because you're black. You can't just deal with them by reading no papers and shit like that. You got to get out really and find out what they're all about.

> You can't deal with them if you ain't got your education and your head together because they got their head together. They got all the money and they know what's going on in the country because they're educated. A lot of the blacks aren't educated. The ones that did graduate from high school graduated from a high school in the slums, where they teaching you slum shit. When you get out of high school and you know how to read, you know how to write, you know arithmetic, adding, subtraction, multiplication, division and all that stuff. You might know a little bit about the history they taught you, that American history shit.

> If you get into college you learn other things. You learn a lot more about the country than you learn in high school.

You can't learn by just staying in the ghetto and staying
around all the same kind, all these poor black people. You got
to get out. You got to get out with these whiteys and get into
their shit.

For Norman Mullen, at least, it is clear that just learning "slum
shit" does not qualify you to deal with "whitey's shit."

It may be their relatively clear and sometimes militant identity
as blacks that enables Josh Miller and Norman Mullen to take the
risks they do—to leave the known discomfort of the ghetto and
venture into the unknown white world. Even Anthony Dobson,
torn between the worlds of the pimp and legitimate jobs, goes
through a series of engagements and withdrawals with the white
world of jobs and education. In some ways the psychological risks
that Josh Miller and Norman Mullen take are far greater than the
physical risks of a beating or imprisonment taken by Douglas
Jones.

Attitudes Toward the Black Community and Black Leaders

There was wide variation in the attitudes of the Pathways
group to black leaders. Brian Henry had difficulty even naming
any; Doug Jones and Andy Garrison gave them little thought. On
the other hand, Josh Miller, Anthony Dobson, and Norman
Mullen identified to some degree with the aspirations of the black
community. Anthony Dobson's refusal to cut his hair in the
approved militant style led to the abrupt termination of his
brief romance with the Panthers. Nevertheless he was clearly concerned about and involved with the black community. Witness
his participation in freedom rides in the South. Josh Miller
exhibited a not uncommon distrust of black leaders who rise from
the community and initially depend on its support but tend to
forget their origins after getting over into the white world beyond
the ghetto.

Norman Mullen managed to combine concern for the black
community with a high degree of self-interest. On the one hand,

he accepted the principle that a well-educated black person from the ghetto had an obligation to help other ghetto blacks find their way out. On the other hand, he added the crucial qualification that this expectation is justified only if it is reasonably lucrative.

You can't just get out of the ghetto and forget about it. That's just impossible. You're never gonna forget what it's like in the ghetto. And no matter what you're doing, I don't think you're gonna forget your people that are in the ghetto. If I got some kind of training that's going to benefit people in the ghetto, that's gonna get them something and make them more wise to what's going on, then I think that's where they should come.

People in urban studies, people in business, if they can get an opportunity to help the people in the ghetto I think they really should do it. A lot of them are doing that, but you can't always find opportunities in the ghetto. When you're going to college you're going to make some money, you understand? You're really not going just to help somebody else, you're going to help yourself.

Now if you can get something out of helping your people too, that's cool. But if you gonna go to college and come back and try to help your people without really making any kind of money that's gonna set you up in the society, then that's just a waste of time.

Josh Miller measured the black activists and community organizers by a tough standard—had they made the lives of black people any better?—and he often found them wanting. One young man even found the murdered Martin Luther King, Jr. less than wholly effective:

At first the newspapers were building him up because he was really accomplishing something. I used to give a damn but the time has changed. I'm older now. At the end he really wasn't doing nothing. He was, in a sense, getting paid for making money off of it. Even if he was living today, his followers would have dwindled.

Others who admired Dr. King testified that they wouldn't want "to end up dead like he did."

Race, Ethnicity, and Class

A colleague who was a roving troubleshooter in the Buffalo, New York, public schools in his days as a graduate student, describes schools, teachers' attitudes, and classroom problems similar to those we found at the Ryan. Most of his time was spent as a pacifier in classes that had been uncontrollable in the predominantly Slavic, totally white, lower-class junior high schools in South Buffalo. He found that corporal punishment, shared stereotypes among many faculty members about the children, considerable puzzlement about what produced students' odd behaviors, and rigid categorizing were widespread. Family reputations determined the school fate of younger siblings among the large Slavic families. The Sustakoskis, for example, were "known trouble-makers," and no matter how meek and submissive an actual Sustakoski might be in reality, he or she was handled with an iron fist and viewed as a ticking time bomb.

Two identical twin boys provided a striking example. Coming from an extremely poor family, one boy was bright, alert, interested in school, and quiet in the classroom. The other was loud, destructive, violent. Yet both boys were perceived by most faculty as identical in attitudes and behaviors as well as in physical characteristics. When our colleague gave the responsive boy the high grades he had earned (while his brother got the F traditionally reserved for both of them), he was called to the principal's office where he was summarily informed that he must have made a mistake and the grade should be "corrected." When he declined either to acknowledge the mistake or make the correction he was informed that "Well, both those kids are exactly alike, they're both fuck-ups, and we're going to get them out by the end of the year." So much for stereotyping. And so much for the twins—both of whom were forced out of school at year's end.

335

Our hunch is that versions of the Black Family Myth, with suitable variations for skin color, ethnicity, and economic level, exist not only in urban slum schools but also in suburban middle-class schools. Rigidity, denial of the here-and-now, teachers' problems in modifying the classroom experience and in obtaining useful detailed knowledge about their students are not confined to the black ghettos, though they are most pervasive and extreme there.

Many of the "injuries" described in our six case studies are injuries of class as well as of race. Yet, we believe that the "injuries" of race are more extensive and more severe than those of class, even if they are sometimes similar in kind. In an earlier publication based on preliminary data from the Pathways project, we compared the responses of two groups of boys who lived across the street from one another in a public housing project in Roxbury. (Rosenthal and Bruce, 1966.) One group consisted of five lower-class white boys; the other consisted of five lower-class black boys.

The replies of these boys to the same set of questions put by the interviewer showed some striking differences between the two groups in how they viewed themselves and their life opportunities. The white boys tended to see themselves as living in an open world where the pathways to success were clearly marked and available to everyone with the will to try. The black boys tended to see themselves as living in a constricted, unpredictable, and often threatening world where the pathways to any kind of success were unclear and unrelated to individual effort.

Our data from both sides of the street conformed with what others have also found: as compared with whites, black youngsters are on balance less hopeful about their own futures and less in control of their own destiny. (DuCette and Wolk, 1972, pp. 493-504.) Even cursory examination of the statistics comparing blacks and whites on family income, occupational level, unemployment, and the like makes it apparent why poor black youngsters are more often burdened with a feeling of helplessness than are their white counterparts.

336

SOME MODEST PROPOSALS FOR CHANGES

Big Implications—and Little

Many social critics of the American scene have proposed big social and educational changes—massive new programs of federal expenditures, major alterations in the distribution of income, large-scale subsidies of private housing for the poor, reconstruction of the inner cities, expensive and extensive educational innovations of many sorts, sizes, and shapes. With some of these suggestions we agree. With others, we disagree. Some might make a difference, others might not. The fact that we do not discuss them in detail should not be taken to mean that we deny their importance. We urgently add our voices to the small chorus calling for an immediate renewal of public concern for the lives of the poor, especially the black poor. We too hope that a change in the social and political climate—not, after all, an impossibility—may lead to such a renewal. Aside from a few brief remarks below, however, we prefer, like good shoemakers, to stick to our last and to draw from the Pathways materials suggestions for changes that flow directly from the findings and out of the experiences of black young people in the Roxbury ghetto. Our suggestions center on the schools because of their accessibility and because of their central role in our findings.

If we cannot write the ultimate formula for humanizing our society, then perhaps we can at least begin to humanize ourselves, to liberate our perceptions and behavior from the myths and stereotypes and actions that have blinded and limited us and harmed others. Although we are not in a position to prescribe in detail how the total educational system should be transformed to better accommodate the developmental needs of children in the ghetto, we nevertheless believe it useful to suggest some modifications in schools and classrooms that ought to make a positive difference in how teachers teach there and children learn there.

Before turning to our modest proposals, however, we want to emphasize our awareness that no classroom, no school, no school system exists in isolation. Each is enmeshed in a series of interlocking bureaucracies that stretch in one direction back to the teacher-training colleges, in another direction to state certifying agencies and boards, and in yet another to the local school system. The federal government, with its diverse agencies, policies, and programs, and the federal courts with their increasingly important rulings about matters previously within the sole purview of the educational system, add yet other levels of complexity.

Many of the problems that we identify in the classroom behaviors or attitudes of teachers on the firing line are a consequence of decisions (or indecisions) made by bureaucrats or administrators far away in time and space. It is not our goal or our intention to point a finger of blame even indirectly at teachers or principals by ignoring the severe limitations on just how much they as individuals can do to change practices embedded in the bureaucratic systems in which all parties to the educational act (including the children) must try to survive.

One area where voices calling for educational changes have been heard (if not obeyed) is in large urban areas with high concentrations of black persons. At the local level increased black political power has had an increasing impact on the local educational system. A good place, then, to begin is by examining this development.

338

BLACK POWER IN LOCAL POLITICS AND EDUCATION: CIVIC VIRTUES

When the inflamed black rhetoric and media-induced white panic about "the black power movement" died down, it became apparent to many that what blacks were "demanding" was startlingly similar to what white groups had demanded and received in years past. Chuck Stone, in his study of the black role in American politics, carefully delineated how the Irish, the Jews, the Italians, and the Poles achieved a measure of political power in our big cities—and how successive generations of these groups benefited from this achievement.

Stone shows in detail how the blacks have captured the mayoralty in many of our largest cities, noting that while "many young blacks are pointing out that political power has passed from the cities to the federal government . . . the fact remains that whoever is mayor of the nation's largest cities is still a political power with which to be reckoned and if he—black or white—does nothing more than control the built-in patronage of municipal jobs . . . and contracts, he must still be regarded as a major source of political influence in the power structure of this country." (Stone, 1970, p. 288) Surely if blacks had earlier played a more significant political role in the municipal administration and educational bureaurcracy of Boston, events at the Ryan might have taken a different and less panic-stricken course.

Stone's recommendations to blacks resemble those given to other groups seeking to improve their economic, social, and political status: unite, use your votes wisely, especially where they can tip elections one way or another, keep a weather eye on your leaders, remember that politics is the art of accommodation and compromise. As Norman Mullen might phrase it, "get your shit together" and pursue some combination of group and self interest.

Most events in American political life occupy a point on the line stretching between what Thorstein Veblen identified as its

339

two polar axioms. On the one hand, "the squeaking wheel gets the grease." On the other hand, "the silent hog eats the swill." Political skill consists of shifting between these stances in the most advantageous way. Black politicians and groups are showing increasing skills in so doing. From the Declaration of Independence through Tammany Hall and Boss Tweed to Boston's James Michael Curley, politics in fact has been the art of who gets what, when, and how. The practical result has been, as blacks and other low-status groups have discovered to their sorrow, who does what to whom.

Josh Miller complained about black leaders who emerged only to treat their black constituencies to a lot of double-talk. Black parents in Roxbury alarmed about the noneducation of their children tried to alter the educational structure at the Ryan. Anthony Dobson hustled a living as a pimp yet at the same time sought the betterment of the black community through political action. These were all beginning attempts to move into the mainstream of American political life.

We suggest that schools and school teachers help these efforts by providing education in genuine civics—not civics in the traditional cliched pieties, but civics as education in the realities and practicalities of how political leverage manages this country and how such leverage can be acquired and used. Lobbies, pressure groups, gerrymandering, ward heeling, voter registration drives and the like should become the meat and potatoes of civics curricula. A few such curricula have been developed for suburban school systems, but virtually nothing has been done for inner-city schools. Students should be trained in how to participate actively in the political process.

It should be remembered that such gains as were made during the 1960's in the education of blacks resulted from political action in which blacks themselves actively participated. On the local scene in Roxbury, it was blacks in the first instance who organized Operation Exodus and the METCO program. Nationally, it was the consistent and long-term political pressure of black leaders that eventually produced the Civil Right Act of

1964 and other federal legislation designed to make equality of opportunity something more than a slogan.

Although the Civil Rights Act and the diverse poverty and educational programs had their limitations and defects, they did open up many opportunities to blacks. Many of the blacks who were able to take advantage of these opportunities appear to have been middle class, with one leg already up the ladder, but through luck and determination some lower-class blacks were also able to get a piece of the action.

Perhaps the sheer scope of the programs—even if they were only a fraction of what was needed—helped insure this. For example, it is estimated that the Upward Bound program in its first year of operation in 1966 was enrolling three percent of the 600,000 disadvantaged youngsters then in high school, or about 18,000 individuals. And Title I of the ESEA Act of 1965 has poured billions of dollars into poor school districts to improve basic skills, although nobody knows for sure how much of this money actually went into good or effective remedial instruction of poor blacks or whites.

We saw these programs at work in Roxbury and at times they worked quite well. If the Jones family was untouched by the programs of the 1960s, all of the Mullens benefited. Norman's brother Junior went to a private school, graduated from college, and is now a working politician; one sister graduated from college and the other is in a college preparatory program; Norman himself is working towards his college degree; and Mrs. Mullen—who despised being on welfare—was able to become a professional in her own eyes by getting a job as a teacher's aide. It is Mrs. Mullen—professional teacher's aide, shrewd observer and critic of education at the Ryan, which her children attended, and initiator of suggestions for constructive change in the schools—to whom we now turn.

WHAT SHOULD BE DONE IN THE SCHOOLS?
MRS. MULLEN SPEAKS

Norman Mullen's mother, who, like Mrs. Henry and other mothers we talked with, deeply regretted her own lack of a chance to become a teacher (". . . I had so much interest in school . . . I'd have been a high school teacher . . . That was my ideal"), laid out for us a program for changes in the Ryan as she discussed the education of her son Norman and his siblings.

After mentioning the increased opportunities that young black people have today compared to those available during her youth in the South, Mrs. Mullen wondered "if Norman knew enough about it . . . I wonder if the teachers talk to him, give him some present idea of what would be offered to him if he'll finish high school and things like that."

Asked what she would do if she were a teacher in the Ryan (this was in 1968—a time of turmoil there of which she was well aware), Mrs. Mullen responded eloquently:

> If I was a teacher, when I first walked into a class, I would walk in with determination. We'd talk about subjects, yes, true enough, but I just wouldn't talk all out of that book. I would teach what's in that book. But I would talk about what's going on in the world today. You got to know that to cope with other parts of your life. I would teach them about the world in which they live and their environment and their surroundings. Teach them the things that they would have to cope with and prepare them how to be able to cope when it comes.

> To talk about their environment, I would tell them you maybe will have to live and learn a lot of conditions that you disapprove of, but you can't take all that into consideration and do just like you would feel about it. You have to abide by some rules and regulations. And I would tell them that all men are created equal. And I think that nobody's brains are

342

stronger than the next person's brains. It's just how they think.

And we would go together to learn together. Not me doing all the teaching. We both can learn, because you never get too old to learn. If you just take a little time, although you are an adult, and listen to what children have to say, you can learn a lot. Ask them for answers and give them answers. Work together, learn more togetherness. We could use that. We could combine it. Combine our own inner thoughts and put them into the books and bring them out, you know.

When you walk in so many classrooms, there's never nothing talked about but from page to page of what's in that book. Not giving a child no idea of what's around him, and what the world has to offer.

Elaborating her theme about the need for relevant and meaningful classroom instruction, she said:

When children are going to school for education they should be taught the value of it. Do not go right into the classroom and say, "This is a history book." Talking about all that past stuff. They should talk about what's today. If we talk about today, yesterday will be in it, too. Read about today and yesterday, and make a comparison right there of today, the happenings of today. And how we can better that condition, so it won't happen as it did yesterday or years ago.

Discussing the ubiquitous discipline problems at the Ryan, Mrs. Mullen noted:

. . . It's a strange thing. There's so many different ways that a child can be disciplined. The worst children can be disciplined. It depends on how a person goes about trying to discipline that child. I have chaperoned down at St. Basil's a lot of kids, and a lot of big, bad fellows are down there. And you could look at them and tell they were bad. But I would push those fellows, and the things that I would say, there wasn't a one disobeyed what I said.

343

And then she went on to describe the kinds of classes, the desirable attitudes of teachers, and the involvement of parents in the schools in terms that few professionals have bettered:

> The first thing I would think of would concern physical education. That's one of the things that—speaking of physical, not mental, right now—I would want a place for physical education. I would want a place for science, a special place for reading, a special place for the class to assemble together.
>
> The next thing would be the preparation of food, because the mind cannot function when the stomach is empty. That's true. A hungry child cannot concentrate.
>
> And I would have English. I would have a place for good listeners. I would have a place for art class. A place for arts and crafts, for imagination. Where they'd be able to design. And I would have a quiet room for music. And a study hall.
>
> I would want willing and active teachers who would try to understand how they live and grow. I would like to have it so that the parents would be free to make suggestions about things that they think the children should have that we hadn't thought of. We would have parents and teachers meetings so parents could speak their own opinions about things. I can't remember that we meet with no teachers . . . We just go and talk about their grades and things. I think we should have special time, special day set aside with all the teachers and parents and the principal and everybody to get together, and not only discuss one child, but discuss education as a whole.

Most of the changes in the Ryan that Mrs. Mullen and many other black parents wanted were small changes designed to humanize the school and to focus education on the acquisition of basic skills of reading, writing, and calculating. The black parents with whom we spoke were skeptical about broadscale innovations and massive educational experiments. They felt that programs like modern math were okay out in the affluent suburbs, where the children would go to college no matter what sort of education they got. For their children—for whom college was more hope than certainty—the black parents wanted a solid basic education and an introduction to a world different from the street, tempered with an understanding of pupils' individual learning problems. A school which recognized parents and their children as human beings with different needs, skills, and desires, and which taught the basic skills, would go a long way toward satisfying Mrs. Mullen and her neighbors.

A GLOSS ON MRS. MULLEN

Mrs. Mullen almost says it all. But we will try to supplement her suggestions with a few others which have emerged from our talks with the Pathways young men and the people among whom they lived.

Our suggestions center on four points:

First, and perhaps foremost, the school should be structured so that teachers are encouraged to avoid stereotyping and rigidly categorizing the pupils. The staff should be trained to look for, perceive accurately, and respond to the diversities of their pupils, rather than to act on presumed similarities.

Second, discipline and classroom order should be overt issues rather than covert closeted traumas that erupt into periodic mini-riots. There should be teacher-training modules and orientation on classroom culture-shock, on cross-cultural communication, and on the specifics of how to cope with likely classroom problems.

Third, a substantial amount of time should be set aside for adequate communication between the staff and individual pupils, between teachers and administrators, between teachers/staff and parents, and between teachers/staff and the other members of the community concerned about education and the schools. Teachers should have the time to *listen* to their students, and should become aware of how important and useful such listening can be.

Fourth, the guidance-and-counseling function, which is often so limited and overloaded in traditional schools as to be more an impediment than an asset, should be expanded enough to give every student realistic advice about genuine opportunities and real-world pitfalls. Guidance personnel and teachers need to teach students how to perceive their real options and how to choose among those options.

Before we elaborate briefly on each of these points, be it noted that we are aware of the likely *costs* of such notions. But let it also be noted that we are equally aware of the all-too-real costs of *not* trying to make things better. Both sets of costs are not only fiscal but human and humane. It has been estimated that it costs more to keep a young person locked up in a prison than it does to send him to a high-priced college and more to rebuild after destructive riots than to prevent them by coping carefully and humanely with their causes. Both in the short-run and in the long-run, the costs of forcing a high rate of unemployment on black ghetto youth are enormous for the lives of the youngsters themselves and their families and for the lives of all of us. It costs the community more to have schools where pupils do not learn and teachers do not teach than to have schools where both are realized in the daily classroom experience.

We will focus on these four topics, letting the ideas and suggestions flow freely. Many of these ideas have been kicking around for years; some have been tried piecemeal. We suggest their systematic and widespread application.

1. *Awareness and Avoidance of Stereotyping and Categorizing*

This has several aspects. First, of course, we must eradicate the myths which are used to avoid looking at the differences among the students and at the realities of their lives. This does not mean that categories and labels cannot be used, but that they should bear a useful, working, correct relationship to the lives of those they purport to describe.

In three remarkable volumes, Nicholas Hobbs and his associates have presented the results of the Vanderbilt University "Project on Classification of Exceptional Children"—results which strongly support our conclusions about the dangers of rigidly categorizing and stereotyping children and the need for sensitive and cautious use of all kinds of labels. (Hobbs, 1974, 1975) Hobbs states the problem clearly:

> . . . classification is serious business. Classification can profoundly affect what happens to a child. It can open doors to services and experiences the child needs to grow in competence, to become a person sure of his worth and appreciative of the worth of others, to live with zest and joy. On the the other hand, classification, or inappropriate classification, or failure to get needed classification—and the consequences that ensue—can blight the life of a child, reducing opportunity, diminishing his competence and self-esteem, alienating him from others, nurturing a meaness of spirit, and making him less a person than he could become. Nothing less than the futures of children is at stake.
>
> (Hobbs, 1975, p. 1)

Hobbs notes that "currently employed classification procedures . . . can be used to discriminate against poor and minority-group children and . . . (are) sometimes used, with more or less conscious intent, to limit their opportunities or to keep them separated from majority-group children." (Ibid, p. 7) We agree with his suggestion that "public and private policies and practices must manifest respect for the individuality of children and appreciation of the positive values of their individual talents and diverse cultural backgrounds." (Ibid, p. 6)

The labels commonly applied to poor black children in some schools have taken on a more sophisticated sound over the years, which has rendered them increasingly pernicious. The new labels may be harder to overcome than the old. If a young man, such as

Norman Mullen, has himself accepted the label of "lazy and shiftless" from his mother and from his teachers, this may limit his effort in high school. But he can (and did) have a sense of control over his future behavior. He can decide to stop being lazy, to commit himself to achievement, to go out and locate every source of available scholarship funding.

But what if Norman had been diagnosed as "minimally brain damaged"—a label which recently has sometimes replaced "lazy and shiftless" as the favorite explanation for low achievement among poor black children? Because minimal brain damage often does not show up clearly on neurological tests, such a pseudomedical "diagnosis" may not be much more scientifically based than the "accurate" observations by middle class white teachers of ten years ago that their poor black pupils were lazy. However, laziness, at least, is amenable to control from within. Minimal brain damage is a permanent condition which cannot be altered. For some, this diagnosis leads to the use of such external controls as drugs or behavior modification. Norman could not have decided to "stop" being minimally brain damaged. And his prospects for achieving the life he wanted might well have been severely limited had he been so diagnosed.

The changes in labels for poor black children who perform badly in school (from "lazy" through "culturally deprived" to "minimally brain damaged" and "hyper-active") appear on the surface to be increasingly sympathetic to the child. The "blame" for his performance has been shifted from himself, to his culture, to a genetic fault over which he has no control. But with the shift of blame has come a loss of control; the individual child and his parents no longer believe that it is within the child's capacity to change his ways, to create for himself a broader pattern of options.

A school oriented to individual differences would make judicious use of available testing and other diagnostic procedures. Anthony Dobson's reading difficulties were evident early in his school career. We suspect, though we cannot prove, that identification of that problem and treatment of it—neither of which is beyond current educational technology—might have made a substantial difference in Anthony's life.

348

Achievement and vocational aptitude tests should be used only with full knowledge about their limitations and then only as partial guides to help schools and teachers understand children and assist children to understand and to help themselves rather than as rigid supposedly scientific measuring rods to classify and pigeonhole depersonalized objects. Henry Dyer, former vice-president of the Educational Testing Service in Princeton, New Jersey, has pointed out that if tests "are perceived as instruments for sorting children into iron-bound categories, they will be used for that purpose. But if they are perceived as supplying basic data needed for helping children learn to cope more and more effectively with the world into which they are growing, then they will be used to provide that kind of help." (Dyer, 1967, pp. 779-780) Dyer has also noted that "Test scores are slippery things, and anyone who uses them without realizing how slippery they are can make serious errors in judgment and do considerable damage to a child's education." Realistic assessment of and training in the uses and misuses of testing should be integral parts of both pre-service and in-service training for teachers, supervisors, and counselors.

2. Discipline and Classroom Order

Discipline should be made an overt part of pre-service and in-service training, removing it from the folklore of the teacher's lounge or the *machismo* of the individual "tough teachers." Both novices and experienced teachers need to learn not only how to deal with disruptive behavior when it occurs; they also need to learn about the various probable *causes* of such behavior as it appears in individuals and groups, and thus have some hope of removing the causes. To this end, in-service courses might be devised for experienced teachers, novices, and student teachers. The purpose of such courses would be to get the participants to analyze the classroom behavior they actually confront from day to day. Such a course might begin with a discussion of the cultures

349

of the community and of the school, exploring what kinds of language, physical behaviors, and situations are likely to produce misunderstandings or difficulties between students and teachers. Such an analysis is important for black as well as for white teachers, because the sources of classroom misunderstandings are often class-based as well as racially-based.

The group could generate a list of *types* of discipline problems that seem to crop up most frequently in their school. They could then choose from among a series of videotapes presenting different disciplinary situations those which are most common in their school. After viewing the tapes, the group could discuss how each of them might handle the situation presented on the tape, and the probable effectiveness of each means of coping. The group could then go on to other kinds of exercises: role play of disciplinary incidents; presentation of actual cases by faculty members; development of motivational devices to supplant disciplinary measures. (For an excellent discussion of techniques of classroom management and control, see Good and Brophy, 1973.)

Exercises can be shaped to the needs of a specific faculty or school. Most important is the dissipation of the "discipline myth"—the notion that discipline, like sex appeal, is something that you either have or you don't, and if you don't, you are irrevocably incapacitated. When teachers become fully aware that discipline is a shared teaching problem which they can learn to cope with, not inherently dissimilar from other teaching problems, some of the emotional load can be removed from the urban classroom scene.

Given such awareness and group support, the young teacher who quit the Ryan after she struck a pupil might not have had to undergo so traumatic an experience—and one so wasteful of her energies and talents and of those of her students. And the liberal teacher who became an overly rigid disciplinarian to survive might have discovered alternative ways to preserve order in the classroom, ways not only more effective but also more satisfying both to himself and to his pupils.

350

Classroom discipline and order should be recognized as a shared problem. In solving the problem teachers need and deserve support from their peers, their supervisors, and the school system. Even if perfect solutions aren't available, at least teachers can be warned against doing things that create or exacerbate problems they most fear.

3. Communication Among the Parties to the Educational Act

In the ideal school, the kinds of linkages and releases of energy that are facilitated by meaningful feedback and genuine communication would lead to the effective deployment of the resources of the total community: teachers, administrators, students, parents, and other interested parties. Shared purposes and involvement and commitment flow from shared information. Notions often filled with overheated rhetoric rather than with substantive content (for example, "relevant" education and "community control") become practical and purposive realities in such an environment. The school is not merely "brought" to the community but is an integral part of the community.

In such a school/community, the Mrs. Mullens might be consultants, putting some of their ideas to work and offering running commentaries on current practices. In such a school, Douglas Jones and his cohorts, rather than being drummed out of the school after being shifted around from one class and one school to the next, might be presented with realistic alternatives that made sense for them. Indeed, it is not beyond belief that Douglas Jones himself might have come up with such alternatives if anyone had ever asked, ideas that would have made school more tolerable for him and made him more tolerable for the school.

Some of the communications problems at the Ryan were created and exacerbated by the social and psychological distances among the participants in the life of the school: middle-class white teachers and lower-class black students; black and white teachers; middle-class black teachers and lower-class black

351

students; black parents, many of whom were born in the South, and Northern-born teachers; adults and young. We do not see the "greening" of the Ryan as an easy task, but surely a significant first step is to recognize the gaps in beliefs, perceptions and life styles that separate many teachers from their students and from their students' families. And a not insignificant second step is to realize that effective communication, like effective discipline, is part of the process of becoming a teacher and of creating an environment conducive to learning. This part of the process can be worked at, learned, taught, and achieved.

4. Guidance and Counseling

The Ryan School had only two guidance counselors for more than 600 children. Two individuals, with all the goodwill in the world, could not have had time to "guide" in any meaningful sense. Instead, they spent their days coping with crises, administering standardized tests, and frantically trying to work out high school placements usually based on inadequate information about both the pupils and the appropriate opportunities available to them. What little time and energy remained was devoted to the few college-bound boys and girls, the ones most likely to reward additional effort. The counselors had few materials, little impetus, and few guidelines to broaden their services to benefit the bulk of their charges.

As a result, few of the young men in our study were ever taught how to plan their own careers. None was treated as a unique individual for whom a specific academic/career plan might have been worked out with the boy himself. Norman Mullen and Brian Henry, as disparate a pair as can be imagined, were lumped together as "smart, artistic" and shoved into Dorchester High, which met the needs of neither. Andy Garrison and Douglas Jones, neither of whom ever disrupted a classroom, were treated as "discipline problems" and got no career guidance at all.

Outside of school, a boy growing up in Roxbury/North Dorchester had few realistic models on whom to pattern a career. They saw professional careers primarily through the distorting lens of the television tube. Perry Mason haranguing the jury lived in Brian Henry's mind as the symbol of professional life; Douglas Jones' mother wanted him to be a doctor, so he could save her life, "like on TV." In the real world, they saw a hard choice between hustling (including pimping, drug dealing, various cons, and robbery) and menial labor (work in the car wash, like Norman Mullen's father or in the factory, like Mr. Garrison). Neither of these occupational models satisfied their aspiration for clean, safe work. But it is what they knew.

What is missing from their immediate experience is the middle range of occupations—the skilled, moderately well-paying work which has been the traditional first rung up the ladder within the lower or working class, the move from unskilled to skilled labor. Some of the Pathways boys were given the opportunity—through prep school and college scholarships—to make the great leap from the lower to the middle class. If they made it, they made it; if they slipped and fell, well—they had been given "every opportunity." But few of them were able to simply climb one rung—to become electricians or keypunch operators or mail sorters whose children would go to college.

The lack of a sense of the middle ground is reflected in the boys' occupational choices. Again and again in the interviews, boys would say that their first career choice was "president," or "lawyer," or, more directly, "millionaire." The second choice, reflecting their pragmatic knowledge of reality, was unexalted— factory worker or stock clerk.

Even when the boys selected, as realistic goals, jobs in the "middle range," they were hampered by inadequate information and misleading counseling. Norman Mullen "decided" to become a court stenographer because of a "college night" description of various possible one and two year programs. But his understanding of court stenography was meager and it was not a clear enough goal to keep him out of his year-long drugged depression. Brian Henry chose an even more plausible occupation— architectural drafting—which would have allowed him to work alone and to use his artistic skills to some extent. But his guidance counselors and his mother pushed him relentlessly toward the college program in a high school which did not even offer the fall-back option of a drafting course if Brian decided (as he, in fact, did) that a four-year college was not for him. Both of these boys managed, on their own, to put together careers. But the guidance structure of the Ryan and of Dorchester High did little to assist them in their efforts. And boys with less capacity to focus their energies, boys like Andy Garrison or Anthony Dobson, never fulfilled their potential or their aspirations.

This pattern should be altered. Guidance counseling is too often the stepchild of the urban school. Men and women with years of training become little more than highly skilled clerks, processing records for hundreds of children. More guidance counseors, selected for their sensitivity to individual differences among black children, could provide the careful, differentiated counseling that Norman Mullen, among others, correctly believed he should have had.

But personnel are not enough. The guidance counselors need to have access to information which allows them to introduce to young people the widest possible variety of options. Counselors should be provided with lists of skilled jobs for which there is a substantial market in their area, including expert projections of the durability of that market. Detailed job descriptions in a format understandable to students should be available from a central clearing house. Such descriptions should be updated and augmented every few years. They could be used in English and social studies classes as well as in guidance offices. The junior high school student could be bombarded with occupational options in school to augment and hopefully correct what he sees on the street and on television. Finally, counselors should have a directory of men and women in many diverse occupations—ranging from lawyers and doctors to skilled craftsmen and laborers—who would be willing to spend a few days showing young people how their jobs work. Each junior high school and high school student could then spend at least a week each year, "checking out" a field which he thinks might be of interest. It is time that the so-called "job-experience programs" touted under the label "career education" be made an educational reality by giving students some "hands-on" experiences in a variety of jobs.

All of these services should be provided for the schools. The counselor could augment these offerings with the advice and example of alumni who have entered a variety of fields with some success—or with none at all. As we learned in the Pathways research, graduates of the Ryan are often eloquent and rational about their school experiences and their subsequent career decisions. They could speak more directly, more acutely, to their successors, perhaps, than anyone else can. Unfortunately, there is not now a guidance counselor in a major city who has the time or the resources to develop such a program.

Our conception of guidance is different from what generally happens in urban schools, although it is often what guidance counselors thought they were being trained for. It is important that counselors move away from the old process of "guiding" students pre-selected by the uncritical use of standardized tests into pre-programmed and all-too-often meaningless (or even nonexistent) slots in what is euphemistically called "the world of work."

Instead, counselors should return to the ancient educational goal of self-knowledge, assisting their students in thinking about themselves, their conditions, and their aspirations. Rather than being victimized by the hustles of matchbook covers and hyped-up television ads, the students would receive accurate descriptions of the realities of the world of work as they related to them. This would replace the ambiguous and fuzzy notions about existing jobs that were displayed by many of the young men we interviewed.

Norman Mullen told us, "When I'm doing something that's creative I put all my energies in it, and I have to be in a certain kind of environment that's gonna make me wanna do things, you know?" The ideal school would provide such an environment.

355

CONCLUSION

We believe in maximizing the opportunities for human beings to grow, to develop, to release and use their energies constructively. We believe that despite a social and economic system that is often biased and oppressive and restricting, individuals and groups can significantly contribute to the enhancement of their own lives and the lives of others. So much for our modest proposals and our high-flown rhetoric. If the reader wants to get at the heart of the matter, let him return to the lives of the six young men and ponder again what *they* are saying to us about human conditions in the ghetto.

Selected References

Allen, Vernon, ed. *Psychological Factors in Poverty.* Chicago: Markham, 1970.

Clark, Kenneth, and Hopkins, Jeannette. *A Relevant War Against Poverty.* New York: Harper & Row, 1969.

Coles, Robert. *The South Goes North.* Boston: Little, Brown, 1968.

DuCette, Joseph, and Wolk, Stephen. "Locus of Control and Levels of Aspiration in Black and White Children." *Review of Educational Research,* vol. 42, no. 4 (Fall 1972) pp. 493-504.

Dyer, Henry S. "Needed Changes to Sweeten the Impact of Testing." *Personnel and Guidance Journal,* April 1967.

Dyer, Henry S. "A Psychometrician Views Human Ability." *Teachers College Record,* April 1960.

Ferman, Louis et al, eds. *Poverty in America.* Ann Arbor: University of Michigan Press, rev. ed., 1970.

Ginzberg, Eli, and Solow, Robert. *The Great Society: Lessons for the Future.* New York: Basic Books, 1974.

Good, Thomas, and Jere Brophy. *Looking in Classrooms.* New York: Harper and Row, 1973.

Hannerz, Ulf. *Soulside.* Lund, Sweden: Berlingska Boktryckeriet, 1969.

Hobbs, Nicholas. *The Futures of Children.* San Francisco: Jossey-Bass, 1975.

Hobbs, Nicholas, ed. *Issues in the Classification of Children.* San Francisco: Jossey-Bass, 1974, two volumes.

Kahn, R. L. et al. *Organizational Stress.* New York: Wiley, 1964.

Ladd, Florence. "Black Youths View Their Environments: Some Views of Housing." *AIP Journal.* March 1972, pp. 108-116.

Liebow, Elliot. *Tally's Corner.* Boston: Little, Brown, 1967.

Malcolm, X. *The Autobiography of Malcolm X.* New York: Grove, 1964.

Marris, Peter, and Rein, Martin. *Dilemmas of Social Reform.* Chicago: Aldine, 2nd ed., 1973.

Minuchin, Salvador et al. *Families of the Slums.* New York: Basic, 1970.

Moynihan, Daniel Patrick. *The Negro Family: The Case for National Action.* Washington, D.C.: U.S. Dept of Labor, 1965.

Moynihan, Daniel Patrick. *The Politics of a Guaranteed Income.* New York: Random House, 1973.

Rainwater, Lee. *Behind Ghetto Walls.* Chicago: Aldine, 1970.

Rainwater, Lee, ed. *Black Experience: Soul.* Chicago: Aldine, 1970.

Rainwater, Lee, and Yancey, William. *The Moynihan Report and the Politics of Controversy.* Cambridge, Mass.: MIT Press, 1967.

Rose, Peter et al. eds. *Through Different Eyes.* New York: Oxford, 1973.

Rosenthal, Robert A., and Bruce, Bernard. "The World Across the Street." *Bulletin of the Harvard Graduate School of Education Association.* vol. XI, no. 2, Fall 1966.

Silverstein, Barry, and Krate, Ronald. *Children of the Dark Ghetto*. New York
Praeger, 1975.

Stack, Carol. *All Our Kin*. New York: Harper & Row, 1974.

Stone, Chuck. *Black Political Power in America*. New York: Delta, 1970,
rev. ed.

Thernstrom, Stephan. *The Other Bostonians*. Cambridge: Harvard Univ.
Press, 1973.

Urofsky, Melvin, ed. *Perspectives on Urban America*. Garden City, New York:
Doubleday Anchor, 1973.

Warner, Sam Bass. *Street Car Suburbs: The Process of Growth in Boston,
1870-1900*. New York: Atheneum, 1969.